Volume 8 Number 2

# economia

Journal of the Latin American and Caribbean Economic Association

Spring 2008

EDITORS

*Eduardo Engel*
*Francisco Ferreira*
*Roberto Rigobon*

LATIN AMERICAN AND CARIBBEAN ECONOMIC ASSOCIATION

BROOKINGS INSTITUTION PRESS
*Washington, D.C.*

Articles in this publication were developed by the authors for the biannual *Economía* meetings. In all cases the papers are the product of the authors' thinking alone and do not imply endorsement by the staff members, officers, or trustees of the Brookings Institution or of LACEA, or of those institutions with which the authors are affiliated.



*Published by*
BROOKINGS INSTITUTION PRESS
1775 Massachusetts Avenue, N.W., Washington, D.C. 20036
www.brookings.edu

ISSN 1529-7470
ISBN-13 978-0-8157-2088-1

For information on subscriptions, standing orders, and individual copies, contact Brookings Institution Press, P.O. Box 465, Hanover, PA 17331-0465. Or call 866-698-0010. E-mail brookings@tsp.sheridan.com. Visit Brookings online at www.brookings.edu/press.

Brookings periodicals are available online through Online Computer Library Center (contact the OCLC subscriptions department at 800-848-5878, ext. 6251) and Project Muse (http://muse.jhu.edu).

Volume 8 Number 2

# economía

Journal of the Latin American and Caribbean Economic Association

Spring 2008

*Editors' Summary* *vii*

PATRICK J. MCEWAN, MIGUEL URQUIOLA, AND EMILIANA VEGAS
*School Choice, Stratification, and Information on School Performance: Lessons from Chile* *1*
Comments by Reynaldo Fernandes and Francisco A. Gallego *28*

NORBERT SCHADY AND MARIA CARIDAD ARAUJO
*Cash Transfers, Conditions, and School Enrollment in Ecuador* *43*
Comments by Ximena Peña and Luis F. López-Calva *71*

ALBERTO CHONG AND HUGO ÑOPO
*The Mystery of Discrimination in Latin America* *79*
Comments by Lucas Ronconi and Miguel Urquiola *108*

ERNESTO LÓPEZ-CÓRDOVA, ALEJANDRO MICCO, AND DANIELKEN MOLINA
*How Sensitive Are Latin American Exports to Chinese Competition in the U.S. Market?* *117*
Comments by Luis F. López-Calva and Peter K. Schott *146*

RAFAEL DI TELLA AND ALEXANDER DYCK
*Cost Reductions, Cost Padding, and Stock Market Prices: The Chilean Experience with Price-Cap Regulation* *155*
Comments by Alexander Galetovic and William W. Hogan *186*

## LATIN AMERICAN AND CARIBBEAN ECONOMIC ASSOCIATION

The Latin American and Caribbean Economic Association (LACEA), or Asociación de Economía de América Latina y el Caribe, is an international association of economists with common research interests in Latin America. It was formed in 1992 to facilitate the exchange of ideas among economists and policymakers.

Membership in LACEA is open to all individuals or institutions professionally concerned with the study of Latin American and Caribbean economies. For membership information, please visit the LACEA website at www.lacea.org and click on "join LACEA."

## ECONOMIA PANEL FOR VOLUME 8, n.2


Luis Henrique Braido, *Fundação Getulio Vargas, Rio de Janeiro*
Luis Felipe López-Calva, *United Nations Development Programme*
Juan Pablo Montero, *Pontificia Universidad Católica de Chile*
Norbert Schady, *World Bank*
Pablo Serra, *Comisión Nacional de Energía, Chile, and Universidad de Chile*
Eric Verhoogen, *Columbia University*


## AUTHORS AND DISCUSSANTS


Maria Caridad Araujo, *World Bank*
Alberto Chong, *Inter-American Development Bank*
Rafael Di Tella, *Harvard University*
Alexander Dyck, *University of Toronto*
Reynaldo Fernandes, *Universidade de São Paulo and INEP, Brazil*
Alexander Galetovic, *Universidad de los Andes and Stanford University*
Francisco A. Gallego, *Pontificia Universidad Católica de Chile*
William W. Hogan, *Harvard University*
Luis F. López-Calva, *United Nations Development Programme*
Ernesto López-Córdova, *Inter-American Development Bank*
Patrick J. McEwan, *Wellesley College*
Alejandro Micco, *Ministry of Finance, Chile*
Danielken Molina, *University of California–San Diego*
Hugo Ñopo, *Inter-American Development Bank*
Ximena Peña, *Universidad de los Andes*
Lucas Ronconi, *University of California–Berkeley*
Norbert Schady, *World Bank*
Peter K. Schott, *Yale University and NBER*
Miguel Urquiola, *Columbia University and NBER*
Emiliana Vegas, *World Bank*

EDUARDO ENGEL
FRANCISCO H. G. FERREIRA
ROBERTO RIGOBON

# Editors' Summary

It has long been understood that economic growth and development are not achieved by brute-force factor accumulation alone. The pursuit of a development path that combines both greater efficiency and social fairness has been high on the agenda for many governments in Latin America during the last decade (if not longer). A preoccupation with equity and efficiency, and the best ways to combine them, also permeates the five papers in this Spring issue of *Economía*.

A possible trade-off between greater efficiency and equal opportunity is central to the debate on school vouchers, for instance. Whereas economists since Milton Friedman have argued that school choice would align provider incentives with the interests of consumers and thus lead to increases in educational quality, a more recent literature points to the possibility that school choice might exacerbate stratification by socioeconomic status across schools. In "School Choice, Stratification, and Information on School Performance: Lessons from Chile," Patrick J. McEwan, Miguel Urquiola, and Emiliana Vegas contribute to this literature in two ways. First, using highly disaggregated, district-level data for Chile and a regression-discontinuity design, they find evidence that the entry of private schools into the education market is not associated with significant increases in test scores but is associated with increases in social stratification. This conclusion is consistent with previous results from the literature, suggesting that greater school choice leads to increased sorting, with no commensurate improvements in average achievement.

Second, McEwan, Urquiola, and Vegas consider the implications of sampling variance (and even of "population variance" over time) for policy schemes that reward or punish schools on the basis of changes in average test scores. Policymakers have focused on these so-called value added (that is, first-differenced) measures of test scores, since test score levels are highly correlated with family socioeconomic status, as a result of the stratification previously discussed. Changes in scores also reflect sampling variation, however, including variation among the specific groups of students starting school in any given year, as well as genuine changes in the quality of the services provided by the schools. Although this issue is unlikely to be a serious problem for large municipalities, it can generate substantial rerankings for individual schools and even for smaller districts, as the authors confirm through a number of statistical tests. These findings suggest that the Chilean debates on school choice, on the ideal design for voucher schemes, and on the precise manner in which data on student achievement can be used to reward or punish schools have contributed to advances in the educational agenda in Latin America but have not yet reached a final conclusion.

The concern with combining equity and efficiency also underlies the "conditional cash transfer revolution" that has transformed social policy in Latin America over the last ten years. The first of these programs began somewhat timidly in Brazil and Mexico in the mid-1990s, yet by 2007 some 80 million individuals across the continent had received government assistance through some form of conditional cash transfer. In "Cash Transfers, Conditions, and School Enrollment in Ecuador," Norbert Schady and Maria Caridad Araujo evaluate the impacts of Ecuador's cash transfer program, known as the *Bono de Desarrollo Humano* (BDH), on school enrollment. A novel aspect of the paper is that it uses differences between the initial program design and the subsequent implementation to assess the relative importance of the conditions (as opposed to the cash itself) in explaining the effects of the program. Given the costs of monitoring and enforcing conditions, this assessment is of considerable policy interest.

Schady and Araujo exploit several idiosyncrasies in the program's design and implementation. First, assignment into treatment and control groups was random in the initial phase of the project. In practice, however, actual treatment did not perfectly coincide with the random assignment. Second, data were collected both before and after the program was implemented, from both treatment and control groups. Third, the program was designed and announced as a conditional transfer program, in which households would receive the transfer conditional on children's school enrollment and attendance, but the condition was not actually enforced in practice, due to administrative constraints.

To overcome the problems associated with selection into the program, Schady and Araujo present before-and-after comparisons and use random assignment as a plausible instrument for program participation. Their results indicate that the program was associated with a large increase in school enrollment. The effect was especially high compared with effects in similar studies in other Latin American countries. Most of the effect seems to be concentrated in transition grades (five or eight years of schooling), when dropout rates are especially high.

The authors then assess the role of the condition in explaining program effects by comparing households that indicated at follow-up that they believed that sending children to school was a requirement of the program (the conditioned households) with households that reported they did not have this perception (the unconditioned households). Although exposure to information about the program cannot be assumed to have been randomly assigned, the results seem to be robust to a variety of specifications, including a comprehensive set of controls, data trimming, and zeroing out of fixed differences between the two groups. The results indicate that most of the program effects seem to be driven by households that believed that there was a school enrollment condition attached to program participation. Interestingly, these reduced-form results are not inconsistent with predictions deriving from structural models of household decisionmaking in the presence of conditioned cash transfers.

There are few better examples of economic behavior that are both inefficient and unfair than discrimination in the labor market, defined as differential hiring or remuneration of workers with identical productivity, on the basis of characteristics such as race or gender. In "The Mystery of Discrimination in Latin America," Alberto Chong and Hugo Ñopo provide a rich overview of the evidence on the prevalence of this behavior in Latin American labor markets. The main theme is that the evidence from different sources paints a number of different pictures. In opinion surveys like Latinobarómetro, Latin Americans overwhelmingly report that discrimination is rampant in their countries. However, delving a little deeper reveals that interviewees and researchers appear to have different interpretations of the term *discrimination*. Interviewees often identify groups such as the poor or the uneducated as the main victims of discrimination.

The authors then turn to the econometric evidence on wage gaps from labor force and household surveys, using a propensity-score matching variant of the Oaxaca-Blinder wage gap decompositions (by ethnicity and gender). An interesting feature of these decompositions is that in addition to the returns and characteristics components, the matching approach yields a term that measures the extent to which the supports of the two groups (on their observed characteristics) overlap. Although this analysis confirms the presence of large wage gaps that cannot be accounted for by acquired human capital characteristics, the authors are careful not to interpret those gaps as providing categorical evidence of discrimination, since many relevant worker characteristics (which may be correlated with race or gender) are not observable through household surveys.

The paper reports on a third (altogether different) type of evidence bearing on discrimination, which arises from experimental attempts to "observe the unobservables." These attempts include randomized field trials in which identical résumés with different genders or class-revealing surnames were sent to prospective employers in Santiago; an experimental study monitoring the Peruvian government's job intermediation service in Lima; and games designed to study stereotypes, played in both Argentina and Peru. Surprisingly, these less conventional approaches suggest a much smaller role for discrimination than is evidenced in the opinion surveys and econometric analyses. Economic agents in Latin America thus seem to act according to economic or monetary incentives rather than on the basis of a propensity to discriminate purely on the basis of preferences. There is some evidence that the population shares beliefs about the potential performance of certain groups, but information and economic incentives trump the propensity to discriminate on the basis of those beliefs. The end result is an unresolved puzzle, in which opinion surveys imply that Latin Americans discriminate often, standard wage-gap decompositions suggest large unexplained wage gaps, and experimental studies point to the possibility that most of those stem from differences in unobserved characteristics. The authors do not claim to have solved the puzzle. By merely laying it out, however, they have contributed to much-needed further research on the true nature of discrimination in Latin America.

Increased efficiency and incentives for productivity growth are often argued to follow from greater trade openness and access to export markets. In the last two decades, however, Latin America has faced increasingly tough competition from other low-cost producers in the developing world, especially China. In "How Sensitive Are Latin American Exports to Chinese Competition in the U.S. Market?" Ernesto López-Córdova, Alejandro Micco, and Danielken Molina use U.S. import data (at the six-digit level) to investigate just how serious that competition has been in trade with the region's main single trading partner. The paper begins by estimating the elasticity of substitution of U.S. imports using detailed trade data over the 1990–2003 period and a two-stage least squares framework. The elasticity estimates for aggregate imports are in line with those of other recent studies. The authors also provide elasticity estimates at the sectoral level, which they use to assess the extent to which Latin American and Chinese goods compete in the U.S. market and to provide forecasts of how alternative policy scenarios could affect Latin American exports to the United States.

López-Córdova, Micco, and Molina simulate three main counterfactual scenarios: a currency revaluation in China, the elimination of U.S. tariffs on Latin American exports under a hemispheric free trade agreement, and the elimination of quotas on apparel and textile exports under the Multi-Fiber Agreement (MFA). They find that a 20 percent appreciation of the renminbi would reduce Chinese exports to the United States by a fifth. Aggregate U.S. imports would decline by 1.7 percent in response to that terms-of-trade shock, and all other regions would have some gain in export share, with Latin America gaining about 0.5 percentage point. Hemispheric free trade would increase Latin America's exports to the United States by around 3 percent. The removal of MFA quotas would lead to a sharp increase in Chinese sales to the United States (40 percent), while Latin America would see its share of the U.S. market decline by around 2 percent (2.5 percentage points). China's gains would come mainly at the expense of other regions.

Privatization has also been promoted as a reform that could engender greater efficiency across many parts of Latin America. The experience of the last decade, however, indicates that the effects of privatization can differ measurably, depending in large part on the quality of the regulatory environment within which the privatized companies operate. This is particularly important in sectors such as electricity, where prices have knock-on effects throughout the economy as well as direct effects on consumer welfare. In the final paper in this issue, "Cost Reductions, Cost Padding, and Stock Market Prices: The Chilean Experience with Price-Cap Regulation," Rafael Di Tella and Alexander Dyck provide an ingenious empirical test for the possibility that firms manipulate their costs to game price regulators. This has long been a concern in the theoretical literature on regulation and on price-cap regulation of monopolies, in particular. The paper reviews the experience of Chile's electricity system, where a price-cap system was introduced in the 1980s. While this form of regulation has become popular as a way of putting price pressure on firms, it may be subject to manipulation through the declaration of higher costs during the review period. This is precisely what Di Tella and Dyck find. Cost reduction appears to be U-shaped, with strong initial cost reduction every four years, coinciding with regulatory reviews. A possible explanation is that firms strategically declare (or actually incur) high costs until the regulator fixes the price, and they only then implement any feasible cost reductions.

To test this interpretation, the authors use stock market data to construct a measure of cumulative abnormal returns for regulated firms around their quarterly announcements, together with a measure of naïve cost expectations that excludes any indication of the occurrence of review periods. In general, cost reports in excess of naïve cost expectations have a negative effect on returns. The exception is cost surprises that occur during review periods, which increase abnormal returns. This is consistent with the hypothesis that strategic firms are successfully gaming the regulators. More generally, the results suggest that stock market information may be useful for complementing current regulatory procedures.

Some final acknowledgements are in order. This sixteenth issue of *Economía* contains two papers that were presented at the panel meeting held May 11–12, 2007, at Yale University's Macmillan Center in New Haven, Connecticut. It also contains three papers discussed at the panel meeting held at Universidad de los Andes in Bogotá, Colombia, on October 3, 2007. As always, thanks are due to all those involved in ensuring the success of those meetings, especially the associate editors of *Economía*, the members of the panel, and the managing editor, Catherine Mathieu-Canuto. The issue benefited enormously from their hard work.

PATRICK J. MCEWAN
MIGUEL URQUIOLA
EMILIANA VEGAS

# School Choice, Stratification, and Information on School Performance: Lessons from Chile

In the early 1980s, Chile implemented a nationwide school choice system, under which the government finances education via a flat per-student subsidy (or voucher) to the public or private school chosen by a family. At present, about 94 percent of all schools (public, religious, and secular private) are voucher funded. More than half of urban schools are private, and most of these operate as for-profit institutions.[1] Since the early 1990s, Chile has also publicized information on school performance and increased per pupil expenditure substantially.

Despite these and other reforms, Chile has found it challenging to improve students' learning outcomes.[2] Hsieh and Urquiola find that the country's relative performance in international tests did not change much between 1970 and 1999.[3] Its performance on the 2000 Programme for International Student Assessment (PISA) is not only much lower than the OECD average but is similar to that of other Latin American countries and low relative to countries with similar income per capita.[4]

McEwan is with Wellesley College; Urquiola is with Columbia University; Vegas is with the World Bank.

For useful conversations and comments, we thank Eduardo Engel, Francisco Ferreira, Francisco Gallego, Alejandra Mizala, and Reynaldo Fernandes. For generous funding, we thank the Institute for Social and Economic Research and Policy (ISERP) at Columbia University. Urquiola is also grateful for support from a National Academy of Education/Spencer Foundation Postdoctoral Fellowship.

1. Elacqua (2006).

2. In much of Latin America—not just Chile—the rapid progress in terms of quantity of education has not been matched by increases in quality, as measured, for example, by test scores (Hanushek and Woessman 2007; Vegas and Petrow 2007).

3. Hsieh and Urquiola (2006).

4. Vegas and Petrow (2007).

Recent discussions and events in Chile reflect disappointment consistent with such findings. For instance, Engel and Navia observe that Chile is doing relatively well in terms of education quantity, but confronts problems with respect to quality.[5] In 2006, student protests resulted in renewed government commitments to address education quality. Additionally, there was surprising agreement among candidates in the last presidential election that education policy should address high levels of inequality.

Chile's experience suggests that we have much to learn about the consequences of education reform, especially school choice, and why it has not resulted in learning gains of the magnitude one might have predicted. This paper addresses these issues in two ways. First, we review the previous literature on the impact of choice in Chile, focusing on the effects on average student achievement and stratification. The reform was implemented nationwide, without an experimental design. Naturally, identifying its causal effect is very difficult and the literature has yet to reach a consensus in this area. To shed additional light on this debate, we present new evidence from a regression-discontinuity design that supports previous findings that school choice—at least as it has been implemented until now—has increased stratification while having little effect on average achievement.

Second, we explore some factors that may explain why the evolution of school quality in Chile has been disappointing. We focus on the difficulties researchers have encountered in generating and interpreting information on school performance. Chile has been at the forefront of measuring, analyzing, and disseminating data on student achievement. Our research suggests three cautionary tales regarding such efforts. First, schools' average test scores are a very good proxy for average student income in Chile, so they are of limited use to either parents or policymakers in terms of identifying especially effective or high value added schools. Second, commonsense approaches to control for parent and student characteristics—such as analyzing school gains between years—yield volatile school rankings. That is, assessments about whether a given school is "good" or "bad" can change substantially between years, misleading parents and policymakers. Third, the presence of test-score volatility complicates the evaluation of education programs that are assigned on the basis of test scores. We show how this volatility in test scores produced misleading estimates of the impact of one of Chile's signature education programs in the early 1990s.

5. Engel and Navia (2006). The authors further note that there is little evidence of improvement either in Chile's own SIMCE tests or in the 1999 and 2003 rounds of the Third International Mathematics and Science Study (TIMSS).

We conclude by discussing the implications of our findings for current education policy in Chile. While we touch on multiple issues, we highlight three conclusions. First, over the past three decades, Chile's school system has improved its users' welfare along many dimensions. At the very least, choice is likely to have raised the welfare of some households by letting them attend schools of their preference. The evolution of aggregate learning outcomes has not been as satisfactory, however. Second, despite concerns regarding the use of test score information for accountability purposes, we argue that the Chilean government should continue to collect and improve the use of student performance data. Third, Chile would be in a position to learn much more if it were willing to credibly evaluate the myriad education initiatives it has introduced.

The rest of the paper proceeds as follows. The next section provides background on Chile's education system and describes the national student assessment system data. We then review evidence on the impact of Chile's school choice scheme on stratification and student achievement. The paper next discusses the challenges of using test score data to assess and improve education quality. Finally, we discuss policy implications.

## Background on Chile's Education System

Prior to the 1981 education reforms, three types of schools existed in Chile: fiscal or public schools were managed by the national Ministry of Education and accounted for about 80 percent of enrollments; unsubsidized private schools did not receive public funding, catered primarily to upper-income households, and accounted for about 6 percent of enrollments; and subsidized private schools did not charge tuition, received limited lump-sum public subsidies, were often religious (mostly Catholic), and accounted for roughly 14 percent of enrollment. This basic structure remained after the 1981 education reform, which had three main components. First, the ministry transferred fiscal school management to more than 300 municipalities, which began to receive a per-student subsidy for every child attending their schools. These schools retained their role as suppliers of last resort: they are not allowed to charge tuition, and they cannot turn away students unless they are overenrolled.[6] Second, subsidized (or voucher) private schools began to receive

6. Primary public schools cannot charge tuition; as of 1994, secondary schools can, but few actually do.

the same per-student subsidy as municipal schools. Unlike the latter, they have wide latitude regarding student selection and, as of 1994, are allowed to charge fees.[7] Third, unsubsidized, tuition-charging private schools have continued to operate without public funding. While they could have started to accept vouchers, the majority of these elite institutions chose not to do so.

By 2003, the two types of private institutions together accounted for about 45 percent of all schools, while voucher schools alone accounted for about 36 percent. In urban areas, these shares were 62 and 48 percent, respectively. As stated, private voucher schools can operate as for-profits, and Elacqua calculates that about 74 percent do so.[8]

Parent-reported data in table 1 confirm substantial differences in the income and fee payments of families in municipal and private schools, especially when compared to the six percent of students enrolled in unsubsidized private sector schools (the data are from a census of fourth grade students). The data also confirm anecdotal impressions and prior research, which suggest that private schools are more likely to subject parents to admissions requirements like exams, interviews, and requests for marriage or baptismal certificates.[9]

In 1988, Chile introduced a national student assessment system known as the *Sistema Nacional de Medición de la Calidad de la Educación,* or SIMCE (the Ministry of Education also administered tests between 1982 and 1984, under a different system). Three features of these data are relevant to our subsequent discussions. First, the SIMCE assesses all students in a single grade—namely, fourth, eighth, or tenth—in a given year. Second, student-level scores and socioeconomic characteristics are only available since 1997, when the Ministry began applying a detailed questionnaire to parents. Previously, test-score data were reported as school averages.[10] Third, the scores of individual students cannot presently be linked across time to form a true panel, which would permit further analyses of school and teacher effectiveness. In the next two sections, we review evidence on the effects of Chile's reforms, all of it using one or more years of the SIMCE assessments.

7. When private subsidized schools charge fees, the per-student subsidy is adjusted downward.

8. Elacqua (2006).

9. Gauri (1998).

10. Student-level data are available for a few years before 1997 but without corresponding information on students or families.

**TABLE 1. Fourth Grade Parent Characteristics in Municipal, Subsidized Private, and Unsubsidized Private Schools, 2005[a]**
Percent

| *Characteristic* | *Municipal* | *Subsidized private* | *Unsubsidized private* |
|---|---|---|---|
| Percent of total students | 50.2 | 43.6 | 6.2 |
| Monthly household income | | | |
| < 100,000 pesos | 35.0 | 14.7 | 0.1 |
| 100,000–200,000 pesos | 41.1 | 32.0 | 0.7 |
| 200,001–300,000 pesos | 12.5 | 18.7 | 1.4 |
| 301,000–400,000 pesos | 5.1 | 11.1 | 2.0 |
| > 400,000 pesos | 6.3 | 24.6 | 95.7 |
| Monthly school fee | | | |
| None | 71.4 | 22.5 | 0.6 |
| 1–4,999 pesos | 17.1 | 10.1 | 0 |
| 5,000–10,000 pesos | 9.8 | 22.8 | 0.2 |
| 10,001–20,000 pesos | 1.4 | 23.8 | 0.2 |
| > 20,000 pesos | 0.3 | 20.8 | 99.0 |
| Parent-reported requirements for school enrollment | | | |
| Civil marriage certificate | 4.8 | 8.8 | 23.1 |
| Church marriage certificate or certificate of baptism | 1.2 | 17.4 | 34.7 |
| Child attended play session | 1.8 | 5.7 | 27.6 |
| Child took entrance exam | 7.6 | 43.4 | 62.7 |
| Parent interview | 12.1 | 33.8 | 74.7 |

Source: 2005 SIMCE test.
a. The 2005 survey tested 259,852 fourth graders and included 233,458 parent responses for income, 232,667 for school fees, and 240,554 for enrollment requirements.

## School Choice and Its Impact on Stratification and Achievement

Economists expect that school choice aligns the incentives of school administrators and teachers with parental demand, thus improving productivity.[11] Recent theories of school markets suggest that choice might also increase stratification by income or other student characteristics. For example, Epple and Romano, on the one hand, and Urquiola and Verhoogen, on the other, present models which, despite emphasizing rather different mechanisms, hold that a system like Chile's would tend to produce sorting in terms of income or ability.[12]

11. Friedman (1955); Chubb and Moe (1990); Hoxby (2000).
12. Epple and Romano (1998, 2002) emphasize peer group effects in a setting in which students differ on both ability and income, while Urquiola and Verhoogen (forthcoming) focus on heterogeneous preferences over class size when students differ only on income.

In this section, we first review the main findings from previous research regarding the effects of choice on education outcomes and stratification in Chile. Second, we present new evidence using an alternate empirical approach focusing on census districts in Chile's Sixth Region.

### *Previous Evidence*

The most common way in which researchers have tried to evaluate the effects of school choice on student learning is by comparing the achievement of students who attend public and private schools. In some countries, though not in Chile, analysts have been able to address this question with the benefit of randomized designs.[13] While the small-scale experiments on which such research relies are well suited to analyzing partial equilibrium questions (such as what would happen to one student's outcomes if she shifted from the public to the private sector), such experiments are not suited to answering general equilibrium questions of the kind raised by Chile's experience (such as what would happen if many students shifted from the public to the private sector).[14] In the absence of true experiments, researchers have adopted quasi-experimental approaches to identify the general equilibrium effects of choice.[15]

In one of the earliest attempts, Hsieh and Urquiola apply a difference-in-differences approach to municipal-level data from 1982 to 1996.[16] The study suggests that municipalities that experienced faster growth in private school market shares show distinct signs of stratification consistent with so-called cream skimming (that is, the middle class exiting public schools) and do not

13. For example, Angrist and others (2002) find beneficial effects of private school scholarships in Colombia. In the United States, the evidence is significantly more mixed. Rouse (1998) finds evidence of rather modest effects in Milwaukee. See also the debate between Howell and Peterson (2002) and Krueger and Zhu (2004). For examples of nonexperimental, private/public comparisons of achievement in Chile, see Aedo and Larrañaga (1994); Bravo, Contreras, and Sanhueza (1999); McEwan and Carnoy (2000); Mizala and Romaguera (2000); McEwan (2001); Contreras (2002); Anand, Mizala, and Repetto (2006); Bellei (2007).

14. McEwan (2000b); Hsieh and Urquiola (2003). More specifically, if some input is behind the private advantage, but is also in fixed supply, then these two analyses can suggest rather different impacts of choice. For example, suppose that peer quality is better in the private sector, and that this generates a causal private advantage. As the private sector expands (as happened in Chile), its peer quality advantage will dissipate, and this could lower average achievement depending on the functional form of peer effects (Hsieh and Urquiola, 2003).

15. For studies that explore the effects of choice on average achievement and stratification in the United States, see Hoxby (2000); Urquiola (2005); Rothstein (2006).

16. Hsieh and Urquiola (2003, 2006).

seem to have experienced higher growth in average outcomes.[17] The key weakness with these estimates—despite the use of some candidate instrumental variables—is that private entry into school markets is endogenous. For instance, if outcomes had been declining in areas where the private sector grew more, these effects would underestimate the salutary effects of competition.

Auguste and Valenzuela analyze the 2000 cross-section of SIMCE data, using distance to a nearby city as an instrument for the private market share.[18] They also find evidence of sorting or cream skimming, but in contrast to Hsieh and Urquiola, they find significant positive effects on achievement. The key assumption in their analysis—that distance affects education outcomes only through its effect on private school entry—is not beyond suspicion, however. It is possible, for example, that more motivated parents migrate toward cities in search of better schools.

Gallego focuses on the 2002 cross-section of SIMCE data, using the density of priests per diocese as an instrument for the number of subsidized schools relative to public schools.[19] He finds substantial effects of the competition proxy on average student achievement. An issue to consider is that priests are unlikely to have ever been randomly allocated. For instance, to the extent that they tend to be concentrated in urban areas, concerns emerge similar to those in Auguste and Valenzuela.[20] Unlike the two previous studies, Gallego does not analyze the effects of private entry on stratification.

All of the above results are reduced form, meaning they are, at best, informative of the net effect of choice on achievement and stratification, and they do not reveal the channels through which these effects might have operated. For instance, stratification could stem from certain schools' actively seeking to screen out poor or low-performing children or from the parents' of such children choosing not to apply to these institutions. The distinction between

17. McEwan (2000a) reports difference-in-differences results on achievement that are consistent with these findings, using a pooled sample of public and private school observations from 1982 to 1996.

18. Auguste and Valenzuela (2006).

19. Gallego (2006).

20. A further issue is that Gallego's instrument, unlike the one used by Auguste and Valenzuela (2006), does not correspond neatly with local school markets. There are currently twenty-six dioceses in Chile (versus more than 300 municipalities, for example). A given market (for example, the capital of a municipality) could have a relatively high number of priests despite being in a low-density diocese.

these processes is subtle and very difficult to identify, and the above strategies provide almost no leverage in this regard.

In short, the literature assessing the effect of school choice on average outcomes in Chile continues to be controversial (less so in the case of the effects on stratification). However, this evidence needs to be considered alongside aggregate levels and trends. If the effects of choice on average school productivity were indeed large, then one would expect Chile's relative performance on international tests to have improved over time.[21] Furthermore, one would expect Chile to outperform other countries with similar levels of gross domestic product per capita. None of these predictions are borne out by empirical research.[22]

## *New Evidence from Census Districts*

Prior research is hard-pressed to identify exogenous variation in the entry of private schools. To cast further light on these issues, we rely on the discontinuous relationship between the size of a local schooling market—proxied by the population of school-aged children—and the probability that a private school enters that market. This approach is motivated by the observation that private schools are more likely to locate in heavily populated areas.[23] By itself, this provides little leverage to identify the causal impact of private school entry, since population is also correlated with variables unobserved by the researcher. However, theory from industrial organization implies a discontinuous relationship between population and private school entry, as private schools pass a profitability threshold.[24] The intuition is that a private school will only enter a market in which a public school already exists if the market is large enough to sustain two schools whose production functions display economies of scale (that is, firms need to be large enough to break even).

Suppose that private schools only enter local markets when the market size exceeds a population threshold. One might assume that local schooling markets—actually small towns—are similar in small intervals on either side of this threshold, both along variables observed by the researcher (such as household incomes) and along those that might be unobserved. To estimate

21. As this paper went to press, results from PISA 2006 were publicized, suggesting Chile might finally be on a trend of relative improvement. We do not analyze those results here owing to timing issues; furthermore, whether this trend is substantial and sustained remains to be seen.

22. Hsieh and Urquiola (2003).

23. Auguste and Valenzuela (2006); Hsieh and Urquiola (2006).

24. Bresnahan and Reiss (1987, 1991).

the impact of private school entry on stratification or achievement, one could therefore compare the outcomes of treated local markets just above the threshold to their untreated counterparts just below.[25] This is a naturally occurring variant of the regression-discontinuity design in which an assignment variable (local market size) and assignment cutoffs (population thresholds) determine whether local markets are treated by private school entry.[26]

The implementation of this approach hinges on identifying local schooling markets. Previous research on Chile almost always aggregates data at the municipal level. These jurisdictions can be large, and they often encompass many dispersed communities that are in fact separate school markets, especially in rural areas. Thus, they are not an adequate unit with which to capture the type of isolated communities that will contain the potentially discontinuous variation required by the research design.[27]

To address this challenge, we collected pilot data on the precise location of primary schools in Chile's Sixth Region, which is located south of Santiago (its geographical extension is 3,200 square miles, about twice the size of Rhode Island).[28] We merged schools' locations with geocoded data from Chile's 2002 population census, including the boundaries of 187 local census districts that fall within thirty-three larger municipalities. Table 2 reports descriptive statistics on the sample. The median census district contains two schools, but 34 percent of them contain only one. Only one district has a private enrollment rate above 60 percent.

Panel A of figure 1 presents two variables on separate *y* axes: household income and average fourth grade (math and language) test scores, both graphed against fourth grade enrollment. In Chile, enrollment in primary grades is close to universal.[29] We may therefore interpret the districtwide fourth grade

25. In practical terms, many authors estimate the average difference in outcomes, local to the threshold, by regressing the dependent variable on smooth polynomials of the assignment variable and a dummy variable indicating values above the threshold (van der Klaauw 2002).

26. The regression-discontinuity design has been applied to a range of issues in the economics of education. In Chile, it has been used to study the impact of the P-900 program, discussed below (Chay, McEwan, and Urquiola 2005), and the effect of delayed primary school enrollment (McEwan and Shapiro 2008).

27. An alternative is to use smaller jurisdictions, such as the more compact *localidad* identified in some Chilean data sets. However, the *localidad* is an informal unit and is thus inconsistently applied by the National Institute of Statistics (INE) and the Ministry of Education.

28. The geographic data collection was funded by Columbia University's Institute for Social and Economic Research and Policy (ISERP) and implemented by a private firm. We also drew on existing geographic data collected by Chile's National Institute of Statistics (INE) and the government of the Sixth Region.

29. Urquiola and Calderón (2006).

**TABLE 2. Descriptive Statistics, Sixth Region Census District Sample**

| *Variable* | *Mean* | *Std. dev.* | *Minimum* | *Maximum* | *No. observations* |
|---|---|---|---|---|---|
| Total fourth grade enrollment | 80.7 | 116.1 | 2.0 | 708.0 | 187 |
| Fourth grade enroll. in public schools | 57.7 | 70.1 | 0.0 | 421.0 | 187 |
| Fourth grade enroll. in subsidized private schools | 19.6 | 56.4 | 0.0 | 478.0 | 187 |
| Fourth grade enroll. in unsubsidized private schools | 3.5 | 18.0 | 0.0 | 161.0 | 187 |
| Number of public schools | 2.2 | 1.5 | 0.0 | 10.0 | 187 |
| Number of subsidized private schools | 0.5 | 1.2 | 0.0 | 11.0 | 187 |
| Number of unsubsidized private schools | 0.1 | 0.4 | 0.0 | 3.0 | 187 |
| Private enrollment rate | 0.103 | 0.148 | 0 | 0.577 | 187 |
| Income | 153.4 | 116.6 | 50.0 | 888.0 | 172 |
| Average test score (math and language) | 238.1 | 21.4 | 192.9 | 311.6 | 172 |
| Relative income (public to total) | 0.92 | 0.19 | 0.14 | 1.00 | 168 |
| Relative mothers' schooling (public to total) | 0.97 | 0.07 | 0.61 | 1.00 | 168 |
| Relative test score (public to total) | 0.98 | 0.04 | 0.78 | 1.00 | 168 |

Source: Authors' calculations, using geocoded school location, census, and SIMCE data for the Sixth Region.

**FIGURE 1. Market Size, Private Enrollment, Income, and Test Scores**

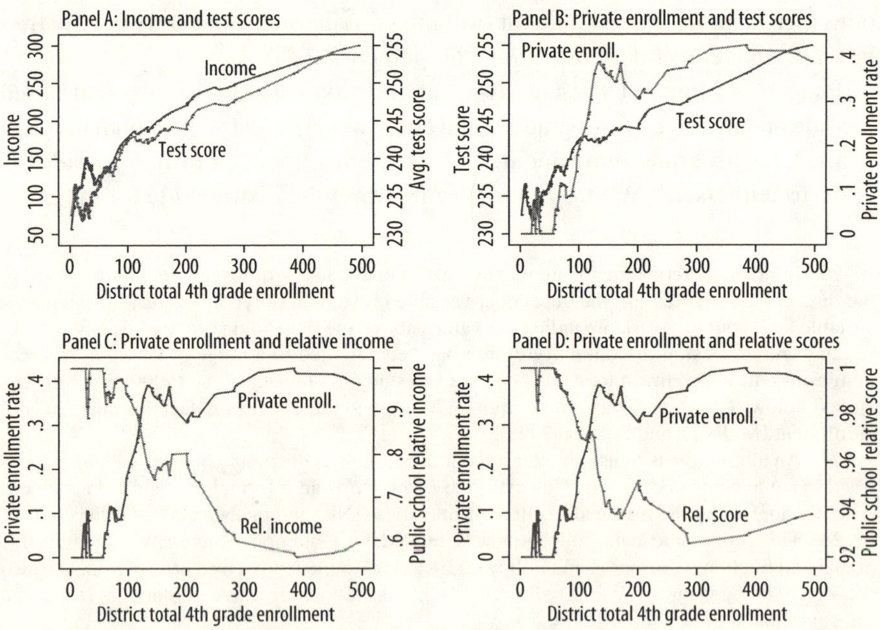


Source: 2002 Census, 2002 SIMCE test, enrollment files, and authors' calculations.

enrollments as a proxy for market size. Both variables rise steadily with district enrollments, suggesting higher average incomes and test scores in larger communities, as observed in many other countries.[30] Furthermore, the overlap between these two lines confirms a correlation between income and test scores.

Panel B copies the segment related to test scores from panel A and adds a segment describing the relation between the private enrollment rate of census districts and our measure of market size. The segment shows that the private share is close to zero in the districts with the fewest students, and it rises sharply in districts with roughly 100 to 150 students. While the change is not altogether discrete, as would be ideal, the share reaches almost 40 percent at around 150 students and remains stable thereafter. The panel provides no evidence of a sharp change in test scores between 100 and 150 students, the vicinity of the relatively sharp rise in private enrollment. If the entry of a more effective private school (and any associated public response) caused school productivity to rise substantially in this range, one might expect test scores and income to diverge in the 100–150 student range. In fact, panel A reveals that they track each other relatively closely in this range.

Panels C and D present evidence that private school entry is associated with discrete changes in the amount of within-market stratification by family income and test scores. In panel C, the *y* axis variables are the private enrollment rate and the ratio of average public student income to the average among all students (so the ratio equals one in census districts with no private schools).[31] Panel C illustrates that this ratio declines sharply in precisely the enrollment range at which private enrollment jumps, suggesting that relatively higher-income students depart public schools once they have a private alternative. In panel D, the same pattern is evident for relative public school test scores.

The evidence in figure 1 suggests that private school entry increases within-district stratification, with no corresponding (sharp) change in average test scores. This finding is consistent with previous evidence from Chile indicating that school choice led to sorting, with no clear improvements in average achievement. We only view the current evidence as suggestive, however, given two caveats. First, it is drawn from a small sample in Chile's Sixth Region, and it remains to be seen whether the patterns would be robust to the inclusion of additional census districts and the use of regression analyses

30. See, for instance, the correlations between market size and socioeconomic status indicated by Angrist and Lavy (1999) and Urquiola (2006) for Israel and Bolivia, respectively.

31. For similar analyses at the municipal level, see Hsieh and Urquiola (2003, 2006).

(which are difficult to conduct with our reduced sample sizes). Second, the evidence is best generalized to small rural communities, although the pattern of results is consistent with evidence from a broader sample and different methods.[32]

## Using Test Scores to Improve Schools: Cautionary Tales

Chile has emerged as a regional leader in the application of standardized achievement tests and the dissemination of their results. For instance, schools' unadjusted average SIMCE scores have been published in Chilean newspapers since the mid-1990s. Economists envision three roles for such information, particularly in a liberalized schooling market. First, test score data may assist parents in choosing effective (or high value added) schools. Second, and more recently, governments have used functions of schools' measured performance to directly allocate rewards, sanctions, and assistance. The most prominent example is the federal No Child Left Behind Act in the United States.[33] In Chile, the Ministry of Education has also used test scores to allocate aid and rewards since the 1990s. For example, schools with low average test scores received additional resources and training in the P-900 program, implemented in the 1990s, while schools with high scores receive merit bonuses under the ongoing *Sistema Nacional de Evaluación de Desempeño de Establecimientos Educacionales* (SNED).[34] Third, economists increasingly use student assessment data to evaluate the impact of education programs and policies. The following subsections describe three reasons why some caution is warranted in using test score data to support each role.

### *Test Score Levels Reflect Socioeconomic Status*

One of the simplest measures of school performance is the unadjusted cross-sectional mean (or level) of students' test scores. This measure undoubtedly contains information on the contribution of schools, but as the Coleman Report and related studies revealed, it also reflects the influence of students' socioeconomic status.[35]

32. Hsieh and Urquiola (2006).
33. Hanushek and Raymond (2005).
34. On the P-900 program, see Chay, McEwan, and Urquiola (2005); on SNED, see Mizala and Urquiola (2008).
35. Coleman and others (1966).

Consequently, in a context of extensive school-based stratification, school rankings based on unadjusted average test score levels might mainly reflect student socioeconomic status. Mizala, Romaguera, and Urquiola examine this issue with eight rounds of SIMCE data between 1997 and 2004, using a sample of 701 schools for which test score and socioeconomic data are consistently available.[36] In each case, schools' average language scores are regressed on mothers' and fathers' schooling and household income.[37] Depending on the year, between 70 and 85 percent of the variation in test scores can be explained by this small set of observable characteristics, suggesting that a ranking based on schools' average test scores may not be very different from one based on students' socioeconomic information. To explore this possibility, the authors consider two hypothetical programs that selected the top fifth of performers using different rules: one ranks schools according to their mean language score in SIMCE data, and the other ranks schools according to average mothers' schooling, reported in the same surveys. They show that these rules agree on the selection or exclusion of about 85 percent of all schools; a similar correspondence results for a program that selected the bottom fifth of performers.

These findings raise two issues. First, it is not clear that schools' test score levels are correlated with their true value added.[38] For example, one might imagine an exceptionally productive school that enrolls predominantly low-income children or, likewise, a rich school with unexceptional administrators and teachers. In such cases, access to information on test score levels may not improve parents' ability to choose the most productive schools. Indeed, it may simply reinforce stratification or reward inefficiency if it encourages parents to choose low value added schools serving wealthy children. This could be entirely consistent with rational parents' desire to improve their children's achievement, however, if they believe that exposure to wealthy peers could improve longer-run outcomes. Second, government accountability programs that purport to identify, reward, or sanction "good" or "bad" schools—that is, those with high or low value added—can misallocate resources if they rely exclusively on test score levels.

36. Mizala, Romaguera, and Urquiola (2007).

37. For complete details on variables and specifications, see Mizala, Romaguera, and Urquiola (2007).

38. Below, we show that schools with lower test score levels in 1988 actually have higher gains in subsequent years (where gain scores are one proxy for schools' value added). However, we suggest that this is an artifact of testing noise and mean reversion, rather than schools' true value added.

**FIGURE 2. School Performance and School Size: Fourth Grade Language Scores**

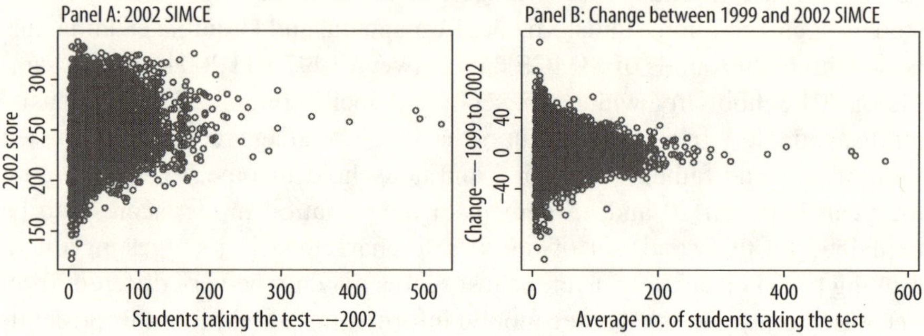


Source: 1999 and 2002 SIMCE language scores and authors' calculations.

### *Controlling for Socioeconomic Status Can Raise Volatility of School Rankings*

A reasonable response to the problems of using unadjusted test scores is to use additional data and methods to control for students' socioeconomic status and obtain a better estimate of schools' value added.[39] One challenging aspect of such analyses is that many family and student variables are unobserved by the researcher, and their omission from statistical specifications potentially biases estimates of school effects. A less well known but nonetheless important challenge, however, is that controlling for socioeconomic status often comes at the expense of introducing volatility into the test score rankings of schools, especially in a stratified school system like Chile's.[40]

What might produce volatility in schools' test performance? First, one-time events, such as a schoolwide illness or distraction on the testing day, could influence test scores.[41] Second, there is sampling variation, since each cohort of students that enters a school is analogous to a random draw from a local population. A school's average performance will thus vary with the specific group of students starting school in any given year. This variance, in turn, depends on the variability of performance in the population from which the school draws its students and the number of students tested.

Chay, McEwan, and Urquiola verify the implication that scores should be more variable in schools with lower enrollment.[42] Figure 2 (panel A) pre-

39. Hanushek and Raymond (2003).
40. Mizala, Romaguera, and Urquiola (2007).
41. Kane and Staiger (2001).
42. Chay, McEwan, and Urquiola (2005).

sents a similar analysis using fourth grade test scores from the 2002 SIMCE. Smaller schools tend to display greater variability in their performance, where school enrollment (on the *x* axis) is measured by the number of fourth grade students who took the test.

Test-score volatility is even more pronounced when we use measures that arguably do a better job of controlling for student socioeconomic status, such as changes in school performance between separate cohorts of fourth graders (1999 and 2002). This measure is appealing to the extent that it controls for time-invariant characteristics of schools, and it better approximates value added.[43] The measure is also relevant since it is used in accountability schemes throughout the world.[44] Panel B in figure 2 shows that the inverse relationship between school size and performance variability becomes even more pronounced—smaller schools on average improved no more or less than larger schools, but their performance is much more volatile.

To explore how volatility in school test scores affects school rankings, we consider a fictitious program that identifies the top 20 percent of schools in each of eight years (see table 3).[45] As a benchmark, suppose that schools' performance does not vary over time. The column labeled "certainty" contains the distribution that one would observe if schools' performance were stable: 80 percent of schools would never appear in the top quintile, and 20 percent would be in this category all eight years. The opposite benchmark supplies the percentages that would be observed if the program were a lottery—that is, if all schools had independent 0.2 probabilities of being selected each year. In this case, one would expect that over the eight years, 17 percent of schools would never get selected. The modal school would end up in the top quintile only once, and no school would be selected every year. The table also summarizes the results that emerge using actual test score levels over eight years. The observed distribution is fairly close to the distribution under stable school performance. This is not surprising given that, as stated, this measure substantially reflects socioeconomic status, and that schools' position in the relative socioeconomic status distribution is relatively stable over time. Finally, the table presents the results of using the eight cross-sections of data to calculate seven observations of changes in mean test scores. The actual distribution in this case is very close to that of a lottery. Over eight years, more than

43. Mizala, Romaguera, and Urquiola (2007) also explore the use of regression residuals left after controlling for observed socioeconomic status.

44. Hanushek and Raymond (2003).

45. This exercise follows Kane and Staiger (2001).

**TABLE 3. Frequencies in Top or Bottom 20 Percent Produced by Different Rankings**

| | *Levels* | | | *Change in test score* | | |
|---|---|---|---|---|---|---|
| *Frequency* | *Certainty* | *Lottery* | *Actual* | *Certainty* | *Lottery* | *Actual* |
| A. No. times school in top 20 percent | | | | | | |
| Never | 80.0 | 16.7 | 59.3 | 80.0 | 21.0 | 16.6 |
| 1 year | 0.0 | 33.6 | 9.1 | 0.0 | 36.7 | 40.0 |
| 2 years | 0.0 | 29.4 | 5.0 | 0.0 | 27.5 | 31.7 |
| 3 years | 0.0 | 14.7 | 5.7 | 0.0 | 11.5 | 10.7 |
| 4 years | 0.0 | 4.6 | 5.3 | 0.0 | 2.9 | 1.4 |
| 5 years | 0.0 | 0.9 | 3.0 | 0.0 | 0.4 | 0.0 |
| 6 years | 0.0 | 0.0 | 3.9 | 0.0 | 0.0 | 0.0 |
| 7 years | 0.0 | 0.0 | 4.1 | 20.0 | 0.0 | 0.0 |
| All 8 years | 20.0 | 0.0 | 4.6 | . . . | . . . | . . . |
| B. No. times school in bottom 20 percent | | | | | | |
| Never | 80.0 | 16.7 | 68.1 | 80.0 | 21.0 | 19.1 |
| 1 year | 0.0 | 33.6 | 5.1 | 0.0 | 36.7 | 34.7 |
| 2 years | 0.0 | 29.4 | 2.3 | 0.0 | 27.5 | 33.5 |
| 3 years | 0.0 | 14.7 | 1.4 | 0.0 | 11.5 | 11.7 |
| 4 years | 0.0 | 4.6 | 3.9 | 0.0 | 2.9 | 1.0 |
| 5 years | 0.0 | 0.9 | 3.9 | 0.0 | 0.4 | 0.0 |
| 6 years | 0.0 | 0.0 | 2.6 | 0.0 | 0.0 | 0.0 |
| 7 years | 0.0 | 0.0 | 5.9 | 20.0 | 0.0 | 0.0 |
| All 8 years | 20.0 | 0.0 | 7.0 | . . . | . . . | . . . |
| C. Schools ever in top and bottom 20 percent | | | | | | |
| Percentage | . . . | . . . | 0.3 | . . . | . . . | 72.5 |

Source: Mizala, Romaguera, and Urquiola (2007).
. . . Not applicable.

80 percent of schools would have been in the top performing group at some point, and more than 70 percent would have been in both the best and worst performing groups.

This last finding suggests that employing measures that better control for socioeconomic status results in an undesirable trade-off. While the school rankings may contain some signal of school effectiveness, the added volatility raises concerns. First, ever-shifting conclusions about the "best" or "worst" schools may lead parents to sort across schools inefficiently. Hanushek, Kain, and Rivkin, for instance, argue that higher student turnover can entail significant negative externalities.[46] Second, teachers and school administrators might begin to respond less to incentive programs whose ex post allocations resemble a lottery.

46. Hanushek, Kain, and Rivkin (2004).

**FIGURE 3. Municipality Size Measured by the Number of Fourth Grade Test Takers, 1990 and 2002**[a]

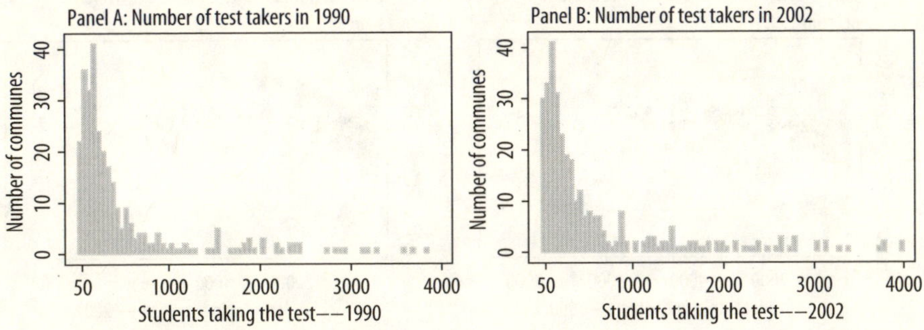


Source: 1990 and 2002 SIMCE test and authors' calculations.
a. For clarity, the figures exclude between five and ten municipalities in which more than 4,000 students took the respective exam.

## *Volatility Concerns Persist with Aggregate Data*

The concerns highlighted above have been raised mostly in the context of school- or classroom-level information. There is consensus that these issues would be mitigated if data were aggregated to higher levels, such as cities or states. The intuition is that averaging across large numbers of schools or students will reduce the influence of one-time, school-specific events, as well as of sampling variation among smaller schools.

In Chile, the municipality is a policy-relevant unit of aggregation at least for public schools, since municipalities are responsible for school management. For this reason, Engel, Mizala, and Romaguera list the most and least improved municipalities in terms of SIMCE performance, and they call on voters to hold their mayors accountable for this performance.[47]

One must single out such "good" or "bad" municipalities with care, however, because volatility concerns persist even with data aggregated to this level. Many municipalities are small as measured by the number of children that take the SIMCE test in a given year. Panel A in figure 3 shows that in 1990, fifty or fewer students took the fourth grade SIMCE test in twenty-one of 315 municipalities, and a hundred or fewer students took it in fifty-four municipalities. While there are also large municipalities (sixty-six had more

47. Eduardo Engel, Alejandra Mizala, and Pilar Romaguera, "Educación municipal: qué tal lo ha hecho su alcalde?" *La Tercera,* 19 September 2004.

**FIGURE 4. Average Language Score and Municipality Size, 1999 and 2002**

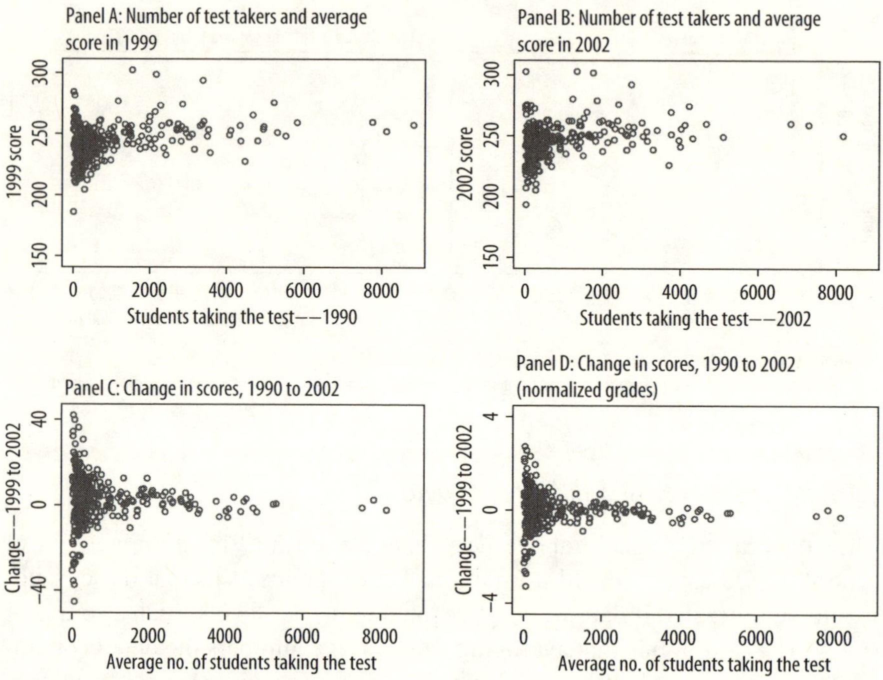


Source: SIMCE, 1990 and 2002, and authors' calculations.

than 1,000 test takers), the data indicate that several municipalities have fewer students than a large school in Santiago.[48] Panel B in figure 3 presents similar data for 2002. Despite a decade's worth of population growth, twenty-six of 337 municipalities had fewer than fifty test takers, and sixty-two had fewer than a hundred.

Figure 4 shows that there is more variation in the performance of smaller jurisdictions than larger ones at the municipal level. Panel A presents the average language score in each municipality in 1999 ordered against the total number of test takers; panel B presents similar evidence for 2002. In both years, the general inverse relationship between size and performance variability is observed. Panel C focuses on the change in scores between 1999 and

48. The mean municipality has approximately 730 students, with a standard deviation of about 1,150.

2002 and shows that, as with school-level data, extreme cases of municipal-level improvement or worsening are most likely found among the smaller jurisdictions.

Table 4 shows that small municipalities dominate in a listing of the ten best and worst municipalities in language performance in 1990 and 2002. In both years, the list of top performers selected from the full sample features municipalities with high levels of income and parental schooling, such as some of the wealthier neighborhoods in Santiago (namely, Providencia, Vitacura, and Las Condes). Some extremely small municipalities like Torres del Paine (in 1990) and Primavera are also among the top performers—with five and seventeen test takers, respectively. Very small municipalities also figure among the worst performers. For comparison, table 4 includes lists that restrict the sample to ninety-seven municipalities with at least 350 students taking the SIMCE in both 1990 and 2002.

Finally, table 5, analogous to the school-level table 3, uses SIMCE test scores for 1990, 1992, 1994, 1996, 1999, and 2002 (that is, the years since 1990 in which the SIMCE was administered at the fourth grade level) to explore the extent to which issues of ranking volatility persist with municipal-level data. The results show that while rankings based on municipalities' absolute scores are relatively stable (even more so than with schools), rankings using changes in scores are still hard to distinguish from a lottery.

### *Volatile School Rankings Can Bias Evaluations*

Economists are increasingly interested in evaluating school interventions that are assigned on the basis of test scores, such as the rewards and sanctions distributed by school accountability programs. The volatility of test-based measures raised in the previous section can affect these evaluations. Consider a ranking of schools by their mean test scores, used to identify the "worst" schools for inclusion in a program. Our discussion suggests that such schools are likely to be disproportionately small, as a result of sampling variation and an unlucky draw of students. Unless the bad luck is systematically repeated in the next year—which is unlikely if random events or sampling variation are the culprit—then we would expect the average score among these schools to bounce back in subsequent years. This mean reversion can easily be mistaken for a positive program effect. In the opposite case, schools with extremely positive scores in one year might dip in the following year, which could be mistaken for a negative program effect. In both cases, common evaluation approaches can over- or underestimate the size of program effects.

**TABLE 4. The Best- and Worst-Performing Municipalities in 1990 and 2002**

| | *Full sample* | | | *Large municipalities* | | | |
|---|---|---|---|---|---|---|---|
| *Year and ranking* | *Municipality* | *Grade* | *No. students* | *Ranking* | *Municipality* | *Grade* | *No. students* |
| 1990 results | | | | | | | |
| 1 | Providencia | 80.5 | 2,197 | 1 | Providencia | 80.5 | 2,197 |
| 2 | Torres del Paine | 79.3 | 5 | 2 | Las Condes | 76.4 | 4,412 |
| 3 | Las Condes | 76.4 | 4,412 | 3 | Ñuñoa | 71.7 | 2,915 |
| 4 | Pumanque | 74.6 | 65 | 4 | La Reina | 71.6 | 1,522 |
| 5 | Primavera | 74.0 | 17 | 5 | Santiago | 68.8 | 7,479 |
| 6 | Ñuñoa | 71.7 | 2,915 | 6 | Punta Arenas | 67.0 | 1,910 |
| 7 | La Reina | 71.6 | 1,522 | 7 | Arica | 66.9 | 3,270 |
| 8 | Navarino | 71.1 | 36 | 8 | Villa Alemana | 66.5 | 1,058 |
| 9 | Porvenir | 70.1 | 87 | 9 | Coyhaique | 65.8 | 876 |
| 10 | Santiago | 68.8 | 7,479 | 10 | Iquique | 65.7 | 2,886 |
| . . . | | | | . . . | | | |
| 306 | Lumaco | 42.9 | 166 | 88 | Monte Patria | 51.7 | 504 |
| 307 | Ercilla | 42.7 | 173 | 89 | Calbuco | 51.6 | 368 |
| 308 | Chaco | 42.3 | 137 | 90 | Paine | 51.1 | 624 |
| 309 | Lonquimay | 41.2 | 172 | 91 | Nueva Imperial | 50.5 | 390 |
| 310 | Quellen | 40.7 | 45 | 92 | La Pintana | 50.5 | 2,343 |
| 311 | Curarrehue | 40.3 | 77 | 93 | Cañete | 50.2 | 674 |
| 312 | Saavedra | 40.1 | 139 | 94 | Collipulli | 49.7 | 438 |
| 313 | Tirua | 39.1 | 246 | 95 | Panguipulli | 48.9 | 603 |
| 314 | Empedrado | 37.4 | 94 | 96 | Los Alamos | 48.6 | 452 |
| 315 | Colchane | 35.1 | 12 | 97 | Longavi | 46.5 | 493 |
| 2002 results | | | | | | | |
| 1 | Vitacura | 303.2 | 1,330 | 1 | Vitacura | 303.0 | 1,330 |
| 2 | Providencia | 299.1 | 1,758 | 2 | Providencia | 299.1 | 1,758 |
| 3 | Primavera | 297.3 | 10 | 3 | Las Condes | 291.9 | 2,733 |
| 4 | Las Condes | 291.9 | 2,733 | 4 | Lo Barnechea | 279.0 | 1,211 |
| 5 | Lo Barnechea | 279.4 | 1,211 | 5 | La Reina | 276.3 | 1,852 |
| 6 | La Reina | 276.3 | 1852 | 6 | Ñuñoa | 274.1 | 2,398 |
| 7 | Navarino | 276.1 | 45 | 7 | Santiago | 272.6 | 4,215 |
| 8 | Ñuñoa | 274.1 | 2,398 | 8 | San Miguel | 267.3 | 1,585 |
| 9 | Santiago | 272.6 | 4,215 | 9 | Concepcion | 267.1 | 3,756 |
| 10 | Hualañe | 271.6 | 149 | 10 | Macul | 262.0 | 1,505 |
| . . . | | | | . . . | | | |
| 324 | Yerbas Buenas | 216.7 | 172 | 88 | Graneros | 233.7 | 486 |
| 325 | Quilaco | 215.7 | 53.5 | 89 | Lo Espejo | 232.5 | 1,503 |
| 326 | S. Juan de la Costa | 215.4 | 143 | 90 | Victoria | 231.6 | 664 |
| 327 | Tolten | 212.7 | 181 | 91 | Padre las Casas | 231.4 | 1,046 |
| 328 | Galvarino | 211.5 | 224 | 92 | Monte Patria | 230.9 | 531 |
| 329 | La Higuera | 210.1 | 59 | 93 | Longavi | 230.0 | 416 |
| 330 | Huara | 209.4 | 28 | 94 | Lautaro | 229.0 | 586 |
| 331 | Til-Til | 209.3 | 279 | 95 | Panguipulli | 226.0 | 596 |
| 332 | Saavedra | 201.9 | 272 | 96 | La Pintana | 225.6 | 3,691 |
| 333 | Colchane | 191.4 | 23 | 97 | Nueva Imperial | 224.0 | 578 |

Source: 1990 and 2002 SIMCE test and authors' calculations.

**TABLE 5. Frequencies in Top or Bottom 20 Percent Produced by Different Rankings, Municipal-Level Observations**[a]

| | *Levels* | | | *Change in relative score* | | |
|---|---|---|---|---|---|---|
| *Frequency* | *Certainty* | *Lottery* | *Actual* | *Certainty* | *Lottery* | *Actual* |
| A. No. times school in top 20 percent | | | | | | |
| Never | 80 | 26.2 | 56.7 | 80 | 32.8 | 32.5 |
| 1 year | 0 | 39.3 | 11.4 | 0 | 41.0 | 34.2 |
| 2 years | 0 | 24.6 | 7.3 | 0 | 20.5 | 20.8 |
| 3 years | 0 | 8.2 | 5.6 | 0 | 5.1 | 6.4 |
| 4 years | 0 | 1.5 | 5.6 | 0 | 1.0 | 2.9 |
| 5 years | 0 | 0.1 | 4.7 | 20 | 0.0 | 3.2 |
| All 6 years | 20 | 0.0 | 8.8 | ... | ... | ... |
| B. No. times school in bottom 20 percent | | | | | | |
| Never | 80 | 26.2 | 57.6 | 80 | 32.8 | 36.6 |
| 1 year | 0 | 39.3 | 14.9 | 0 | 41.0 | 36.6 |
| 2 years | 0 | 24.6 | 8.5 | 0 | 20.5 | 23.7 |
| 3 years | 0 | 8.2 | 6.1 | 0 | 5.1 | 3.2 |
| 4 years | 0 | 1.5 | 3.8 | 0 | 1.0 | 0.0 |
| 5 years | 0 | 0.1 | 6.1 | 20 | 0.0 | 0.0 |
| All 6 years | 20 | 0.0 | 2.9 | ... | ... | ... |

Source: SIMCE tests (1990, 1992, 1994, 1996, 1999, and 2002) and authors' calculations.

... Not applicable.

a. Panel A refers to a hypothetical program that would select the top 20 percent of municipalities, and panel B presents an analogous exercise for a program that would select the bottom 20 percent. Columns 1 and 4 describe the distribution that would be observed over the six years under "certainty," for test score levels and changes, respectively. Columns 2 and 5 provide the distribution that would be obtained if the program were a lottery, for levels and changes, respectively.

In the early 1990s, Chile's 900 Schools Program (or P-900), later renamed and modified by the Ministry of Education, consisted of a targeted intervention to a group of schools that received improvements in infrastructure, instructional materials, teacher training workshops, and after-school tutoring workshops for children not performing at grade level.[49] The program's initial assignment, in the 1990 school year, was primarily based on 1988 SIMCE test scores. Schools in thirteen regions were ranked from best to worst. Separate cutoff scores were established for each region, and schools that scored below the cutoff score were preselected to participate, although some were subsequently removed.[50]

Panel A in figure 5 illustrates a stylized version of the assignment rule by plotting, on the *x* axis, the average score of each school in the year used to determine school rankings (called the prescore) and, on the *y* axis, the treatment status of the school, which takes a value of 0 or 1. The prescores range

49. Chay, McEwan, and Urquiola (2005).

50. This removal has important methodological implications that we gloss over here; they are discussed at length in Chay, McEwan, and Urquiola (2005).

**FIGURE 5. Hypothetical Assignment of P-900 Schools and Effects on Test Scores**

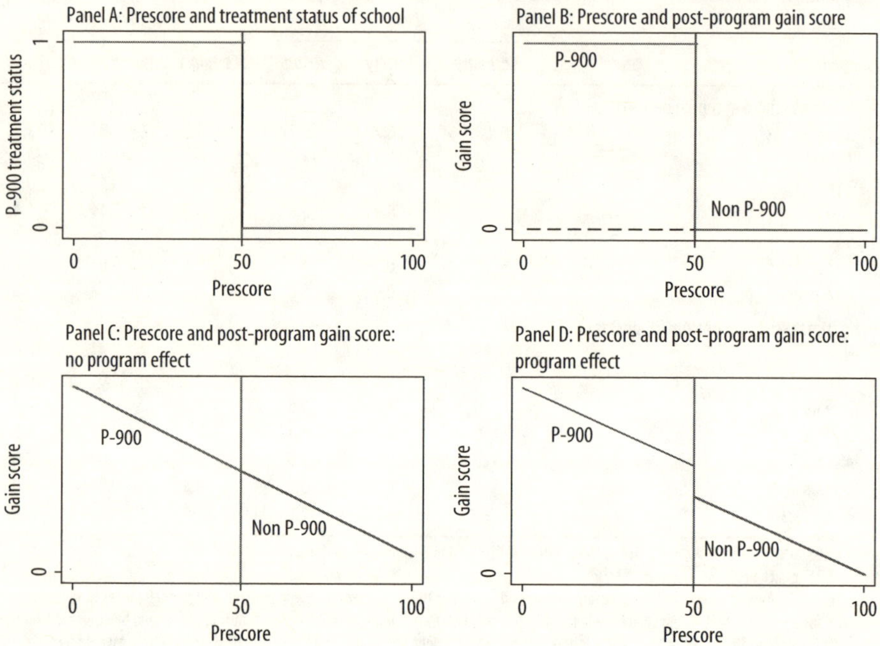


Source: Chay, McEwan, and Urquiola (2005).

from 0 to 100, and we arbitrarily choose 50 as the program cutoff, such that all schools with prescores of 50 or less are treated with the P-900 program, and the rest are not.

P-900 has been praised as one of the most successful school interventions in the developing world, and the literature reflects a perception that it substantially raised the achievement of treated schools.[51] Specifically, previous research finds that treated schools' average test scores improved more than those of untreated schools, a result obtained from a difference-in-differences specification. For example, the 1988 to 1990 changes in scores imply program effects that are equivalent to 0.3 and 0.5 standard deviations in math and language, respectively. For 1988 to 1992 gain scores, the implied P-900 effects are 0.5 and 0.7 standard deviations, respectively. For these estimates to have a causal interpretation, the differences in the gain scores of treated and untreated schools must be entirely due to the program. Panel B of fig-

51. See, for example, García-Huidobro (1994, 2000).

**FIGURE 6. Gain Scores by 1988 Average Score Relative to the Regional Cutoff**

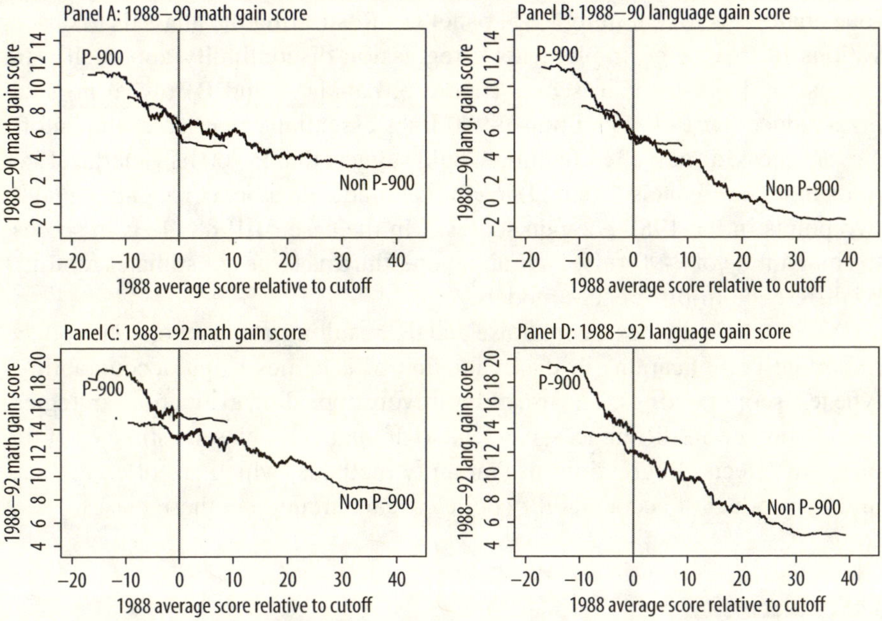


Source: Chay, McEwan, and Urquiola (2005).

ure 5 illustrates a scenario in which this may be the case. The *y* and *x* axes display the post-program gain score and the prescore, respectively. Here, the vertical distance between the two line segments is the added gain among P-900 schools (that is, the treatment effect), and a causal interpretation of the effect may be justified. In contrast, if schools with lower prescores have higher gain scores even in the absence of P-900, then the program effect may be closer to zero. This is the case in panel C of figure 5, which shows no break in the relation between the gain score and the prescore close to the assignment cutoff. However, a difference-in-differences specification would erroneously identify a positive treatment effect. Finally, panel D illustrates a break in test scores close to the assignment cutoff, consistent with a program effect.

Using a regression-discontinuity approach to consider the actual evidence, we plotted unweighted smoothed values of schools' gain scores against their 1988 prescores (relative to their respective regional cutoff), distinguishing between P-900 and untreated schools; the results are presented in figure 6. We find a negative relation between gain scores and 1988 scores, which is consistent with substantial mean reversion. To the extent that P-900 had an effect, we should observe a break in these relationships close to the cutoff (one analogous to that in figure 5, panel D). Restricting the analysis to observations in this range implements a regression-discontinuity approach. The graphs for 1988–90 gain scores (figure 6, panels A and B) reveal no such break, since the P-900 and non-P-900 lines essentially overlap at the cutoff. Nevertheless, a "naïve" evaluation would suggest that P-900 had a large effect in its first year. Panels C and D, in contrast, indicate a break roughly equal to two points in the 1988–92 gain scores.[52] In the case of 1988–92 gain scores, the magnitude of P-900 effects is about one-third as large as estimates returned by difference-in-differences models.

We conclude that test score noise and the resulting mean reversion produce important complications in the evaluation of schemes using accountability-type test score rankings. The use of intuitively appealing evaluation strategies, like difference-in-differences, can lead to dramatically biased estimates of the program effects. Regression-discontinuity methods, which are often the natural by-product of accountability policies, can circumvent these biases.

## Policy Discussion

The last three decades have been remarkable for education in Chile. In the 1980s, the military government introduced a large-scale school choice initiative. Since 1990, successive democratically elected center-left administrations have chosen not to alter the essential features of that scheme, but rather have focused on increasing resources and launching a series of initiatives. These include the following: targeted programs to raise quality in schools serving the poor, extending the years of mandatory basic education to twelve and ensuring that all first-grade entrants remain in schools throughout the twelve-year cycle, lengthening the school day, raising teacher pay, improving infrastructure, reforming the national curricula, establishing national standards, and introducing performance assessment systems for students, teachers, and schools.

Together, these policies have undoubtedly raised some households' welfare and improved school quality along many dimensions. Anyone visiting a

52. In fact, two types of breaks are visible in these figures: those at the cutoff and those for treated and untreated schools with overlapping 1988 scores (our initial regression evidence will capture both). Their magnitudes are generally similar. This reflects the fact that the assignment discontinuities (figure 6) are imperfect, leading to fuzziness across the cutoff score.

public or private school in Chile can see as much—relative to much of the region, classes take place reliably, many teachers seem to be satisfied with their work, and the infrastructure is adequate, even in rural areas. This reflects Chile's economic growth, but it also reflects the resources and effort expended on schools. Additionally, many households have taken advantage of choice to shift their children into subsidized private schools, and based on revealed preference, this must have improved their welfare.

Despite these advances and for reasons not yet fully understood, Chile's education system has made insufficient progress in improving student learning, as measured by test scores. Stratification probably increased over the period, and the associated perceptions of inequality were likely exacerbated when, beginning in 1994, private subsidized schools were allowed to charge supplementary tuition. Not surprisingly, schools with higher-income children tended to avail themselves of this opportunity to expand their funding.

The failure of the reforms to substantially raise learning outcomes and reduce school-based inequality has produced widespread dissatisfaction. Chile is perhaps the only country in Latin America where a majority of citizens list education quality and equity as one of their main political concerns, and education issues are regularly featured in the media. Indeed, these concerns were the main reason students called for a nationwide secondary-level student strike that took place in May and June of 2006. In 2007, a number of measures to raise the quality and equity of education were announced, including the creation of a Superintendency of Education responsible for quality assurance; a substantial increase in the value of the voucher subsidy; a change in the voucher design to begin differentiating its value according to students' socioeconomic status (tied with the introduction of further school accountability measures); and a significant overhaul of the laws that regulate the system, aimed at prohibiting publicly financed schools from selecting students, requiring more stringent reporting on the use of public funds, and prohibiting the operation of schools on a for-profit basis.

In the resulting policy debate, perhaps the single most controversial issue has been the proposal to eliminate private schools' ability to operate for profit. The existing evidence does not suggest that this policy would produce high returns in terms of education quality. Just as shifting large numbers of children into for-profit schools seems to have had a limited impact on average test scores, stripping those schools of their ability to profit is unlikely to lead to a large change. Furthermore, a key challenge in raising quality seems to be providing schools (as well as parents and students) with adequate incentives, and to the extent that for-profit schools might be responsive to well-specified incentives, it seems worth keeping them in existence. In addition, as Engel has noted, schools can devise ways to conceal profits.[53]

A second measure, changing the voucher design such that it is higher for children of lower socioeconomic status, was recently approved by Chile's Parliament. This preferential subsidy (as it is called in Chile) is intended to discourage cream skimming and increase accountability based on student learning outcomes (as opposed to just attendance).[54] It seems a promising avenue for raising quality and equity, although the literature does not provide much direct guidance on its potential impact and its details have not been fully worked out (particularly with respect to the precise gradient between socioeconomic status and the size of subsidies).

An additional proposal that would affect stratification involves prohibiting student selection by schools in grades one through eight. As stated above, selective admissions are widespread in Chile, particularly among private schools, which rely on tools ranging from testing to requiring marriage and baptismal certificates. At present, the details of this proposal are still to be worked out (for instance, whether to allow sibling preference, how the policy would address religious schools, and how compliance would be monitored), and its ultimate impact is difficult to predict given our incomplete knowledge of the channels through which stratification comes about.[55] Nevertheless, this initiative also seems worth exploring, not least because reducing stratification might improve the ability of the system to evaluate school performance. At the same time, its eventual impact on stratification is hard to gauge. For instance, some stratification happens naturally as a result of the interaction between residential sorting and the fact that children of primary age typically do not travel far to attend school. Furthermore, such segregation is potentially exacerbated in Chile by the existence of add-on tuition. Finally, much caution is needed in implementing this policy because the proposal could affect the ability of the very best public secondary schools (which rely on testing

53. Eduardo Engel, "El lucro y las políticas públicas," *La Tercera,* 15 April 2007.

54. Schools that received additional funding for lower socioeconomic status children would have to sign agreements with the Ministry of Education stipulating specific student learning goals, to which they would be held accountable.

55. Similar regulatory issues exist for publicly funded and privately managed charter schools in the United States. The majority of state-specific charter school laws explicitly require schools to admit students by lottery if their applications exceed available positions, although exceptions are often made for siblings of current students (McEwan and Olsen 2007). The conduct of many such lotteries is self-monitoring, in that they are conducted, by law or custom, in a public forum.

selection generally at the seventh grade) to excel. Some observers have noted that selective public schools have contributed to social mobility in Chile.[56]

As the Chilean government moves forward in education reform, it will need to continue to collect, disseminate, and use information on school performance. While the findings in this paper indicate reasons for caution in this regard, it is still the case that generating appropriate incentives for schools requires the use of high-quality performance data.[57] Chile would therefore do well to invest more in data collection and analysis. For instance, it could gather information on student-level gains or produce filtered estimates in the manner discussed by Kane and Staiger (although the theory and practice on how to calculate these is limited, even in the United States).[58] None of these strategies is likely to provide a silver bullet solution to the challenges described, but they might improve the quality and usefulness of school performance information.

Finally, an important issue not receiving much attention in the current debate is the need for Chile to do more to assess its own education policies and initiatives. Whenever possible, evaluations should be planned and designed in conjunction with policies, and they should employ experimental or high-quality quasi-experimental methods.[59] Over the past decades, Chilean administrations have shown imagination in designing and implementing education reform, but they have been less inclined to rigorously evaluate these initiatives. Given the universal difficulty in designing effective education policy, this must change if Chile is to optimize its ability to improve interventions and increase their impact on school quality and equity.

56. Alejandra Mizala and Pablo González, "La LOCE y la calidad de la educación," *La Tercera,* 15 April 2007.

57. Mizala and Urquiola (2008).

58. Kane and Staiger (2001).

59. Shadish, Cook, and Campbell (2002).

# Comments

**Reynaldo Fernandes:** Chile has undergone considerable reform of the educational system in the last twenty-five years. In the early 1980s, the government implemented a nationwide voucher system, in which the management of public schools was transferred from the Ministry of Education to the municipalities. Under this system, municipal schools receive a per-student subsidy and are not allowed to charge tuition or turn away students unless overenrolled. Subsidized private schools receive the same per-student subsidy as municipal schools, but they have wide latitude regarding student selection and are allowed to charge fees (after 1994). Since the end of Augusto Pinochet's military government in the early 1990s, Chile has been governed by the same political coalition, which has given continuity to the effort of improving education in the country. This has led to substantial increases in the per-pupil expenditure, the dissemination of information on school performance, and other policy measures.

In 2000, Chile participated in the Program for International Student Assessment (PISA), with the expectation that the results would reflect the effects of years of investment in the sector. The PISA results were disappointing, however. Chilean students' performance was much lower than European and Asian students and similar to that of students in other Latin American countries, such as Brazil and Mexico. While there is thus no evidence that the Chilean education reform has improved students' average test score, there is evidence that the voucher system has contributed to increased stratification, in the sense that students with better socioeconomic status have transferred from public schools to private ones.

McEwan, Urquiola, and Vegas address these issues, contributing to the literature in two distinct aspects: they present new evidences that Chilean education reform has increased stratification and has had little effect on students' average achievement; and they explore factors that may explain why the evolution of school quality in Chile has been disappointing. In this comment, I focus on the second contribution.

The market mechanism assumes that efficient firms can be expanded or replicated, which pushes inefficient firms out of the market. If Chilean students' low performance on the PISA test is due to inefficient schools, then the market mechanism is not working in the voucher system implemented in the country. However, the relation between low performance and schools' inefficiency is not evident. Students' performance on standardized tests depends both on school quality and on external factors such as students' socioeconomic status. School quality, in turn, depends on the schools' efficiency in managing their resources and on the total amount of available resources. Thus, low performance cannot automatically be identified with school inefficiency. Given that Chile expanded the freedom of school choice and increased per-pupil expenditures, one could expect an improvement on test scores. McEwan, Urquiola, and Vegas show that this is not the case. Their evidence suggests that the Chilean voucher system did not contribute to increasing schools' efficiency. The question is, why not?

To address this question, several factors need to be explored, but the authors focus on just one: "the difficulties researchers have encountered in generating useful information on school performance." While the measurement problem is a serious one for establishing an accountability program (with rewards and punishments) and for assessing the program's effectiveness, its importance for orienting parents in school choice is not very clear. The response to the failure of education reform in Chile must be obtained elsewhere.

## Imperfection of the Quality Measure and School Accountability Programs

The practice of evaluating schools according to their students' performance on standardized tests is becoming more frequent worldwide. It is also common to allocate rewards, sanctions, and assistance based on these results. Since it is important to show teachers and parents the reasons why their schools are being rewarded or punished, simple indicators are desirable. This may explain why students' mean test scores are among the most widely used performance measures by school accountability programs. Other measures used are mean test score variations between two periods of time (a measure of progress) and mean test score variation for students' cohorts in different grades (a measure of value added).

The literature on school accountability emphasizes two potential problems in using scores on standardized tests: distortion of incentives and gaming. In the case of the former, the problem lies in the fact that schools have multiple goals, whereas the measures used focus on only a few. Schools are therefore motivated to concentrate their efforts on those aspects required by the programs. In the case of gaming, schools might adopt strategies to change test scores without improving teaching quality. Strategies might include training and motivating students to participate in the tests or excluding low-proficiency students from the tests or from the school.

McEwan, Urquiola, and Vegas suggest that scores on standardized tests are imperfect measures of the restricted goals that they are intended to evaluate, even when no gaming is present. A math test is an imperfect tool for assessing a school's capacity to provide good learning to its students because it reflects not only school effort, but also the influence of family and friends, the students' inherent abilities, and random error. The authors highlight that test scores are measures with a lot of noise since the variance of error is very large, especially among small schools.

McEwan, Urquiola, and Vegas suggest there is a trade-off in the extent to which rankings generated using test score measures are either very similar to rankings based purely on students' socioeconomic status or very volatile from year to year. This is indeed a serious problem for school accountability programs, since rewarding or punishing schools based on the socioeconomic status of their students or based on a lottery would have undesirable consequences for the incentive structure of the schools' accountability programs. For example, schools that perform poorly on achievement tests because they receive low-income students may be discouraged from improving teaching quality, since school ranking does not reflect all the effort made. Similarly, programs that focus on rewarding the "best" schools or punishing the "worst" do not motivate larger schools. Smaller schools are more likely to be among the top or bottom schools, since error variance decreases as the number of students rises.[1]

Error variance also creates some difficulties for evaluating programs' effectiveness using standard procedures such as difference-in-differences analysis. In any given year, the schools with the lowest performances tend to be overrepresented among the schools achieving a low value of error. Thus,

1. Kane and Staiger (2002).

the mean reversion process would tend to increase the mean performance of the schools with the lowest performances, disregarding any change in schools quality.

## Imperfection of the Quality Measure and School Choice Process

Suppose that three measures of students' performance on standardized tests are available for each school: mean test score, value added, and mean test score variation between two subsequent years. Further suppose that the variance of error is very small and that it may not be taken into account. If policymakers have to choose one of these measures to implement a school accountability program, the majority would probably go with value added. Some might opt for mean test score variation, but very few would choose mean test scores, since punishing schools because they have low-income students simply is not reasonable. Mean test scores might not be a bad choice, however, for parents deciding on a school for their children. Value added measures do not represent what most people consider a good school. A school that has low-performing students and produces good value added could be a bad choice for a student with high learning capacity.

Students' mean test scores may be a good guide for orienting school choice. First, top schools tend to combine good students and good quality, while bottom schools tend to have both bad students and bad quality. Students who want to transfer from a low-performing school to a high-performing school are probably doing the right thing. Second, the family's options do not include all schools, but rather are generally restricted to the few that are closest to home. In this case, the separation of school effects and student effects is not the main issue, because socioeconomic status tends to be very similar for families living in the same neighborhood. If that is not the case, it may be relatively easy for the families to separate the two effects. The families probably have more information on schools than the econometrician, who lives far from their reality.

If schools want to attract more and better students, they need to raise their students' mean test score. Better quality schools will probably have an advantage in this process. While the market mechanism may cause stratification, one could expect that it would raise students' mean performance substantially. If this mechanism does not work in Chile, it is probably not because the families lack information on the quality of schools.

**Francisco A. Gallego:** This interesting and ambitious paper addresses a variety of topics related to the school system in Chile. The paper presents a literature review on the Chilean voucher system and its effects on school quality and stratification; new evidence on the correlation between school entry and outcomes using a regression-discontinuity design in a Chilean region with relatively low school entry and a relatively large share of rural population; a detailed discussion on the degree of informativeness of most available measures of school outcomes in Chile; and a policy discussion on the present and the future of the Chilean voucher system, with implications for other countries. The paper highlights the key findings that the school system in Chile has not fulfilled its implicit promise of increasing quality and that the reforms have accentuated stratification. I agree with these two stylized facts. The new evidence using regression-discontinuity design supports these facts, but neither the interpretation of the results nor its policy implications are obvious. In turn, the section on information is really interesting and shows that simply providing information may not produce big impacts on school quality. I do not have major comments on this section, so I concentrate on the other parts of the paper. Finally, I agree with most of the policy implications presented, although I would shift the emphasis somewhat.

I organize my comments in two sections. First, my comments on the actual implementation of the quasi-voucher system in Chile stress a couple of missing pieces in the analysis. Second, I discuss briefly the policy implications presented in the paper.

## The Quasi-Voucher System in Chile

I agree with the propositions that school quality in Chile could be better and that the actual implementation of the voucher system has been an important cause of the high degree of stratification in schools.[1] However, I would stress two additional points not present in the paper. First, the Chilean experience of choice is not the only way of implementing school choice and is certainly subject to many improvements. In this sense, the Chilean voucher system is not really a textbook version of the Friedman-style voucher system (which is why I call it just a quasi-voucher system).[2] Second, I disagree somewhat with the

1. Many of the ideas presented in this section are based on Gallego and Sapelli (2007a, 2007b).

2. Moreover, some key features of the system changed from 1981 to 2007; see Gallego (2006).

authors' reading of the available literature.[3] Very little causal evidence is available to answer many questions, and given the nature of what is available, it is really hard to learn much more with the methodologies used so far.[4] In addition, evidence is still lacking on the cost effectiveness of the Chilean voucher system. Even if quality did not rise relative to the prevoucher system, enrollment seems to have improved (although there is no evidence on this), and little is known about costs in conterfactual scenarios. The rest of this section explores three key issues for understanding the actual evolution of the voucher system and its impacts on quality and stratification.

## *The Actual Value of the Voucher*

From a conceptual point of view, publicly financed education in Chile is provided through a quasi-market for a heterogeneous product. There is fundamental heterogeneity because production costs vary with students' socioeconomic status. As we economists well know, the key incentive mechanism in a voucher system should be the value of the per-student voucher. In the simplest model, $p$ is the value of the per-student voucher, $c(q)$ is the unit cost of providing quality $q$, and $c(.)$ is increasing in $q$. If there is free entry in the market, $p = c(q)$, and the value of the voucher pins down quality. A higher value of the voucher thus implies higher quality. Then, a low value of the voucher may well explain the low quality observed in Chile—as in the case of an $\varepsilon$ voucher in which the value of the voucher is close to zero.

Table 6 presents the annual value of the per-student voucher in Chile. It is currently about U.S.$1,200 (in constant 2005 PPP-adjusted dollars), which is equivalent to about 11.3 percent of per capita GDP. The value dropped in the late 1980s to about $600 (about 15 percent of per capita GDP). To provide a benchmark, the table also lists the value of selected U.S. voucher programs. The median for a group of programs is U.S.$2,400 (about 28 percent of per capita GDP). The value of the Chilean voucher is thus quite low by international standards. Moreover, there is a consensus in Chile that the value of the voucher is not enough to provide a minimum acceptable school quality.[5]

3. Larrañaga (2004) and Sapelli (2003) provide alternative recent surveys of the Chilean voucher system. Additional references on the effectiveness of vouchers and public schools include Sapelli and Vial (2002, 2003, 2005, 2006).

4. As the authors argue, the key weakness of many papers in this literature is "that private entry into school markets is endogenous." One must therefore be extremely careful in deriving causal interpretations of some empirical regularities found in this and other papers.

5. Gallego and Sapelli (2007b).

**TABLE 6. Voucher Value in Several Programs**

| *Program* | *Percent of per capita GDP* | *Value of voucher*[a] |
|---|---|---|
| Chile | | |
| 1982 | 53.19 | 1,019 |
| 1985 | 32.55 | 686 |
| 1990 | 14.12 | 606 |
| 1995 | 11.21 | 733 |
| 2000 | 12.06 | 1,010 |
| 2005 | 11.32 | 1,265 |
| Selected U.S. programs | | |
| Charlotte, North Carolina | 9.01 | 1,669 |
| Cleveland, Ohio | 24.01 | 2,455 |
| Dayton, Ohio | 10.90 | 1,178 |
| Florida | 34.43 | 3,927 |
| Milwaukee, Wisconsin 1990 | 31.00 | 2,402 |
| Milwaukee, Wisconsin 1998 | 37.27 | 4,611 |
| Average | 24.44 | 2,707 |
| Median | 27.5 | 2,429 |

Source: Author's calculations.
a. In constant 2005 PPP-adjusted U.S. dollars (purchasing power parity).

As previously discussed, the value of the voucher does not depend on students' socioeconomic status. So if the per-student voucher is low on average, it should be even lower for poor students. In equilibrium, these students are probably segregated in low-quality public schools, because both public and voucher schools with excess demand will select "cheap" students.

All in all, both the observed low quality and the stratification may be consequences of the established prices (which are too low, particularly for poor students) and not of school choice per se. Interestingly, current policies that will increase the voucher disproportionately for poor students may provide good experiments for studying the relevance of my story to explain the outcomes of the Chilean quasi-voucher system.

### *The Role of Self-Selection and Self-Stratification vis-à-vis Selection from the Supply Side*

Many arguments and policy proposals relate the stratification we observe in Chile to selection from the supply side, because regulations allow overenrolled public and voucher schools to freely select students—that is, private schools are able to cream skim students. As previously discussed, these overenrolled schools have incentives for selecting according to student costs.

Moreover, voucher and secondary public schools may charge a top-up fee above the voucher.

The question is how big cream skimming from the supply side is. I am not sure it is as extensive as the arguments in the paper imply. First, the school-entry cohort is significantly smaller today than during the peak in the mid-1990s: the school-entry cohort in 2001–05 was 11 percent smaller than in 1996–2000, and it will be 15 percent smaller in fifteen years. Many schools—especially middle-class schools—have excess supply. Second, survey evidence suggests that 93 percent of parents say they send their kids to the school they wanted.[6] This figure is probably biased upward, but the order of magnitude is suggestive. Finally, a group of researchers and I recently carried out a survey of parents in three regions in Chile. The results reveal that 89 percent of parents apply to just one school (the average number of schools to which parents apply is 1.16), and only about 7.5 percent of parents applied to a school and were not accepted.[7] Moreover, of the students that applied to a school and were not accepted, about 40 percent ended up in voucher schools.[8]

This evidence as a whole suggests that selection from the supply side is not as extensive as commonly thought. An alternative explanation is that there is self-selection: studies show that parents like to be with peers who are similar to them.[9] Moreover, equilibrium self-selection is relevant in both selective and nonselective schools.[10]

The policy implications of self-selection are different from the policy implications of school selection. Prohibiting school selection will not decrease stratification significantly if self-selection is what matters the most.

6. Centro de Estudios Públicos (2006).

7. The numbers increase to 1.26 school applications per student and 12 percent of students who applied to a school and were not accepted in the Santiago Metropolitan Area, which has the highest penetration of voucher schools. Similarly, the percentage of students who applied to a school and were rejected and then ended up in voucher schools is 41 percent.

8. The low number of applications may be a consequence of selection from the supply side. In equilibrium, parents might not apply to schools that they expect are going to reject their kids. However, if this argument is of first-order importance, it would imply that these sophisticated parents must be really rational when they choose schools, which contradicts one of the most important arguments against school choice, and that currently used measures of school selectivity may be severely biased.

9. Elacqua, Schneider, and Buckley (2006); Gallego and Hernando (2007). For the theoretical rationale for this class of preferences, see Rayo and Becker (2007). Luttmer (2005) presents experimental evidence, and Chakrabarti (2005) includes related evidence for the voucher program in Milwaukee, Wisconsin.

10. Gallego and Hernando (2007).

### *The Impact of Nonvoucher Public Programs*

Arguments outlining the potential benefits of a voucher system are based on the assumption that schools have hard budget constraints. In reality, public schools in Chile tend to receive explicit transfers from other programs and implicit transfers to finance school deficits.[11] At least some public schools, therefore, have soft budget constraints This should have an impact on the incentives created by the voucher. This theoretical argument seems to be supported by the data. Public schools that operate under relatively soft budget constraints do not react to interschool competition, whereas schools that operate under hard budget constraints react strongly.[12] In contrast, Gallego and Hernando similarly find that only voucher schools with low market power (in the quality dimension) offer high quality, while public schools do not react to this incentive.[13]

## Policy Implications

The value of the voucher needs to be increased, but with different values for different socioeconomic groups.[14] This could increase average quality, decrease stratification, and improve the set of schools available to poor students. However, the necessary differentiation in the additional increase for poor students seems to be greater than current policy proposals. Simulations suggest that the value of the voucher should at least be doubled for poor students and should not increase for about 20 percent of students.[15] Thus, it may not be realistic to expect that small increases in the value of the voucher will generate big impacts on quality for poor students, because the increase in the voucher value may not be sufficient to foster acceptable levels of quality.

A second issue that emerges from the previous discussion is that parents strongly value both distance and quality when choosing schools.[16] Moreover, quality seems to be a superior attribute and distance an inferior attribute. This

11. See Serrano and Berner (2002), for instance.

12. Gallego (2006). In that paper, I extensively discuss some valid concerns about the identification strategy (that is, that "priests are unlikely to have ever been randomly allocated"). I present evidence against those concerns and thus in support of the strategy.

13. Gallego and Hernando (2007).

14. Aedo and Sapelli (2001) were the first authors to argue in favor of this proposal.

15. Gallego and Sapelli (2007b). The simulations use the following target: move all students to at least 0.50 standard deviation above current average test scores.

16. Gallego and Hernando (2007).

implies that low-quality schools may survive by being close to students, and this will be especially true for poor students. Thus, the education system needs to incorporate an exit mechanism, through a Superintendence or other institutional arrangement, for schools below some minimum quality level.

Finally, regulations that protect bad public schools from competition should be eliminated. In the current context, the increase in the voucher could easily be used just to finance deficits, without a clear impact on school quality.

## Conclusion

McEwan, Urquiola, and Vegas raise a number of issues on the effects of a voucher system and information on school quality and stratification. The Chilean case provides an interesting experience that includes elements of a voucher system as well as some key distortions to this system. How these elements and distortions affect average quality and stratification is the key research question from an academic and policy perspective. Moreover, there is room for new research using more theoretically motivated semistructural empirical studies.[17] I look forward to seeing more research on this and other topics from the authors.

17. Urquiola and Verhoogen (forthcoming) is an excellent example.

## References


Aedo, Cristian, and Osvaldo Larrañaga. 1994. "Sistemas de entrega de los servicios sociales: la experiencia chilena." In *Sistemas de entrega de los servicios sociales,* edited by Cristian Aedo and Osvaldo Larrañaga, pp. 33–74. Washington: Inter-American Development Bank.

Aedo, Cristian, and Claudio Sapelli. 2001. "El sistema de vouchers en educación: una revisión de la teoría y evidencia empírica para Chile." *Estudios Públicos* 82 (otoño): 35–82.

Anand, Priyanka, Alejandra Mizala, and Andrea Repetto. 2006. "Using School Scholarships to Estimate the Effect of Government Subsidized Private Education on Academic Achievement in Chile." Working Paper 220. Santiago: University of Chile.

Angrist, Joshua, and Victor Lavy. 1999. "Using Maimonides' Rule to Estimate the Effect of Class Size on Scholastic Achievement." *Quarterly Journal of Economics* 114(2): 533–75.

Angrist, Joshua, and others. 2002. "Vouchers for Private Schooling in Colombia: Evidence from a Randomized Natural Experiment." *American Economic Review* 92(5): 1535–558.

Auguste, Sebastian, and Juan Pablo Valenzuela. 2006. "Is It Just Cream Skimming? School Vouchers in Chile." Buenos Aires: Fundación de Investigaciones Económicas Latinoamericanas.

Bellei, Cristian. 2007. "The Private-Public School Controversy: The Case of Chile." PEPG Working Paper 05-13. Harvard University, Program on Education Policy and Governance.

Bravo, David, Dante Contreras, and Claudia Sanhueza. 1999. "Rendimiento educacional, desigualdad y brecha de desempeño privado público: Chile 1982–1997." Working Paper 163. Santiago: University of Chile, Department of Economics.

Bresnahan, Timothy F., and Peter C. Reiss. 1987. "Do Entry Conditions Vary across Markets?" *Brookings Papers on Economic Activity* (special issue): 833–71.

———. 1991. "Entry and Competition in Concentrated Markets." *Journal of Political Economy* 99(5): 977–1009.

Centro de Estudios Públicos. 2006. "Estudio nacional de opinión pública, junio–julio 2006. Tema especial: educación." Santiago.

Chakrabarti, Rajashri. 2005. "Do Vouchers Lead to Sorting under Random Private School Selection? Evidence from the Milwaukee Voucher Program." Harvard University.

Chay, Kenneth, Patrick J. McEwan, and Miguel Urquiola. 2005. "The Central Role of Noise in Evaluating Interventions That Use Test Scores to Rank Schools." *American Economic Review* 95(4): 1237–258.

Chubb, John, and Terry M. Moe. 1990. *Politics, Markets, and America's Schools.* Brookings.

Coleman, James S., and others. 1966. *Equality of Educational Opportunity.* U.S. Department of Health, Education, and Welfare, Office of Education.

Contreras, Dante. 2002. "Vouchers, School Choice, and the Access to Higher Education." Working Paper 845. Yale University, Economic Growth Center.

Elacqua, Gregory. 2006. "Enrollment Practices in Response to Vouchers: Evidence from Chile." Occasional Paper 125. Columbia University, Teachers College, National Center for Study of Privatization in Education (www.ncspe.org/publications_files/OP125.pdf [31 August 2007]).

Elacqua, Gregory, Mark Schneider, and Jack Buckley. 2006. "School Choice in Chile: Is It Class or the Classroom?" *Journal of Policy Analysis and Management* 25(3): 577–601.

Engel, Eduardo, and Patricio Navia. 2006. *Que gane el "más mejor."* Santiago: Random House Mondadori.

Epple, Dennis, and Richard E. Romano. 1998. "Competition between Private and Public Schools, Vouchers, and Peer-Group Effects." *American Economic Review* 88(1): 33–62.

———. 2002. "Educational Vouchers and Cream Skimming." Working Paper 9354. Cambridge, Mass.: National Bureau of Economic Research.

Friedman, Milton. 1955. "The Role of Government in Education." In *Economics and the Public Interest,* edited by Robert A. Solo. Rutgers University Press.

Gallego, Francisco A. 2006. "Voucher-School Competition, Incentives, and Outcomes: Evidence from Chile." Pontificia Universidad Cátolica de Chile, Instituto de Economía.

Gallego, Francisco A., and Andrés Hernando. 2007. "School Choice in Chile: Looking at the Demand Side." Pontificia Universidad Cátolica de Chile, Instituto de Economía, and Harvard University.

Gallego, Francisco A., and Claudio Sapelli. 2007a. "El esquema de financiamiento de la educación en Chile: una evaluación." *Revista de Pensamiento Educativo* 40(1): 263–84.

———. 2007b. "Financiamiento y selección en educación: algunas reflexiones y propuestas." *Puntos de Referencia* 286 (septiembre): 1–12. Santiago: Centro de Estudios Píblicos.

García-Huidobro, Juan Eduardo. 1994. "Positive Discrimination in Education: Its Justification and a Chilean Example." *International Review of Education* 40(3–5): 209–21.

———. 2000. "Educational Policies and Equity in Chile." In *Unequal Schools, Unequal Chances: The Challenges to Equal Opportunity in the Americas,* edited by Fernando Reimers, pp. 160–78. Harvard University Press.

Gauri, Varun. 1998. *School Choice in Chile.* University of Pittsburgh Press.

Hanushek, Eric A., John F. Kain, and Steven G. Rivkin. 2004. "Disruption versus Tiebout Improvement: The Costs and Benefits of Switching Schools." *Journal of Public Economics* 88(9–10): 1721–746.

Hanushek, Eric A., and Margaret E. Raymond. 2003. "Lessons about the Design of State Accountability Systems." In *No Child Left Behind? The Politics and Practice of Accountability,* edited by Paul Peterson and Martin West, pp. 127–51. Brookings.

———. 2005. "Does School Accountability Lead to Improved Student Performance?" *Journal of Policy Analysis and Management* 24(2): 297–327.

Hanushek, Eric A., and Ludger Woessmann. 2007. "The Role of School Improvement in Economic Development." Working Paper 12832. Cambridge, Mass.: National Bureau of Economic Research.

Howell, William G., and Paul E. Peterson. 2002. *The Education Gap: Vouchers and Urban Schools.* Brookings.

Hoxby, Caroline M. 2000. "Does Competition among Public Schools Benefit Students and Taxpayers?" *American Economic Review 90*(5): 1209–238.

Hsieh, Chang-Tai, and Miguel Urquiola. 2003. "When Schools Compete, How Do They Compete? An Assessment of Chile's Nationwide School Voucher Program." Working Paper 10008. Cambridge, Mass.: National Bureau of Economic Research.

———. 2006. "The Effects of Generalized School Choice on Achievement and Stratification: Evidence from Chile's Voucher Program." *Journal of Public Economics* 90(8–9): 1477–503.

Kane, Thomas J., and Douglas O. Staiger. 2001. "Improving School Accountability Measures." Working Paper 8156. Cambridge, Mass.: National Bureau of Economic Research.

———. 2002. "The Promise and Pitfalls of Using Imprecise School Accountability Measures." *Journal of Economic Perspectives* 16(4): 91–114.

Krueger, Alan B., and Pei Zhu. 2004. "Another Look at the New York City School Voucher Experiment." *American Behavioral Scientist* 47(5): 658–98.

Larrañaga, Osvaldo. 2004. "Competencia y participación privada: la experiencia chilena en educación." *Estudios Públicos* 96 (primavera): 107–44.

Luttmer, Erzo F. P. 2005. "Neighbors as Negatives: Relative Earnings and Well-Being." *Quarterly Journal of Economics* 120(3): 963–1002.

McEwan, Patrick J. 2000a. *The Impact of Vouchers on School Efficiency: Empirical Evidence from Chile.* Ph.D. dissertation, Stanford University.

———. 2000b. "The Potential Impact of Large-Scale Voucher Programs." *Review of Educational Research* 70(2): 103–49.

———. 2001. "The Effectiveness of Public, Catholic, and Non-Religious Private Schools in Chile's Voucher System." *Education Economics* 9(2): 103–28.

McEwan, Patrick J., and Martin Carnoy. 2000. "The Effectiveness and Efficiency of Private Schools in Chile's Voucher System." *Educational Evaluation and Policy Analysis* 22(3): 213–39.

McEwan, Patrick J., and Robert Olsen. 2007. "Admissions Lotteries in Charter Schools." Wellesley College and the Urban Institute.

McEwan, Patrick J., and Joseph S. Shapiro. 2008. "The Benefits of Delayed Primary School Enrollment: Discontinuity Estimates Using Exact Birth Dates." *Journal of Human Resources* 43(1): 1–29.

Mizala, Alejandra, and Pilar Romaguera. 2000. "School Performance and Choice: The Chilean Experience." *Journal of Human Resources* 35(2): 392–417.

Mizala, Alejandra, Pilar Romaguera, and Miguel Urquiola. 2007. "Socioeconomic Status or Noise? Tradeoffs in the Generation of School Quality Information." *Journal of Development Economics* 84: 71–75.

Mizala, Alejandra, and Miguel Urquiola. 2008. "Parental Choice and School Markets: The Impact of Information Approximating School Effectiveness." Columbia University.

OECD (Organization for Economic Cooperation and Development). 2000. Programme for International Student Assessment (PISA) Database. Paris (www.pisa.oecd.org).

———. 2003. Programme for International Student Assessment (PISA) Database. Paris (www.pisa.oecd.org).

Rayo, Luis, and Gary S. Becker. 2007. "Evolutionary Efficiency and Happiness." *Journal of Political Economy* 115(2): 302–37.

Rothstein, Jesse. 2006. "Good Principals or Good Peers? Parental Valuations of School Characteristics, Tiebout Equilibrium, and the Incentive Effects of Competition among Jurisdictions." *American Economic Review* 96(4): 1333–350.

Rouse, Cecilia Elena. 1998. "Private School Vouchers and Student Achievement: An Evaluation of the Milwaukee Parental Choice Program." *Quarterly Journal of Economics* 113(2): 553–602.

Sapelli, Claudio. 2003. "The Chilean Voucher System: Some New Results and Research Challenges." *Cuadernos de Economía* 40(121): 530–38.

Sapelli, Claudio, and Bernardita Vial. 2002. "The Performance of Private and Public Schools in the Chilean Voucher System." *Cuadernos de Economía* 39(118): 423–54.

———. 2003. "Peer Effects and Relative Performance of Voucher Schools in Chile." Working Paper 256. Pontificia Universidad Cátolica de Chile, Instituto de Economía.

———. 2005. "Private vs. Public Voucher Schools in Chile: New Evidence on Efficiency and Peer Effects." Working Paper 289. Pontificia Universidad Cátolica de Chile, Instituto de Economía.

———. 2006. "Performance of Voucher Schools in Chile: Efficiency, Resources or Sorting?" Pontificia Universidad Cátolica de Chile, Instituto de Economía.

Serrano, Claudia, and Heidi Berner. 2002. "Chile: un caso poco frecuente de indisciplina fiscal (bailout) y endeudamiento encubierto de la educacion municipal." Working Paper R-446. Washington: Inter-American Development Bank.

Shadish, William R., Thomas D. Cook, and Donald T. Campbell. 2002. *Experimental and Quasi-Experimental Designs for Generalized Causal Inference*. Boston: Houghton Mifflin.

Urquiola, Miguel. 2005. "Does School Choice Lead to Sorting? Evidence from Tiebout Variation." *American Economic Review* 95(4): 1310–326.

———. 2006. "Identifying Class Size Effects in Developing Countries: Evidence from Rural Bolivia." *Review of Economics and Statistics* 88(1): 171–77.

Urquiola, Miguel, and Valentina Calderón. 2006. "Apples and Oranges: Educational Enrollment and Attainment across Countries in Latin America and the Caribbean." *International Journal of Educational Development* 26(6): 572–90.

Urquiola, Miguel, and Eric Verhoogen. Forthcoming. "Class Size and Sorting in Market Equilibrium: Theory and Evidence." *American Economic Review.*

Van der Klaauw, Wilbert. 2002. "Estimating the Effect of Financial Aid Offers on College Enrollment: A Regression-Discontinuity Approach." *International Economic Review* 43(4): 1249–286.

Vegas, Emiliana, and Jenny Petrow. 2007. *Raising Student Learning in Latin America.* Washington: World Bank.

NORBERT SCHADY
MARIA CARIDAD ARAUJO

# Cash Transfers, Conditions, and School Enrollment in Ecuador

Investments in human capital in childhood are generally believed to be critical for adult well-being. Children who have higher educational attainment are more productive as adults, earn higher wages, and have better health status than children with less education. In country after country, governments have sought to devise effective policies to increase school enrollment. In this context, cash transfer programs have expanded dramatically in many developing countries, especially in Latin America. These are often conditional cash transfer programs, in which eligible households are given transfers conditional on compliance with certain requirements. In most countries, households are required to send school-aged children to school and to take younger children for regular visits to health centers, where they receive nutritional supplements and growth monitoring. The best known of these programs is *Oportunidades* (formerly Progresa) in Mexico, although similar programs have also been implemented in a number of other Latin American countries.

This paper evaluates the impact of a cash transfer program in Ecuador, the *Bono de Desarrollo Humano* (BDH), on school enrollment. This is a large program—in 2004, the BDH budget was approximately 0.7 percent of gross domestic product (GDP). Eligibility for BDH transfers is determined by a proxy means test known as the Beneficiary Identification and Selection

Schady and Araujo are with the World Bank.

This research would not have been possible without the collaboration of our colleagues in the Secretaría Técnica del Frente Social in Ecuador. We also thank Orazio Attanasio, Pedro Carneiro, Quy-Toan Do, Daniel Dulitzky, Francisco Ferreira, Deon Filmer, Jed Friedman, Sebastián Galiani, Paul Gertler, Mauricio León, Karen Macours, David McKenzie, Ren Mu, Christina Paxson, Juan Ponce, Martin Ravallion, Carolina Sánchez-Páramo, Laura Schechter, and Renos Vakis for many useful comments.

System, or Selben. In theory, the 40 percent of households with the lowest Selben score are eligible for monthly transfers.[1]

The analysis in this paper is divided into two parts. The first part assesses the overall impact of the BDH on school enrollment. During an expansion of the BDH coverage, program administrators undertook an experimental evaluation of the program's impact. A sample of households that had not previously received transfers was selected and randomly divided into treatment and control groups. Data on both groups were collected at baseline, before households started to receive BDH transfers, and follow-up, approximately one and a half years later. We use this experimental study design to show that BDH transfers significantly increased school enrollment. These results complement earlier findings of positive effects of cash transfer programs on enrollment in Mexico, Colombia, Nicaragua, and Honduras.[2]

The second part of the paper provides evidence on the relative importance of transfers and conditions (or perceived conditions) in explaining the positive BDH program effects on enrollment. Conditions attached to transfers introduce a kink in the budget constraint, and their effect depends on whether this compels households to behave differently than they would have done otherwise.[3]

The BDH was originally modeled on *Oportunidades*. Program administrators intended to condition transfers on school enrollment and attendance, among other things. Local elected leaders (the heads of the *Juntas Parroquiales*) were encouraged to hold town-hall-style meetings in which the BDH was presented as a compact between the state and beneficiaries—the state agreed to transfer resources to poor households, and these households, in turn, agreed to send their children to school. The BDH program also briefly aired a series of radio and television spots that explicitly linked transfers with school enrollment, and some BDH administrators appear to have stressed the enrollment requirements when they signed up households for transfers. In practice, however, the BDH did not monitor the schooling condition because of administrative constraints, and it thus did not penalize households whose children were out of school. Nevertheless, the BDH information campaign had an

1. The BDH transfer was $15 a month at the time these data were collected; it was doubled to $30 a month in early 2007.

2. On Mexico, see Schultz (2004) and Behrman, Sengupta, and Todd (2005); on Colombia, see Attanasio and others (2005); on Nicaragua, see Maluccio and Flores (2004); on Honduras, see Glewwe and Olinto (2004).

3. See Das, Do, and Özler (2005) for an illustration.

effect: in the follow-up survey used in this paper, approximately a quarter of respondents stated that they believed that sending children to school was a BDH program requirement.

We compare the impact of the program among conditioned households (that is, those who told survey enumerators that school enrollment was a BDH requirement) and unconditioned households (those who told enumerators that there was no enrollment requirement attached to transfers). Our estimates show that program effects on enrollment are only significant among conditioned households. Because exposure to the information campaign was not assigned randomly, these comparisons are not experimental. However, the effects we estimate are insensitive to adding a large number of controls, trimming the data, and sweeping out fixed differences between conditioned and unconditioned households. We therefore argue that the larger program effect among conditioned households most likely has a causal interpretation. These results complement evidence from a variety of structural and microsimulation models for Mexico and Brazil, all of which conclude that conditions attached to transfers explain the bulk of the effect of conditional cash transfer programs on school enrollment.[4]

The rest of the paper is structured as follows. The next section briefly describes the BDH, the sample frame, and the data. The paper then presents our results on overall program effects, while a subsequent section focuses on the differences between conditioned and unconditioned households. The final section concludes.

## Background and Study Design

Ecuador is a lower-middle-income country. In 2004, its per capita GDP was $1,435 in constant 2000 U.S. dollars, or $3,595 in PPP-adjusted constant 2000 U.S. dollars, about half the population-weighted Latin American average. Inequality is high (the Gini coefficient is 0.44), although not especially so by Latin American standards. Poverty is widespread. An estimated 18 percent of the population lives on less than a dollar per person per day, and more than 40 percent live on less than two dollars per day.[5]

The net enrollment rate in primary school in Ecuador is 90 percent. The net enrollment rate in secondary school is substantially lower, however, at

4. On Mexico, see Todd and Wolpin (2006); Attanasio, Meghir, and Santiago (2005); de Janvry and Sadoulet (2006); on Brazil, see Bourguignon, Ferreira, and Leite (2003).

5. World Bank (2004).

45 percent. Overall enrollment rates changed very little between 1990 and 2001: calculations based on the 1990 and 2001 population censuses indicate that the net primary enrollment rate increased from 88.9 to 90.1, while the net secondary enrollment rate rose from 43.1 to 44.7.[6] In part because of this stagnation in enrollment rates, the Ecuadorian government has given high priority to identifying policies that increase the coverage of the education system, especially at the secondary level.

There is no gender disparity in educational attainment in Ecuador; enrollment rates are marginally higher for girls than for boys. The mean level of schooling of the adult population ages fifteen and older is 6.5 years. On average, educational outcomes in Ecuador are comparable to those of other countries with similar income levels. As is the case in many other countries, however, educational outcomes vary by household socioeconomic status. For example, heads of households above the poverty line have approximately four more years of schooling than those below the poverty line in urban areas and three more years in rural areas.[7]

This paper focuses on the *Bono de Desarrollo Humano* (BDH) program, which grew out of an earlier program known as the *Bono Solidario.* The *Bono Solidario* was created in 1999, in the midst of an economic crisis. The purpose of the program was to make cash transfers to poor households, but eligibility criteria were not clearly defined. As a result, many of the households that received transfers were not poor, and many poor households were not covered by the program.

Since 2003, the BDH program has taken steps to retarget transfers to the poor. To this end, the government developed a composite welfare index based on information on household composition, education levels, dwelling characteristics, and access to services, aggregated by principal components. This index is known as the Beneficiary Identification and Selection System, or Selben. The Selben covers around 90 percent of households in rural areas in Ecuador and about the same percentage of households in selected urban areas that were judged to have a high incidence of poverty. Households surveyed by the Selben are ranked by their Selben score. In theory, 40 percent of households in Ecuador are eligible for $15 monthly transfers by the BDH, based on their low Selben scores. However, until recently the government did not have the budget to make transfers to all households in the first two Selben quintiles, so expansion of the coverage of benefits has been gradual.

6. Vos and Ponce (2005).
7. World Bank (2004).

BDH transfers are made to women, and they can be collected at any branch office of the largest network of private banks (*Banred*) or from the National Development Bank (*Banco Nacional de Fomento*). In terms of magnitude, the monthly $15 BDH transfer accounts for approximately 9 percent of the pre-transfer expenditures of the median household in the study sample. As a point of comparison, *Oportunidades* transfers accounted for about 20 percent of average household expenditures in Mexico.[8] Although the BDH program and the *Bono Solidario* program that preceded it have been the subject of much controversy and policy discussion in Ecuador, the impact of these programs on schooling has not been systematically evaluated.[9]

## *Sample Frame*

The sample for the BDH program evaluation, which we use for our analysis in this paper, was drawn from the Selben rosters for four of the twenty-two provinces in the country: Carchi, Imbabura, Cotopaxi, and Tungurahua. All four provinces are in the highland region of the country. The sampling framework followed a two-stage process: parishes were randomly drawn from within these provinces, and a sample of 1,488 households was then selected from within the parishes. Of these households, 1,306 had school-aged children (ages six to seventeen) at the time of both the baseline and follow-up surveys, as well as baseline data for all of the variables used in this paper. (One exception is parental education, which is missing in a small number of cases in which the respondent did not know the education of a child's parent when the parent did not live in the household.) This sample of 1,306 households, which includes 2,875 school-aged children, is the basis for the analysis in this paper. None of the households in the sample had received BDH or *Bono Solidario* transfers prior to the program evaluation. At the request of program administrators, households near the cut-off between the first and second Selben quintiles were over-represented, as were households with older children; all of the households were drawn from the first and second Selben quintiles.

8. Skoufias (2005).

9. León, Vos, and Brborich (2001) analyze the impact of the *Bono Solidario* program on consumption poverty, and León and Younger (2007) focus on the impact of the *Bono Solidario* on child health. Both papers find significant but modest program effects, but their analyses are not experimental. Rather, they are based on comparisons between *Bono Solidario* recipients and nonrecipients in the 1998–99 *Encuesta de Condiciones de Vida* (ECV), a nationally representative household survey, and may therefore be subject to biases associated with endogenous program placement or take-up.

At the time the evaluation was launched, the BDH budget was insufficient to cover all households in the first and second Selben quintiles. Half the households in the evaluation sample were randomly assigned to a treatment group that would be eligible for BDH transfers, and the rest were assigned to a control group that would not be eligible for transfers for the first two years. We refer to the first group as lottery winners and the second group as lottery losers. Lottery losers were taken off the roster of households that could be activated for BDH transfers. As shown below, however, a substantial share of these households nonetheless received BDH transfers, an issue we address in our estimates of program impact.

Because of the criteria for selection into the BDH evaluation, households in the study sample are poorer than other households in Ecuador. Table 1 reports the means and standard deviations for selected characteristics of households in the study sample at baseline, of all households in the parishes included in this study, and of all households in the country whose Selben score places them in the first or second quintile. The samples for these calculations are limited to households with children ages six to seventeen. Averages for the parishes in the study sample are based on the 2001 Population Census; national averages for households in the first two Selben quintiles are based on the 1998–99 *Encuesta de Condiciones de Vida* (ECV), a multipurpose household survey. Table 1 suggests that households in the sample are noticeably poorer than the average household in their parishes: a comparison of the first and second columns in the table shows that they are less likely to have water from a network, less likely to have a flush toilet, and more likely to have a dirt floor, while the heads of household have lower education levels. This is not surprising given that the means in the second column include both households in the first and second Selben quintiles and other households. A comparison of the first and third columns suggests that households in the evaluation sample are also somewhat poorer than the average household eligible for the BDH in Ecuador, perhaps because the parishes in the evaluation sample are poorer, on average, or because they are more unequal.

### Data

The main sources of data used in this paper are the baseline and follow-up surveys designed for the BDH evaluation. Both surveys were carried out by an independent firm that had no association with the BDH program, namely, the Catholic University of Ecuador. The baseline survey was collected between

**TABLE 1. Comparison of the Evaluation Sample with National and Parish-Level Averages[a]**

| *Household characteristic* | *Impact evaluation sample at baseline* | *All households in evaluation parishes* | *All BDH-eligible households in Ecuador* |
|---|---|---|---|
| *A. Household-level variable* | | | |
| Household size | 5.77 | 4.19 | 5.84 |
| | (1.84) | (1.51) | (2.26) |
| No. rooms in house | 2.61 | 3.31 | 2.47 |
| | (1.20) | (2.32) | (1.20) |
| Water from network | 0.45 | 0.78 | 0.69 |
| | (0.50) | (0.41) | (0.47) |
| Has toilet | 0.24 | 0.72 | 0.66 |
| | (0.43) | (0.45) | (0.49) |
| Has dirt floor | 0.28 | 0.18 | 0.20 |
| | (0.45) | (0.39) | (0.41) |
| Age of household head | 44.96 | 42.70 | 43.89 |
| | (9.33) | (12.94) | (12.83) |
| Education of household head | 4.47 | 7.03 | 5.11 |
| | (2.77) | (5.02) | (3.48) |
| Household head is male | 0.85 | 0.77 | 0.82 |
| | (0.36) | (0.42) | (0.38) |
| Household head is literate | 0.83 | 0.91 | 0.81 |
| | (0.38) | (0.29) | (0.39) |
| Household head is indigenous | 0.16 | 0.17 | 0.11 |
| | (0.36) | (0.38) | (0.33) |
| *B. Child-level variable* | | | |
| Age | 11.41 | 11.72 | 10.78 |
| | (3.09) | (3.46) | (3.12) |
| Mean years of completed schooling | 4.41 | 5.08 | 3.76 |
| | (2.60) | (3.03) | (2.65) |

a. The table presents means and standard deviations (in parentheses). Calculations for the first column are based on the impact evaluation sample; those for the second column are based on the 2001 population census; those for the third column are based on the 1998–99 *Encuesta de Condiciones de Vida* (ECV). All estimates are based on households with children aged six to seventeen.

June and August 2003, and the follow-up survey was collected between January and March 2005.

The survey instrument included a roster of household members and information on, among other things, the level of schooling attained, marital status, and languages spoken by all adults; school enrollment, grade progression, and work of all children ages six to seventeen; an extensive module on household expenditures, which closely followed the structure of the 1998–99 ECV; and a module on dwelling conditions, ownership of durable goods, and access to public services. We aggregated expenditures into a consumption aggregate, appropriately deflated with regional prices of a basket of food items collected at the time of the surveys; durable goods and dwelling conditions were aggregated by principal components into a composite indicator of household assets.[10] The main outcome measure in this paper is a dummy variable that takes the value of one if a child is enrolled in school in the current school year.[11]

The follow-up evaluation survey included a module on access to and perception of the BDH program. Ninety-seven percent of households in the sample had heard of the BDH program, and 61 percent stated that they received transfers. The survey also asked respondents whether they believed that households had to comply with any requirements or conditions to receive transfers. Respondents were not prompted for answers, but 27 percent stated that "ensuring that children attend school" was a prerequisite to receive BDH transfers. We refer to these households as conditioned households in the analysis; they include both lottery winners (55 percent of all conditioned households) and lottery losers (45 percent).[12]

10. The indicator is based on the number of rooms in the house, dummy variables for earth floors, access to piped water, and access to a flush toilet (three variables), and count variables for the number of household durables based on responses to twenty-two separate questions in the survey. Results are similar when a simple count of household assets, rather than principal components, is used to aggregate these variables or if the measures of household conditions and assets are not aggregated at all but enter individually in the regressions. See Filmer and Pritchett (2001) for a discussion of these methods.

11. One concern is that households that received BDH transfers could have lied about their enrollment status. This concern is not particular to this evaluation—it could be an issue for any evaluation of a program that requires beneficiaries to comply with certain conditions and for which data are collected on the basis of household survey responses; see, for example, Schultz (2004) and Behrman, Sengupta, and Todd (2005) on *Oportunidades* and Ravallion and Wodon (2000) on the Food for Education program in Bangladesh. While we cannot fully rule out such concerns, they are unlikely to be a serious problem for our analysis for a number of reasons. During training, enumerators were instructed that they should not identify themselves as associated with the BDH program or its evaluation under any circumstances; if questioned, enumerators were to state that the information given by respondents would in no way affect eligibility for social programs, including the BDH program. Compliance with these instructions was verified during spot visits in the field. Moreover, questions about the BDH program were included in the last module of the survey, well after questions about household characteristics and (critically) schooling of children. Finally, households could also have lied about whether they had received BDH transfers. This appears not to have been the case, however, since their answers match up very closely with banking records on transfers, as shown in footnote 14.

12. The percentage of conditioned households in our sample is close to that found in other data sources. In a nationwide household survey carried out in December 2005, respondents were asked whether they believed that households had to comply with any requirements to receive BDH transfers: 26.0 percent answered that BDH beneficiaries were expected to ensure that children enroll in school and attend regularly. The question was worded in exactly the same way in the December 2005 nationwide survey and in the January–March 2005 survey used in this paper. One important difference is that the December 2005 survey asked this question only of households that reported receiving BDH transfers. In the January–March 2005 survey, 32.9 percent of

We obtained data from *Banred* on total BDH transfers collected by households in the sample between January 2004 and July 2005. This allows us to construct two measures of BDH treatment—one based on household survey responses and one based on banking records.[13] Discrepancies between the two sources of data are minor, and the estimated program effects are similar regardless of whether treatment status is defined with the household data or the banking records.[14]

One possible concern with this evaluation is anticipation effects among households assigned to the control group. Households in this group were not told they would receive BDH transfers in the future. Nevertheless, although it is not easy for an individual household to learn its Selben score, some lottery losers may have concluded that they were eligible for transfers on the basis of their score. If consumption is smoothed over time, households in the control group may have increased their spending on schooling in anticipation of future transfers. Insofar as this is the case, the program effects reported here are likely to be lower-bound estimates of the BDH impact.

Attrition over the study period was low: 94.1 percent of households were reinterviewed. Among households that attrited, most had moved and could not be found (4.2 percent), while in a few cases no qualified respondent was available for the follow-up survey despite repeat visits by the enumerator

households receiving BDH transfers believed there was an enrollment requirement. We thank Mauricio León for help with calculations based on the December 2005 survey.

13. When a BDH beneficiary attempts to collect a transfer at a bank, her national identification number is used to check whether she is eligible for transfers, and a record is made of the amount of money she receives. The national identification numbers of respondents and other adults in the household were collected in the baseline and follow-up surveys, and the private banks in *Banred* provided data on the payments made to all persons with these identification numbers, on a monthly basis. A household is defined as treated using the banking records if a member withdrew BDH funds at least once. Transfers can be collected on a monthly basis, or they can accumulate for up to four months. In the study sample, 92 percent of households who ever withdrew transfers according to the banking records did so at least ten times over the nineteen-month period, and more than three-quarters of recipient households received a total amount equivalent to nineteen monthly transfers.

14. Of the 1,306 households in the sample, 493 (38 percent) are untreated by both measures, and 672 (51 percent) are treated by both measures. Only 22 households (2 percent) appear as treated in the banking records but not the household survey, and 121 (9 percent) appear as treated in the household survey, but not the banking records. The national identification number was used to merge the surveys and the banking records. Discrepancies could arise if enumerators failed to collect the identification numbers of all household members or made errors copying the numbers. In addition, the banking records do not cover the small share of households (approximately 2 percent) who collect transfers from the National Development Bank, rather than the consortium of private banks in *Banred*.

(1.0 percent) or the respondent refused to participate in the survey (0.5 percent). There is no relation between assignment to the study groups and attrition, and baseline differences between attrited and other households in per capita expenditures, assets, maternal education, and paternal education are small and insignificant. Attrited children were less likely to be enrolled at baseline, although this is largely driven by the fact that they were older.[15] Attrition is most likely to introduce biases in estimation when there are large differences between attrited and other households or when attrition is correlated with treatment status, and there is little evidence that this is the case in our data.

### *Descriptive Statistics at Baseline*

We begin by assessing the extent to which the randomized experiment worked. Table 2 summarizes the baseline characteristics of lottery winners and losers and of transfer recipients and nonrecipients. The table shows that there are no significant differences between lottery winners and losers in any of a large number of variables. At baseline, lottery winners and losers are essentially indistinguishable in terms of enrollment, grade attainment, child work, gender, per capita expenditures, assets, parental education, and household size. These comparisons make clear that the random assignment to treatment and control groups was successful.

Although random assignment was successful, there is unfortunately a very imperfect match between assignment to a study group and receipt of BDH transfers. Program take-up among lottery winners was 78 percent; lack of information, the cost of traveling to a bank, and stigma may all have discouraged some households from receiving transfers. More worryingly, 42 percent of households assigned to the control group received transfers. The precise reasons for this substantial contamination are unclear. Conversations with BDH administrators suggest that the list of households that had been randomly excluded from the program was not immediately passed on to operational staff activating households for transfers. This situation was corrected after a few

15. In a regression of a dummy variable for attrited households on a dummy variable for lottery winners, the coefficient is 0.054, with a robust standard error of 0.057. In a simple regression of baseline enrollment on a dummy variable for attrited households, the coefficient is –0.083, with a robust standard error of 0.038. When a set of unrestricted child age dummies is included in the regression, the coefficient on the dummy variable for attrited children becomes insignificant: The coefficient is –0.033, with a robust standard error of 0.034. On the other hand, a joint test shows that the age dummies are clearly significant ($p$ value of less than 0.001).

**TABLE 2. Baseline Differences between Lottery Winners and Losers and between BDH Recipients and Nonrecipients**[a]

| | *Difference by lottery status* | | *Difference by receipt of BDH transfers* | |
|---|---|---|---|---|
| *Explanatory variable* | *Mean of lottery losers* | *Difference between lottery losers and winners* | *Mean of nonrecipient households* | *Difference between nonrecipient and recipient households* |
| Probability that child is enrolled | 0.770 | −0.003 | 0.787 | 0.052*** |
| | (0.423) | (0.021) | (0.409) | (0.017) |
| Child age | 11.72 | 0.045 | 11.63 | −0.173* |
| | (2.82) | (0.094) | (2.83) | (0.102) |
| Child is male | 0.486 | −0.030 | 0.497 | −0.009 |
| | (0.500) | (0.020) | (0.500) | (0.019) |
| Log of per capita expenditures | 3.39 | 0.020 | 3.38 | −0.040 |
| | (0.541) | (0.023) | (0.521) | (0.033) |
| Asset index | 0.041 | 0.015 | 0.023 | −0.029 |
| | (0.877) | (0.058) | (0.827) | (0.070) |
| Father's education | 4.92 | 0.029 | 5.08 | 0.477** |
| | (2.73) | (0.147) | (2.62) | (0.187) |
| Mother's education | 3.87 | 0.144 | 4.02 | 0.574*** |
| | (2.93) | (0.150) | (2.90) | (0.213) |
| Household head is male | 0.881 | 0.013 | 0.877 | 0.003 |
| | (0.323) | (0.022) | (0.329) | (0.021) |
| Household head is indigenous | 0.168 | 0.029 | 0.156 | 0.006 |
| | (0.374) | (0.024) | (0.363) | (0.027) |
| Household head is literate | 0.843 | −0.032 | 0.875 | 0.044 |
| | (0.364) | (0.021) | (0.331) | (0.032) |
| Household size | 6.33 | 0.051 | 6.40 | 0.249** |
| | (1.98) | (0.123) | (1.87) | (0.122) |

* Statistically significant at the 10 percent level.
** Statistically significant at the 5 percent level.
*** Statistically significant at the 1 percent level.

a. All means refer to baseline values. Sample size is 2,875 for all variables except for father's education ($n = 2{,}748$) and mother's education ($n = 2{,}827$). Standard errors (in parentheses) are adjusted for within-parish correlation.

weeks, but withholding transfers from households that had already begun to receive them was judged to be politically imprudent.

Table 2 reveals clear differences between households that received BDH transfers and those that did not. Children in households that received transfers were significantly more likely to be enrolled at baseline than children in nonrecipient households; the fathers of these children had 0.48 more years of schooling, on average, and their mothers had 0.57 more years. Both of these differences are large, amounting to about one-fifth of a standard deviation, and significant. The heads of households that received transfers were also significantly more likely to be literate. Finally, households that received transfers were larger than households that did not. Selection into the BDH program (as opposed to selection by the lottery) appears to be nonrandom.

## Overall Estimates of BDH Program Impact

We begin our analysis with a reduced-form model that focuses on differences in outcomes between households randomly assigned to the treatment group (rather than households that received BDH transfers in practice) and households randomly assigned to the control group (rather than households that did not receive transfers):

$$Y_{it} = \alpha_c + \mathbf{X}_{it-1}\beta + Z_i\delta + \varepsilon_{it}, \quad (1)$$

where $Y_{it}$ is a dummy variable that takes on the value of one if child $i$ is enrolled in school at the time of the follow-up survey; $\alpha_c$ is a set of canton-level fixed effects; $\mathbf{X}_{it-1}$ is a vector of baseline child and household characteristics; $Z_i$ is a dummy variable that takes the value of one if a family was a lottery winner; and $\varepsilon_{it}$ is the regression error term. The parameter $\delta$ is an exogenous lottery effect that relies only on the random assignment.

It is also possible to run regressions in which the dependent variable is the change in enrollment between baseline and follow-up. Incorporating baseline enrollment in the estimation helps sweep out any unobserved heterogeneity across households that may have persisted despite random assignment. This alternative specification is as follows:

$$Y_{it} - Y_{it-1} = \alpha_c + \mathbf{X}_{it-1}\beta + Z_i\delta + \varepsilon_{it}. \quad (2)$$

In both cases, we present results for four specifications, corresponding to different numbers of controls. The first specification includes no controls and is equivalent to unadjusted mean differences between lottery winners and losers; the second specification includes controls for child age and gender; the third specification includes an extended set of controls for baseline child and household characteristics; and the fourth specification supplements these controls with twenty-seven canton-level fixed effects.[16] The stability of the

16. The controls for child age are dummy variables corresponding to each year of age. The extended set of controls includes parental education, per capita expenditures, the composite measure of household wealth, dummy variables for whether paternal or maternal education is missing, dummy variables for whether a household head is indigenous, literate, and male (three separate variables), a dummy variable for rural households, and a measure of the number of household members.

coefficient on lottery winners—both as more controls are added and across specifications that define the dependent variable in terms of levels (as in equation 1) or changes (as in equation 2)—is an important check on the identification strategy.

As an alternative to reduced-form regressions, we use the randomized selection into study groups as an instrument for the actual receipt of BDH transfers:

$$Y_{it} - Y_{it-1} = \alpha_c + X_{it-1}\varphi + T_i\lambda + v_{it}, \quad (3)$$

where $T_i$ is a dummy variable that takes the value of one if a household received BDH transfers and is instrumented with assignment by the lottery, $Z_i$. By construction, assignment into treatment and control groups is orthogonal with the error term, $v_{it}$, and therefore satisfies the exclusion restriction.[17]

Despite contamination of the control group and less-than-complete take-up by lottery winners, assignment by the lottery is a strong predictor of BDH treatment. In a regression of treatment on lottery status, with no controls, the coefficient is 0.347, with a robust standard error of 0.040; when the extended list of controls and canton fixed effects are added, the coefficient is 0.361, with a standard error of 0.037.

### *Main Results of Program Impact*

The main results on the overall BDH program impact on enrollment are presented in tables 3 and 4. Table 3 reports the results from the reduced-form, linear probability model (ordinary least squares). In panel A, the dependent variable is enrollment at follow-up, while in panel B, the dependent variable is the change in enrollment between baseline and follow-up. In both cases, the main coefficient of interest is that on the dummy for lottery winners.

The table shows that the probability that a child is enrolled in school at the time of the follow-up survey is 3.2 to 4.0 percentage points higher among lottery winners than lottery losers. The estimates of program effects are stable across specifications, as one would expect given the random assignment by the BDH lottery. The stability of the coefficient on lottery losers does not stem from the lack of the explanatory power of the additional covariates. For example, in the specifications in panel A, the $R$ squared rises from 0.001 in the specification with no controls to 0.256 in the specification that includes the full list of controls and canton fixed effects. Also, results are similar

17. Imbens and Angrist (1994).

**TABLE 3. The Impact of BDH Transfers on School Enrollment: Reduced-Form Models[a]**

| *Explanatory variable* | *(1)* | *(2)* | *(3)* | *(4)* |
|---|---|---|---|---|
| *A. Dependent variable: Enrollment at follow-up* | | | | |
| BDH lottery winner | 0.032* | 0.040** | 0.037** | 0.039** |
| | (0.019) | (0.017) | (0.016) | (0.016) |
| Child is male | | 0.050*** | 0.053*** | 0.054*** |
| | | (0.018) | (0.017) | (0.017) |
| Log of per capita expenditures | | | 0.053*** | 0.078*** |
| | | | (0.018) | (0.017) |
| Asset index | | | 0.016 | 0.016 |
| | | | (0.011) | (0.011) |
| Father's education | | | 0.015*** | 0.015*** |
| | | | (0.005) | (0.006) |
| Mother's education | | | 0.022*** | 0.021*** |
| | | | (0.005) | (0.005) |
| Household size | | | −0.001 | −0.002 |
| | | | (0.007) | (0.006) |
| Child age dummies | No | Yes | Yes | Yes |
| Canton dummies | No | No | No | Yes |
| $R^2$ | 0.001 | 0.175 | 0.237 | 0.256 |
| *B. Dependent variable: Change in enrollment between baseline and follow-up* | | | | |
| BDH lottery winner | 0.035* | 0.034* | 0.035** | 0.037** |
| | (0.018) | (0.017) | (0.017) | (0.018) |
| Child is male | | 0.030** | 0.029* | 0.031** |
| | | (0.015) | (0.015) | (0.015) |
| Log of per capita expenditures | | | −0.025 | −0.026 |
| | | | (0.017) | (0.019) |
| Asset index | | | 0.014 | 0.015 |
| | | | (0.009) | (0.009) |
| Father's education | | | 0.005 | 0.005 |
| | | | (0.004) | (0.004) |
| Mother's education | | | 0.000 | 0.000 |
| | | | (0.003) | (0.004) |
| Household size | | | −0.005 | −0.007 |
| | | | (0.006) | (0.006) |
| Child age dummies | No | Yes | Yes | Yes |
| Canton dummies | No | No | No | Yes |
| $R^2$ | 0.002 | 0.046 | 0.054 | 0.064 |

* Statistically significant at the 10 percent level.

** Statistically significant at the 5 percent level.

a. The specifications in columns (3) and (4) also include dummy variables for whether father's education or mother's education is missing and for whether the household head is male, indigenous, or literate (three separate variables). Sample size is 2,875 in all regressions. Standard errors (in parentheses) are adjusted for within-parish correlation.

**TABLE 4. The Impact of BDH Transfers on School Enrollment: Two-Stage Least Squares[a]**

| *Explanatory variable* | *(1)* | *(2)* | *(3)* | *(4)* |
|---|---|---|---|---|
| BDH lottery winner | 0.101* | 0.099* | 0.100** | 0.103** |
| | (0.052) | (0.050) | (0.050) | (0.048) |
| $R^2$ | | 0.041 | 0.047 | 0.057 |

* Statistically significant at the 10 percent level.

** Statistically significant at the 5 percent level.

a. The dependent variable is the change in enrollment between baseline and follow-up. Specification (1) includes no controls; specification (2) includes a set of single-year child age dummies and a dummy for child gender; specification (3) supplements this with variables for baseline log per capita expenditures, the asset composite, father's education, mother's education, dummy variables for whether father's education or mother's education is missing, household size, and dummy variables for whether the household head is male, indigenous, or literate (three separate variables); specification (4) also includes a set of canton fixed effects. In all specifications, the dummy variable for whether a household received transfers is instrumented with random assignment by the BDH lottery. The sample size is 2,875 in all regressions. Standard errors (in parentheses) are adjusted for within-parish correlation.

when the dependent variable is defined in levels at follow-up (panel A) or in changes (panel B). We therefore focus on the specification in changes for the rest of the paper.

Table 4 presents comparable results from the structural, two-stage least squares model. In this case, the main coefficient of interest is on children in households that received BDH transfers, which is instrumented with the randomized assignment by the lottery. These regressions show that BDH transfers resulted in an increase in enrollment of approximately 10 percentage points among complier households.[18] This is a large effect compared with estimates for other programs in Latin America. For example, Schultz estimates that *Oportunidades* had an impact on the enrollment of children in first through eighth grades of between 3.4 and 3.6 percentage points, while Attanasio and others conclude that *Familias en Acción* had an impact of approximately 10 percentage points on the enrollment of children age twelve to seventeen in rural areas and 5 percentage points in urban areas, with no impact among younger children.[19] We do not have a satisfactory explanation for the large magnitude of the BDH effects. Households in our sample tend to be very poor—median per capita expenditures at baseline were just under two dollars per capita per day and less than about one dollar per capita per day for about 10 percent of the households in the sample. However, households

18. Additional results (unreported but available on request) show that the coefficients are similar if the *Banred* banking records are used to construct the variable for BDH transfers (rather than the answers provided by households in the follow-up survey, as in the table) or if estimation is done by joint bivariate probit, rather than two-stage least squares.

19. Schultz (2004); Attanasio and others (2005).

who benefited from *Oportunidades* in Mexico also appear to have been very poor. Hoddinott, Skoufias, and Washburn estimate that per capita expenditures in the *Oportunidades* control localities in 1998 were 189 pesos, or approximately US$0.61 a day at prevailing exchange rates.[20] Cross-country comparisons of expenditure levels are hazardous for a variety of reasons, including differences in purchasing power and in expenditure modules across surveys, but it does not appear at first glance that households in the BDH evaluation sample are a great deal poorer than those who benefited from *Oportunidades* in Mexico. Moreover, the amount of the transfer in *Oportunidades* accounted for approximately 20 percent of the consumption of the average household, versus 9 percent in our sample, which only makes the large magnitude of the BDH program effects on enrollment all the harder to explain. Another possible explanation for the difference in magnitudes in the estimated effects across countries is related to estimation choices. Instrumental variables estimates such as those we report for the BDH apply only to households whose likelihood of receiving transfers was affected by the BDH lottery—what Angrist, Imbens, and Rubin call compliers.[21] These compliers cannot be easily identified from the data without additional assumptions, but they may have characteristics that made their enrollment choices particularly sensitive to transfers.[22]

### *Heterogeneity of Treatment Effects*

We next assess possible heterogeneity of BDH treatment effects by school grade, gender, place of residence, maternal education, and per capita expenditures. We first focus on differences by school grade. We begin by estimating the rate of continuation from one grade to another, using information on the years of schooling completed by young adults in the baseline survey.[23] Specifically, we calculate the fraction of these young adults who report having completed exactly a given number of years of schooling—for example, the fraction of adults who have completed exactly one year of schooling, exactly two years, and so on. The continuation rate is then given by the difference in these proportions of adults across adjacent grades. Figure 1 summarizes the results. The figure reveals sharp drops in the continuation rate in

20. Hoddinott, Skoufias, and Washburn (2000, p. 49).
21. Angrist, Imbens, and Rubin (1996).
22. See Angrist (2004) for a discussion.
23. We define young adults as those aged nineteen to twenty-four, but our results are very similar with other age ranges.

**FIGURE 1. Continuation Rate, by School Grade**

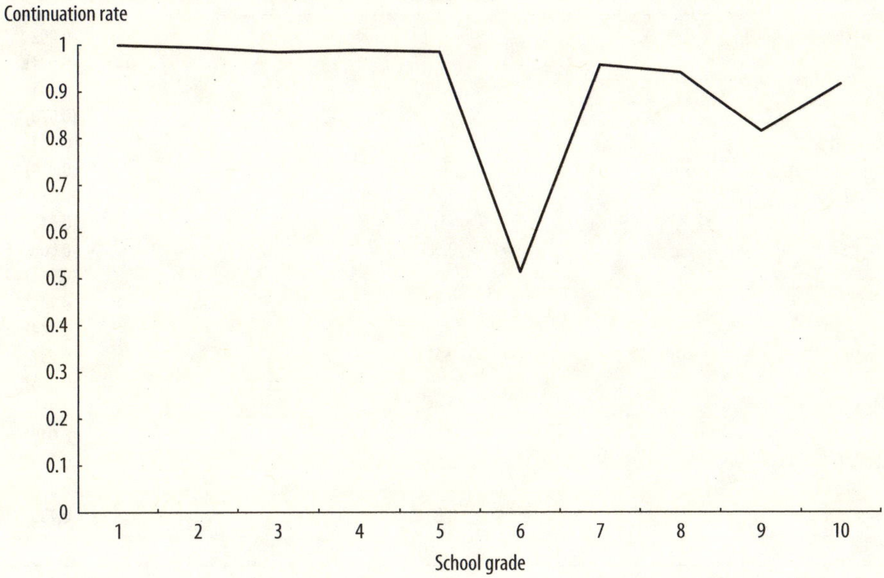


Source: Authors' calculations, based on the 2003 evaluation survey.

sixth grade (the last year of primary school) and ninth grade (the last year of lower secondary school). One might therefore expect that the BDH effects would be largest at these transition grades in which, absent the program, the likelihood of dropping out of school is large.

To assess the heterogeneity of BDH program effects by school grade, we use information on the highest grade attained by children at baseline. For children who were enrolled in school, the highest grade attained and the grade in which a child was enrolled at baseline are closely related. For example, we can infer that a child who was enrolled in school and whose highest grade attained was fifth grade was enrolled in sixth grade at baseline. We therefore generate ten dummy variables, corresponding to the attainment of no grades through the attainment of ninth grade at baseline.[24] We then run separate regressions

24. Both the baseline and follow-up surveys collected schooling information only for children between the ages of six and seventeen; we thus have only a handful of children who have attained more than nine grades at baseline.

**TABLE 5. Heterogeneity of Treatment Effects, by Baseline Grade[a]**

| *Grade* | *Continuation rate* | *Coefficient* |
|---|---|---|
| No schooling | | −0.002 |
| | | (0.031) |
| First | 0.999 | 0.001 |
| | | (0.020) |
| Second | 0.994 | −0.031 |
| | | (0.019) |
| Third | 0.984 | −0.031 |
| | | (0.041) |
| Fourth | 0.988 | 0.009 |
| | | (0.043) |
| Fifth | 0.984 | 0.113** |
| | | (0.044) |
| Sixth | 0.513 | 0.032 |
| | | (0.026) |
| Seventh | 0.956 | −0.007 |
| | | (0.049) |
| Eighth | 0.940 | 0.125*** |
| | | (0.046) |
| Ninth | 0.814 | 0.130* |
| | | (0.068) |

* Statistically significant at the 10 percent level.
** Statistically significant at the 5 percent level.
*** Statistically significant at the 1 percent level.
a. The dependent variable in all specifications is the change in enrollment between the baseline and follow-up surveys. The variable "grade" refers to the highest grade completed at the time of the baseline survey. The continuation rate is calculated on the basis of adults aged nineteen to twenty-four at the time of the baseline survey. All specifications include a set of single-year child age dummies and a dummy for child gender. Standard errors (in parentheses) are adjusted for within-parish correlation. Sample size varies by grade.

that limit the sample to children who have achieved a given number of years of schooling at baseline. These regressions include the age and gender dummies, but they do not include the extended set of controls and canton fixed effects, given the small sample sizes for some grades.

The results in table 5 indicate that BDH program effects are concentrated among children who were likely to face transition grades between the two surveys. For children who had completed exactly five years of schooling at baseline, the BDH program effect is 0.113 (with a standard error of 0.044); for those who had completed eight years of schooling, it is 0.125 (with a standard error of 0.046). For all other children, the program effect on enrollment is insignificant at the 5 percent level or higher, although it is borderline significant for children who had completed exactly nine years of schooling at baseline. This pattern of results, whereby BDH program effects on enrollment are concentrated among children in school grades in which the prob-

**TABLE 6. Heterogeneity of Treatment Effects, by Baseline Characteristics[a]**

| *Baseline characteristic* | *Baseline enrollment* | *Coefficient* | *Test of equality (p value)* |
|---|---|---|---|
| Gender | | | |
| Boys | 0.784 | 0.027 | 0.631 |
| | | (0.022) | |
| Girls | 0.753 | 0.042 | |
| | | (0.024) | |
| Place of residence | | | |
| Urban | 0.784 | 0.049*** | 0.150 |
| | | (0.018) | |
| Rural | 0.753 | 0.022 | |
| | | (0.019) | |
| Maternal education | | | |
| Low | 0.693 | 0.028 | 0.479 |
| | | (0.022) | |
| High | 0.866 | 0.042** | |
| | | (0.016) | |
| Per capita expenditures | | | |
| Low | 0.729 | 0.045** | 0.417 |
| | | (0.021) | |
| High | 0.807 | 0.024 | |
| | | (0.022) | |

** Statistically significant at the 5 percent level.

*** Statistically significant at the 1 percent level.

a. The dependent variable in all specifications is the change in enrollment between the baseline and follow-up surveys. All specifications include a set of single-year child age dummies and a dummy for child gender. Sample size is 2,875 in all regressions. Standard errors (in parentheses) are adjusted for within-parish correlation.

ability of continuing to the next grade was relatively low, is similar to results for *Oportunidades* in Mexico, where program effects on enrollment are concentrated among children enrolled in sixth grade at baseline.[25]

We next focus on possible differences in BDH program effects based on gender, place of residence (urban or rural), maternal education (incomplete primary or less versus completed primary or more), and baseline per capita expenditures (above or below the median). The results of these calculations are presented in table 6. Each of these comparisons is based on a regression with a main effect (for example, a main effect for girls) and two interactions (for example, an interaction between lottery winners and girls and an interaction between lottery winners and boys). The table also includes a row for the baseline enrollment levels; these are useful for assessing whether larger BDH treatment effects are found among groups with the biggest margin for

25. Schultz (2004); de Janvry and Sadoulet (2006).

improvement. Finally, the last column of the table presents the results of an *F* test of the equality of coefficients on the two interaction effects. For example, in the first comparison, we report the *p* value on an *F* test of the equality of the coefficient on the interaction between lottery status and girls and the coefficient on the interaction between lottery status and boys.

As the table shows, we find no clear evidence of heterogeneity across these dimensions of the data. The point estimates are larger for girls than for boys, for urban than for rural areas, for more educated mothers than for less educated mothers, and for poorer households. None of these differences are statistically significant, however.

## Program Effects among Conditioned and Unconditioned Households

The second part of the paper focuses on differences in outcomes between conditioned and unconditioned households, as described above. Recall that conditioned households are those that told enumerators that they believed the BDH transfers had a schooling requirement, whereas unconditioned households told enumerators that transfers did not have a schooling requirement. We begin by limiting the sample to lottery winners, and we then compare the outcomes for conditioned and unconditioned households after adjusting for observable differences in a variety of ways. The first estimator is based on a linear regression that includes a dummy variable for conditioned households (among lottery winners):

$$Y_{it} - Y_{it-1} = \alpha_c + \mathbf{X}_{it-1}\eta + C_i\psi + \varepsilon_{it}, \quad (4)$$

where $C_i$ is a dummy variable that takes the value of one if the respondent told the enumerator that the transfers had a schooling requirement and zero otherwise.

Linear regression models rely heavily on extrapolation to impute potential (or counterfactual) outcomes. This may introduce biases if the distribution of the covariates $\mathbf{X}_{it-1}$ is very different for conditioned and unconditioned households. We therefore present results based on two alternative methods to correct for observable differences between conditioned and unconditioned households. Both of these are recent developments in the literature on matching estimators.[26] The first of these is a bias-adjusted matching estimator

26. For a thoughtful review, see Imbens (2004).

proposed by Abadie and Imbens.[27] This estimator uses nearest-neighbor matching to match treated and control households on the basis of their covariates; it then adjusts for any remaining differences in the distribution of the covariates with regression techniques. Abadie and Imbens show that this bias-corrected matching estimator performs well in practice.[28] The second estimator relies on a reweighting scheme for the data, as proposed by Hirano, Imbens, and Ridder.[29] To calculate the weights, a dummy variable for conditioned households is regressed on their baseline characteristics (again for lottery winners):

$$C_i = \alpha + \mathbf{X}_{it-1}\gamma + \omega_i. \qquad (5)$$

This regression is then used to predict the probability that a household is conditioned, $\pi_i$, also known as the propensity score.[30] Hirano, Imbens, and Ridder show that giving conditioned households a weight of $1/\pi_i$ and unconditioned households a weight of $1/(1 - \pi_i)$ produces a fully efficient estimator of the Average Treatment Effect, with conservative standard errors.[31] To further adjust for observable differences between conditioned and unconditioned households, we also experiment with trimming the sample to remove the 10 percent of households with the lowest propensity score and the 10 percent with the highest score.

It is also possible to use information on lottery losers in the estimation. Since conditioned households are found among both lottery winners and losers, we can estimate a difference-in-differences specification:

$$Y_{it} - Y_{it-1} = \alpha_c + \mathbf{X}_{it-1}\beta_1 + C_i\beta_2 + Z_i\delta_i + \left(Z_iC_i\right)\delta_2 + \varepsilon_{it}. \qquad (6)$$

27. Abadie and Imbens (2002).

28. Abadie and Imbens (2002). Another recent application is McKenzie, Gibson, and Stillman (2006).

29. Hirano, Imbens, and Ridder (2003).

30. To avoid values of the propensity score below zero or above one, we estimate equation 5 by probit rather than ordinary least squares (OLS). The regression does not include canton fixed effects, as there are three cantons in which no household was conditioned. The probit algorithm automatically drops these from the sample when canton fixed effects are included in the regression, and no weights would be generated for these households. Our results are not sensitive to this choice. The coefficients for the weighted regressions reported below are very similar to those obtained when households in these cantons are dropped from the sample, weights are estimated on the basis of a regression that includes canton fixed effects, and weighted regressions are run on this smaller sample.

31. Hirano, Imbens, and Ridder (2003). Recent applications include Hirano and Imbens (2002); Chen, Mu, and Ravallion (2006); Filmer and Schady (2008).

The main parameter of interest is $\delta_2$, which denotes the difference-in-differences estimate of the effect of the perceived enrollment requirement among lottery winners.[32] This specification allows us to sweep out any fixed differences between conditioned and unconditioned households, which could help reduce any remaining sources of bias. However, multiple differencing of this sort can also reduce the signal-to-noise ratio of the estimates and make the point estimates less precise.

### *Comparisons between Conditioned and Unconditioned Households at Baseline*

We begin by comparing the characteristics of conditioned and unconditioned households separately for lottery winners and losers.[33] Table 7 reveals a number of significant differences between conditioned and unconditioned households at baseline. Children in conditioned households were more likely to be enrolled in school than children in unconditioned households; the parents of these children have more schooling and are less likely to be illiterate than their unconditioned counterparts; and conditioned households tend to have more household members. Some of these differences are large. For example, conditioned households have between 0.57 and 0.66 more years of paternal schooling and between 0.68 and 0.69 more years of maternal education than unconditioned households.

Table 8 summarizes baseline differences between conditioned and unconditioned households within the sample of lottery winners after matching and reweighting.[34] For the purpose of the table, all of the covariates have been normalized to have zero mean and unit standard deviation. The sample in panel A includes all lottery winners, while the sample in panel B trims the 10 percent of households with the highest propensity scores and the 10 percent with the lowest scores. The first and second columns report the standardized means of a given variable for conditioned and unconditioned households; the third column reports the raw difference between these values; the fourth column

32. Since the dependent variable in equation 6 is defined as changes in enrollment between baseline and follow-up, this model could also be written as a triple-difference specification, moving $Y_{it-1}$ to the right-hand side of the equation, and interacting it with the parameters $C_i$, $Z_i$, and $Z_iC_i$.

33. The sample size for these comparisons and for the regressions in table 9 is slightly smaller than for our earlier analysis because in thirty-five households, including seventy-four school-aged children, respondents did not answer questions about knowledge and perceptions of the BDH program. Differences between households that did not answer these questions and other households in terms of baseline parental education, per capita expenditures, assets, child enrollment, age, and gender are not significant.

34. Abadie and Imbens (2002); Hirano, Imbens, and Ridder (2003).

**TABLE 7. Baseline Differences between Conditioned and Unconditioned Households[a]**

| | Lottery winners | | Lottery losers | |
|---|---|---|---|---|
| *Explanatory variable* | *Mean of conditioned households* | *Difference* | *Mean of unconditioned households* | *Difference* |
| Probability that child is enrolled | 0.819 | 0.077*** | 0.823 | 0.068** |
| | (0.385) | (0.028) | (0.383) | (0.025) |
| Child age | 11.60 | −0.171 | 11.24 | −0.565*** |
| | (2.78) | (0.147) | (2.84) | (0.179) |
| Child is male | 0.475 | −0.016 | 0.480 | −0.049 |
| | (0.500) | (0.029) | (0.500) | (0.033) |
| Log of per capita expenditures | 3.37 | −0.024 | 3.55 | −0.073 |
| | (0.523) | (0.053) | (0.502) | (0.059) |
| Asset index | 0.014 | −0.037 | −0.032 | −0.072 |
| | (0.836) | (0.071) | (0.781) | (0.090) |
| Father's education | 5.39 | 0.659*** | 5.36 | 0.572* |
| | (2.70) | (0.247) | (2.37) | (0.291) |
| Mother's education | 4.35 | 0.681** | 4.29 | 0.689** |
| | (3.04) | (0.320) | (2.62) | (0.288) |
| Household head is male | 0.877 | −0.006 | 0.844 | −0.028 |
| | (0.329) | (0.030) | (0.363) | (0.031) |
| Household head is indigenous | 0.147 | −0.030 | 0.098 | −0.057 |
| | (0.355) | (0.043) | (0.298) | (0.041) |
| Household head is literate | 0.877 | 0.046 | 0.920 | 0.061* |
| | (0.329) | (0.033) | (0.271) | (0.036) |
| Household size | 6.44 | 0.145 | 6.51 | 0.344* |
| | (1.93) | (0.203) | (1.80) | (0.176) |

* Statistically significant at the 10 percent level.
** Statistically significant at the 5 percent level.
*** Statistically significant at the 1 percent level.
a. All means refer to baseline values. Sample size is 1,472 for lottery winners and 1,329 for lottery losers. Standard errors (in parentheses) are adjusted for within-parish correlation.

provides the average difference in the matched pairs, after matching with the bias-corrected matching estimator; the fifth column provides the average difference between conditioned and unconditioned households when conditioned households are given a weight of $1/\pi_i$ and unconditioned households are given a weight of $1/(1 - \pi_i)$.[35]

35. The matching estimates are based on matching with the four nearest neighbors, although our results are not sensitive to this choice. For example, the estimated program effect for the full sample of lottery winners reported in table 9 is 0.088 (with a standard error of 0.020). When matching is performed using only one neighbor, the value is 0.091 (with a standard error of 0.020), and when matching is performed using sixteen neighbors, the estimate is 0.086 (with a standard error of 0.020).

**TABLE 8. Baseline Differences between Conditioned and Unconditioned Households after Matching and Reweighting Lottery Winners**[a]

| | *Average* | | *Difference* | | |
|---|---|---|---|---|---|
| *Explanatory variable* | *Conditioned* | *Unconditioned* | *Raw* | *Matching* | *Reweighting* |
| *A. Full sample* | | | | | |
| Enrollment | 0.124 | –0.057 | 0.181 | 0.061 | –0.070 |
| Child age | –0.042 | 0.019 | –0.061 | 0.019 | 0.027 |
| Child is male | –0.023 | 0.010 | –0.033 | –0.046 | –0.029 |
| Log of per capita expenditures | –0.029 | 0.015 | –0.044 | –0.057 | 0.021 |
| Asset index | –0.031 | 0.011 | –0.043 | –0.041 | 0.008 |
| Father's education | 0.194 | –0.074 | 0.268 | 0.055 | –0.044 |
| Mother's education | 0.180 | –0.072 | 0.252 | 0.082 | –0.033 |
| Household head is male | –0.014 | 0.004 | –0.017 | 0.009 | 0.018 |
| Household head is indigenous | –0.056 | 0.024 | –0.080 | –0.042 | –0.027 |
| Household head is literate | 0.094 | –0.034 | 0.128 | 0.024 | 0.047 |
| Household size | 0.053 | –0.020 | 0.073 | 0.030 | –0.028 |
| Mean difference | | | 0.111 | 0.042 | 0.032 |
| *B. Trimmed sample* | | | | | |
| Enrollment | 0.148 | 0.018 | 0.129 | 0.043 | 0.040 |
| Child age | –0.078 | –0.022 | –0.056 | 0.026 | –0.030 |
| Child is male | 0.010 | 0.012 | –0.002 | –0.011 | –0.004 |
| Log of per capita expenditures | 0.005 | –0.002 | 0.008 | –0.028 | –0.001 |
| Asset index | 0.016 | 0.081 | –0.065 | –0.064 | –0.040 |
| Father's education | 0.088 | –0.042 | 0.129 | 0.068 | 0.005 |
| Mother's education | 0.058 | –0.072 | 0.130 | 0.093 | 0.020 |
| Household head is male | 0.103 | 0.068 | 0.035 | 0.010 | 0.033 |
| Household head is indigenous | –0.024 | –0.002 | –0.022 | –0.034 | 0.016 |
| Household head is literate | 0.060 | 0.052 | 0.008 | –0.008 | –0.069 |
| Household size | 0.076 | 0.042 | 0.035 | 0.004 | 0.023 |
| Mean difference | | | 0.056 | 0.035 | 0.026 |

a. The sample is limited to lottery winners. All variables have been standardized to have zero mean and unit standard deviation. The first two columns present the means for conditioned and unconditioned households, respectively; the third column reports the difference in these raw means; the fourth column reports the difference after bias-corrected nearest-neighbor matching (Abadie and Imbens 2002); the fifth column reports the difference after reweighting with a transformation of the propensity score (Hirano, Imbens, and Ridder 2003). Sample sizes are 1,472 for the full sample and 1,178 for the trimmed sample.

Table 8 shows that the average raw difference between conditioned and unconditioned households in the full sample is equal to 0.111 standard deviations. Trimming removes approximately half of the average imbalance in the samples; the bias-corrected matching estimator removes approximately two-thirds of the difference in the covariates; and the reweighting scheme removes approximately three-quarters of the imbalance in the samples. In sum, both estimators make conditioned and unconditioned households very closely comparable in terms of their observed covariates, especially when they are combined with judicious trimming of the sample.

**TABLE 9. BDH Effects on Enrollment at Follow-up, Conditioned and Unconditioned Households[a]**

| *Method and sample* | *Coefficient* | *No. observations* |
|---|---|---|
| *A. Lottery winners only* | | |
| OLS | | |
| Full sample | 0.062* | 1,472 |
| | (0.034) | |
| Trimmed sample | 0.059 | 1,178 |
| | (0.038) | |
| Matching | | |
| Full sample | 0.076*** | 1,472 |
| | (0.026) | |
| Trimmed sample | 0.072*** | 1,178 |
| | (0.028) | |
| Reweighting | | |
| Full sample | 0.079** | 1,472 |
| | (0.036) | |
| Trimmed sample | 0.069* | 1,178 |
| | (0.039) | |
| *B. Lottery winners and losers* | | |
| Difference-in-differences | | |
| Full sample | 0.060 | 2,801 |
| | (0.051) | |
| Trimmed sample | 0.072 | 2,236 |
| | (0.061) | |

* Statistically significant at the 10 percent level.
** Statistically significant at the 5 percent level.
*** Statistically significant at the 1 percent level.
a. Standard errors (in parentheses) are adjusted for within-parish correlation.

## *The Effect of Conditions Attached to Transfers*

Table 9 reports the results of comparing the school enrollment behavior of conditioned and unconditioned households. The table includes the results for the four different estimation methods, with and without data trimming. Panel A includes lottery winners only and reports the coefficient on conditioned households. Panel B includes lottery winners and losers and reports the coefficient on the interaction between lottery winners and conditioned households. All specifications include the extended list of controls and canton fixed effects.

The table shows that the change in enrollment between baseline and follow-up is 6 to 8 percentage points higher among households that believed the BDH transfers had an enrollment requirement than among other households. The parameters are robust to different estimation methods and to trimming of the data. In some specifications, in particular the difference-in-differences specification, the point estimates are not significant at conventional levels. However, the point estimates from this specification are very close to those from the specifications in which the sample is limited to lottery winners.

Finally, we discuss one more possible concern with our estimates of the effect of the perceived condition on enrollment. Consider a case in which two kinds of households are eligible for BDH transfers—type A households, which enroll their children in school, and type B households, which do not. Despite this difference in behavior, both types of households receive transfers. Type A households may continue to believe that transfers are conditional, but type B households quickly realize that transfers are not conditional—after all, they continue to receive transfers even though their children are not in school. In this situation, the causality flows (at least in part) from school enrollment to awareness of the condition, and the parameter on the condition in the enrollment regression would not have a causal interpretation.

In an attempt to rule out this possibility, we performed the following validation exercise. If causality flows from school enrollment to the perceived condition, we would expect that the association between the condition and enrollment would be highest for households with children enrolled in the earliest grades in primary school at baseline, since enrollment rates are very high at that level of schooling. If, on the other hand, causality flows from the perceived condition to school enrollment, we would expect that the association would be highest for children enrolled in the transition grades, in which, absent the transfers, the likelihood of dropping out of school is large. As shown above, children who had completed exactly five or eight years of schooling at baseline were most likely to be enrolled in transition grades with a high dropout rate (sixth and ninth grades, respectively). The validation exercise therefore compares the effect of the condition on enrollment for children in lower primary grades and those in transition grades.

For this purpose, we use the difference-in-differences specification that includes both the lottery winners and the lottery losers. When the sample is limited to children who had completed exactly five or eight years of schooling at baseline, the coefficient on the interaction between lottery winners and conditioned households is 0.194 (with a standard error of 0.113); when the sample is limited to children who had completed no more than four years of schooling at baseline, the coefficient is 0.021 (with a standard error of 0.037). The association between the perceived condition and enrollment is thus large and significant for children in transition grades (where the margin for positive program effects is large), but it is absent for those in lower primary grades (where this margin is very small). We conclude from these checks that it is very unlikely that the results in table 9 are substantially biased by reverse causality.

## Conclusion

Policymakers throughout the developing world have long sought to identify programs that build the human capital of the poor. Remarkably little is known, however, about the effect of policies on educational outcomes.[36] This paper adds to a growing literature illustrating that cash transfer programs in Latin America have had positive, and in some cases large, effects on school enrollment. The results for the *Bono de Desarrollo Humano* (BDH) program in Ecuador are based on the random assignment of households into treatment and control groups based on a lottery. Despite substantial contamination of the control group, our reduced-form estimates imply that school-aged children in households that were BDH lottery winners were 3.2 to 4.0 percentage points more likely to be enrolled in school than children in households that were lottery losers. The results are robust to defining the dependent variable in levels or changes, and they are insensitive to the addition of a large number of controls.

The results in this paper also contribute to an ongoing discussion about the extent to which the effects of conditional cash transfer programs on enrollment are a result of the income effects or the transfer conditions.[37] The *Economist* recently stated that "cash transfers, with strings attached, are a better way of helping the poor than many previous social programs."[38] To date, however, there is no experimental or quasi-experimental evidence on this point. In Ecuador, schooling requirements were announced, but never enforced. Nevertheless, approximately one-quarter of the households in our sample (as well as in other data) believed that parents were expected to enroll their children in school to be eligible for BDH transfers. We compare the impact of transfers among these conditioned households with those found among unconditioned households. These estimates suggest that the impact of the BDH program on enrollment was only significant among households that believed there was a

36. Glewwe (2002).

37. A recent five-day international conference on conditional cash transfers held in Istanbul, for example, featured a heated debate between advocates of conditional and unconditional cash transfers. See World Bank's website "Conference Sessions: Day 2 Session (June 27, 2006)" (http://info.worldbank.org/etools/ICCT06/D2_S2new.htm).

38. "Poverty in Latin America: New Thinking about an Old Problem," *Economist,* 17–23 September 2005, pp. 36–38.

schooling requirement associated with the transfers. Although these comparisons are not experimental, they are insensitive to the addition of a large number of controls, to estimates that difference out fixed unobservable differences between conditioned and unconditioned households, and to various ways of trimming and reweighting the data. We conclude that differences in the response to the BDH program between conditioned and unconditioned households are likely to have a causal interpretation.

In Ecuador, enrollment conditions were never monitored, and households that did not enroll their children in school were not penalized. Does this mean that administrators of cash transfer programs can simply announce a schooling requirement and expect that parents will enroll their children in school because they are afraid they could otherwise be disqualified from transfers? The results for Ecuador suggest that such a strategy may work in the short term—at least, for that fraction of households that can be convinced there is an enrollment requirement. We suspect, however, that the effect of an unenforced condition will gradually dissipate as households realize that they will not be penalized if they do not send their children to school and then adjust their behavior accordingly.

# Comments

**Ximena Peña:** The well-measured success of the Mexican *Oportunidades* cash transfer program, formerly known as Progresa, has led many countries to design similar programs, including rigorous evaluation schemes. This paper evaluates the impact of Ecuador's *Bono de Desarrollo Humano* (BDH) on the school enrollment of children aged six to seventeen. Two special characteristics of the BDH implementation make its evaluation challenging and the results, in turn, quite interesting.

First, treatment is potentially endogenous since unmeasured characteristics may affect both the likelihood of receiving transfers and enrollment. The program originally followed an experimental design in which lottery winners received transfers and lottery losers were to be incorporated into the program at a later date, thereby providing a control. At baseline, there were no significant differences between lottery winners and losers in a wide set of covariates, including enrollment. Actual treatment, however, differed from the random assignment: 22 percent of lottery winners did not take up the program, while 42 percent of lottery losers received transfers. This translates into significant differences between treatment and control groups in several covariates at baseline, notably enrollment. In determining the impact of BDH on enrollment, the authors estimate the Intent to Treat and regress school enrollment at follow-up against the lottery outcome in addition to the appropriate controls. Their results suggest that the Intent to Treat increased enrollment by 3.2 to 4.0 percent. They get very similar results when they repeat the estimation using changes in enrollment between baseline and follow-up as the dependent variable. With the same dependent variable, they use the lottery outcome to instrument for actual treatment and estimate the effects using two-stage least squares. They find an increase in enrollment of between 9.2 and 11.4 percentage points. These results are large compared with other findings in the literature, especially since they are not focusing on the specific age groups for which impacts are highest. In other countries, transfers have the strongest impact on enrollment at stages with high dropout rates; the authors similarly find that the impacts are highest among children facing transition grades (five or eight completed years of schooling) when school abandonment is high. Other than transition grades, impact is only significant at nine completed years of schooling. The program is thus ineffective at increasing enrollment at other stages of education.

Second, even though transfers were delivered with no strings attached, around one-fourth of the treatment group believed attendance was mandatory. Conditions on school enrollment and attendance were included in the program design and advertised at informational town-hall-style meetings, in radio and television spots, and at sign-up. In practice, however, conditions were never monitored and noncomplying households were not penalized. Nevertheless, the follow-up survey revealed that 27 percent of beneficiaries believed that school attendance was a prerequisite to receiving transfers. Using only lottery winners, the authors estimate the effect of conditionality on enrollment. Since the distribution of covariates differs at baseline between conditioned and unconditioned households, the authors control for selection on observables in several ways, including a bias-adjusted matching estimator, a reweighting scheme, and data trimming to remove 20 percent of the sample with the highest and lowest propensity scores. They find that enrollment is 5 to 8 percent higher in conditioned than in unconditioned households. The paper would benefit if these results were translated into a more easily comparable measure, such as net differences in enrollment rates or years of schooling.

Based on the wording of the perceived conditioning—namely, ensuring that children attend school—the program seems to have additional effects on attendance that are impossible to measure using existing data. This aspect should be included in a future follow-up survey, to facilitate the evaluation of other impacts of the program.

Exploring several factors would strengthen the paper's results. First, can the results be generalized? The four regions chosen for the study are in the highlands. Are they representative of the country as a whole? Second, the estimation strategy does not explicitly consider the effects of the precursor to the BDH, called *Bono Solidario,* which was a poorly targeted unconditional cash transfer program. Even though families who received *Bono Solidario* transfers were excluded from the sample, its effects are present. An effort should be made to address this. For example, was the program evenly spread in the regions evaluated? Third, the Colombian experience shows that the targeting instrument (Sisben) can be manipulated. It would be relevant to know whether this is a problem for Selben and whether that poses additional challenges for the present evaluation. Finally, the wrinkle in the BDH program implementation offers a unique opportunity to explore the importance of costly conditionality. While the presented results are interesting, I am left wondering about the implications for optimal program design. Is the additional impact on schooling worth the cost of having strings attached to the program?

The proliferation of evaluations of cash transfer programs has provided a lot of information on the impact on several outcomes, such a nutrition, child labor, and school enrollment. However, the generated information has not been used in the same measure to adjust program design. This is mainly due to the misalignment of the required changes and politicians' incentives. If academics do not push harder to use the body of results to fine-tune the programs, millions of dollars devoted to impact evaluations will continue to translate into academic publications only, and not into the desired maximum benefits for the poor.

**Luis F. López-Calva:** Norbert Schady and Maria Caridad Araujo's paper represents an important step forward in understanding the effects of conditional cash transfer programs in Latin America and the behavioral responses of households that receive them. This is not a trivial issue considering that almost 80 million people in Latin America and the Caribbean were beneficiaries of such subsidies in 2007.

The paper uses a randomized study design to analyze the impact of the *Bono de Desarrollo Humano* (BDH), a conditional cash transfer program, on school enrollment among poor children in Ecuador. The authors present two main results, namely, that the BDH program had a large, positive impact on the school enrollment of poor Ecuadorean children and that the program effects are significantly larger among a minority of households that believed the transfers had a school-enrollment requirement. The reason the paper establishes a group of people who "believed" the transfer was conditioned is that the conditionality was not really enforced, though the implementation created the perception among certain households that it would be.

The paper deals with a difficult set of problems that makes traditional impact-evaluation methodologies less appropriate. First, the program instituted a randomized design that was violated in practice, which could potentially affect the validity of the assessment. To address this challenge, the authors wisely exploit an originally random design as an instrument for intervention. The results are quite robust, and the instrument seems appropriate. Thus the data are not really experimental, but there is an initial lottery that can be used as an instrument, highly correlated with treatment. Second, as already mentioned, the program's conditionality was not enforced. Some households, however, perceived the transfer to be subject to a specific behavior. While this represents a problem for the analysis from a traditional perspective, it opens the possibility of discussing new issues, previously unexplored in conditional cash transfer program evaluations, as explained below.

The econometrics consist mainly of setting up a reduced-form model, then adding controls and the instrument for treatment in a two-stage least squares model. The authors could strengthen the study by controlling for supply-side issues, to expand their exploration of the heterogeneous results among people receiving the transfer. The survey includes access to services, for example, so they may be able to examine the effect of distance to the school. While the fixed effects for the community may already be accounting for that factor, trying specifications in which supply-side characteristics vary across households could be useful, if available. Assessments of these interventions systematically assume that the supply side is homogeneous, but this assumption could obscure important factors in the program's outcome.

An important issue raised in the paper involves the quality of targeting under decentralized selection schemes. Ecuador's centralized design started with a randomized selection, which later was not followed by the operators in the field. One criticism of randomization is that under a limited budget, a program should start by including the poorest. These critics believe that a decentralized decision mechanism based on discretionary selection would best accomplish this goal, since field operators have more information for selecting the poorest among eligible households. For the case of Ecuador, Schady and Araujo compare the socioeconomic characteristics of lottery winners and losers in the original design with those of actual recipients and nonrecipients. They find that randomization would have resulted in a more progressive (or neutral) selection than the discretionary selection by operators.

One caveat that bears mentioning has to do with conditioned versus unconditioned households, in terms of their perceptions. Those beneficiaries whose perceptions are conditioned have obvious incentives to declare enrollment. The paper correctly addresses this concern given the existing information. The authors claim, however, that this problem arises in all databases like this, yet in other cases, like *Oportunidades* in Mexico after 2003, there is an administrative record that allows verification.

The evidence in the paper is generally convincing. The authors satisfactorily solve the methodological challenges, and the effects are economically relevant. They need to extend their evaluations beyond traditional impact-evaluation analysis, however. Their analysis could be used to address deeper questions, where feasible. For example, in the area of child labor, the normative arguments in academic and policy realms can be summarized as a debate over preferences versus constraints. Conditional cash transfers relax the household's budget constraint but impose a condition on the behavioral response. This implies that, for several valid reasons, the desired response may not be socially optimal, or even individually welfare improving, from a standard long-run perspective. In policy circles, the question is whether the conditionality is justifiable, or whether the relaxation of the cash constraint is sufficient to generate the behavioral response the policymakers are trying to induce. Until recently, this question has been addressed empirically. Alvarez, Devoto, and Winters show that conditionality may play a role as an effective screening device, and it becomes a useful tool for policymakers.[1] They also show, however, that supply-side issues (related to health service providers in the case of *Oportunidades* in Mexico) may be a factor for dropouts from the program.

Schady and Araujo find that many so-called unconditioned households increased enrollment (the presumably desired result), while some conditioned households did not. What could explain the differential response? Do households that responded in the desired direction have access to other markets, like credit? Are there supply-side issues that can explain such differences? The impact evaluation literature assumes that supply-side issues, other context-related constraints, and access to other markets are either homogeneous across households or controlled for through appropriate specifications. Experiments like the one analyzed here, featuring a cash transfer and heterogeneous responses presumably as a result of perceptions, may be useful for better understanding the rationale for conditionality or even the need for it in the absence of certain local characteristics. In several countries, opposition to conditional cash transfer schemes has been based on one of two arguments—either a rights-based approach that challenges targeting and conditionality, or the notion that imposing conditions is paternalistic and ignores that households would respond to the transfers in a way that is individually and socially desirable. Evidence like that presented in this paper supports the view that conditionality may be a good idea given that, even when preferences are not an issue, financial constraints are not the only hurdles that beneficiaries must overcome. Even more important, understanding what factors are contributing to the differential response to transfers would help policymakers design more comprehensive interventions to enhance household welfare and achieve socially optimal long-run outcomes.

1. Alvarez, Devoto, and Winters (2008).

## References


Abadie, Alberto, and Guido W. Imbens. 2002. "Simple and Bias-Corrected Matching Estimators for Average Treatment Effects." Technical Working Paper 283. Cambridge, Mass.: National Bureau of Economic Research.

Alvarez, Carola, Florencia Devoto, and Paul Winters. 2008. "Why Do Beneficiaries Leave the Safety Net in Mexico? A Study of the Effects of Conditionality on Dropouts." *World Development* (forthcoming).

Angrist, Joshua D. 2004. "Treatment Effect Heterogeneity in Theory and Practice." *Economic Journal* 114(3): C52–C83

Angrist, Joshua D., Guido W. Imbens, and Don Rubin. 1996. "Identification of Casual Effects Using Instrumental Variables." *Journal of the American Statistical Association* 91(434): 444–55.

Attanasio, Orazio, Costas Meghir, and Ana Santiago. 2005. "Education Choices in Mexico: Using a Structural Model and a Randomized Experiment to Evaluate Progresa." Working Paper EWP05/01. London: Institute for Fiscal Studies.

Attanasio, Orazio, and others. 2005. "How Effective Are Conditional Cash Transfers? Evidence from Colombia." Briefing Note BN54. London: Institute for Fiscal Studies.

Behrman, Jere R., Piyali Sengupta, and Petra E. Todd. 2005. "Progressing through Progresa: An Impact Assessment of a School Subsidy Experiment in Mexico." *Economic Development and Cultural Change* 54(1): 237–75.

Bourguignon, Francois, Francisco Ferreira, and Phillippe Leite. 2003. "Conditional Cash Transfers, Schooling, and Child Labor: Micro-Simulating Brazil's *Bolsa Escola* Program." *World Bank Economic Review* 17(2): 229–54.

Chen, Shaohua, Ren Mu, and Martin Ravallion. 2006. "Are There Lasting Impacts of a Poor-Area Development Program?" Washington: World Bank, Development Research Group.

Das, Jishnu, Quy-Toan Do, and Berk Özler. 2005. "Reassessing Conditional Cash Transfer Programs." *World Bank Research Observer* 20(1): 57–80.

De Janvry, Alain, and Elisabeth Sadoulet. 2006. "Making Conditional Cash Transfer Programs More Efficient: Designing for Maximum Effect of the Conditionality." *World Bank Economic Review* 20(1): 1–30.

Filmer, Deon, and Lant Pritchett. 2001. "Estimating Wealth Effects without Expenditure Data—or Tears: An Application to Educational Enrollments in States of India." *Demography* 38(1): 115–32.

Filmer, Deon, and Norbert Schady. 2008. "Getting Girls into School: Evidence from a Scholarship Program in Cambodia." *Economic Development and Cultural Change* 56(3): 619–56.

Glewwe, Paul. 2002. "Schools and Skills in Developing Countries: Education Policies and Socioeconomic Outcomes." *Journal of Economic Literature* 40(2): 436–82.

Glewwe, Paul, and Pedro Olinto. 2004. "Evaluating the Impact of Conditional Cash Transfers on Schooling: An Experimental Analysis of Honduras' PRAF Program." University of Minnesota.

Hirano, Keisuke, and Guido W. Imbens. 2002. "Estimation of Causal Effects Using Propensity Score Weighting: An Application to Data on Right Heart Catheterization." *Health Services and Outcomes Research Methodology* 2(3–4): 259–78.

Hirano, Keisuke, Guido W. Imbens, and Geert Ridder. 2003. "Efficient Estimation of Average Treatment Effects Using the Estimated Propensity Score." *Econometrica* 71(4): 1161–89.

Hoddinott, John, Emmanuel Skoufias, and Ryan Washburn. 2000. "The Impact of PROGRESA on Consumption: Final Report." Washington: International Food Policy Research Institute.

Imbens, Guido W. 2004. "Nonparametric Estimation of Average Treatment Effects under Exogeneity: A Review." *Review of Economics and Statistics* 86(1): 4–29.

Imbens, Guido W., and Joshua D. Angrist. 1994. "Identification and Estimation of Local Average Treatment Effects." *Econometrica* 62(2): 467–75.

León, Mauricio, Rob Vos, and Wladymir Brborich. 2001. "¿Son efectivos los programas de transferencias monetarias para combatir la pobreza? Evaluación de impacto del *Bono Solidario* en el Ecuador." Quito: Sistema Integrado de Indicadores Sociales del Ecuador.

León, Mauricio, and Stephen D. Younger. 2007. "Transfer Payments, Mother's Income, and Child Health in Ecuador." *Journal of Development Studies* 43(6): 1126–143.

Maluccio, John A., and Rafael Flores. 2004. "Impact Evaluation of a Conditional Cash Transfer Program: The Nicaraguan *Red de Protección Social.*" FCND Brief 184. Washington: International Food Policy Research Institute.

McKenzie, David, John Gibson, and Steven Stillman. 2006. "How Important is Selection? Experimental versus Non-Experimental Measures of the Income Gains from Migration." Policy Research Working Paper 3906. Washington: World Bank.

Ravallion, Martin, and Quentin Wodon. 2000. "Does Child Labor Displace Schooling? Evidence on Behavioral Responses to an Enrollment Subsidy." *Economic Journal* 110(462): C158–C75.

Schultz, T. Paul. 2004. "School Subsidies for the Poor: Evaluating the Mexican Progresa Poverty Program." *Journal of Development Economics* 74(1): 199–250.

Skoufias, Emmanuel. 2005. "Progresa and Its Impacts on the Welfare of Rural Households in Mexico." Report 139. Washington: International Food Policy Research Institute.

Todd, Petra E., and Kenneth I. Wolpin. 2006. "Using Experimental Data to Validate a Dynamic Behavioral Model of Child Schooling: Assessing the Impact of a School Subsidy Program in Mexico." *American Economic Review* 96(5): 1384–417.

Vos, Rob, and Juan Ponce. 2005. "Meeting the Millennium Development Goal in Education: A Cost-Effectiveness Analysis for Ecuador." Working Paper 402. The Hague: Institute of Social Studies.

World Bank. 2004. *Ecuador: Poverty Assessment.* Washington.

ALBERTO CHONG
HUGO ÑOPO

# The Mystery of Discrimination in Latin America

Conventional wisdom holds that Latin America is a highly discriminatory society. This belief is hardly surprising given the history of ethnic and class conflicts in the region and the plethora of anecdotal evidence reinforcing this notion. However, whereas it cannot be argued that many societies in the region do, in fact, discriminate, the crucial questions have barely been broached. Understanding the extent of such discrimination and exploring the channels through which it operates deserve special attention.

How widespread is discrimination in Latin America? The primary opinion survey in the region, Latinobarómetro, explores discriminatory perceptions for representative samples of the population of eighteen countries.[1] As shown in figure 1, when individuals were asked in 2001 who they think suffers the most from discrimination, they consistently and overwhelmingly highlighted the poor, followed by indigenous peoples and Afro-descendants. This pattern is consistent across countries in the region. In all the countries surveyed, poverty is perceived as being the main driver of discrimination, with responses varying from 14 percent in the case of Panama to 49 percent in the case of Nicaragua. Figure 2 illustrates these results for the countries surveyed.

These results, however, are not entirely consistent with the answers to a similarly worded question asked only a few years later. Starting in 2004, the same Latinobarómetro survey asked Latin Americans why they think people

Chong and Ñopo are with the Inter-American Development Bank.

Sebastián Calonico, Lucas Higuera, Gianmarco León, and Vanessa Rios provided excellent research assistance. Rafael di Tella, Carmen Pagés, Claudia Piras, Lucas Ronconi, and Miguel Urquiola contributed valuable comments. Some sections of this paper have circulated under the title "Discrimination in Latin America: An Elephant in the Room?"

1. The countries surveyed by Latinobarómetro are Argentina, Bolivia, Brazil, Colombia, Costa Rica, Chile, the Dominican Republic, Ecuador, El Salvador, Guatemala, Honduras, Mexico, Nicaragua, Panama, Paraguay, Peru, Uruguay, and Venezuela. For more information on the Latinobarómetro Corporation and its surveys, see its website (www.latinobarometro.org).

**FIGURE 1. Groups Affected by Discrimination in Latin America, 2001[a]**

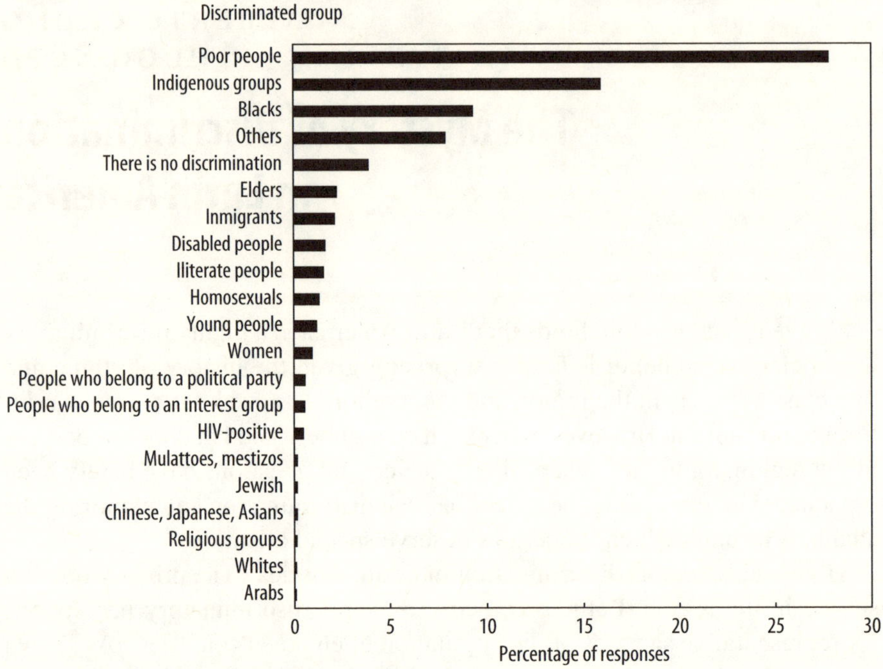


Source: Latinobarómetro (2001).

a. The figure reports responses to the following 2001 Latinobarómetro survey question: "From what you have known or heard, which groups do you think experience the most discrimination, or do you think that there is no discrimination?"

in their country are not treated equally. One out of every three Latin Americans pointed to poverty as the basis for unequal treatment, but in a departure from the earlier poll, individuals did not identify ethnic and racial characteristics as the second and third top reasons for discrimination. Rather, they cited lack of education and lack of connections as the basis for unequal treatment. One interpretation of these results is that Latin Americans now consider economic factors more important than social factors in explaining unequal treatment, although responses vary by country. Figure 3 shows the ranking of reasons for the whole region, and figure 4 shows how the perceived reasons for unequal treatment vary from one country to another. While poverty is considered the number one cause of discrimination in the Dominican Republic and Nicaragua, lack of education tops the list of reasons in Guatemala. Lack of connections, which ranks third in the region overall, is viewed as the most important reason for unequal treatment in Mexico, Colombia, and Panama.

**FIGURE 2. Perceptions of Discrimination by Poverty, by Country[a]**

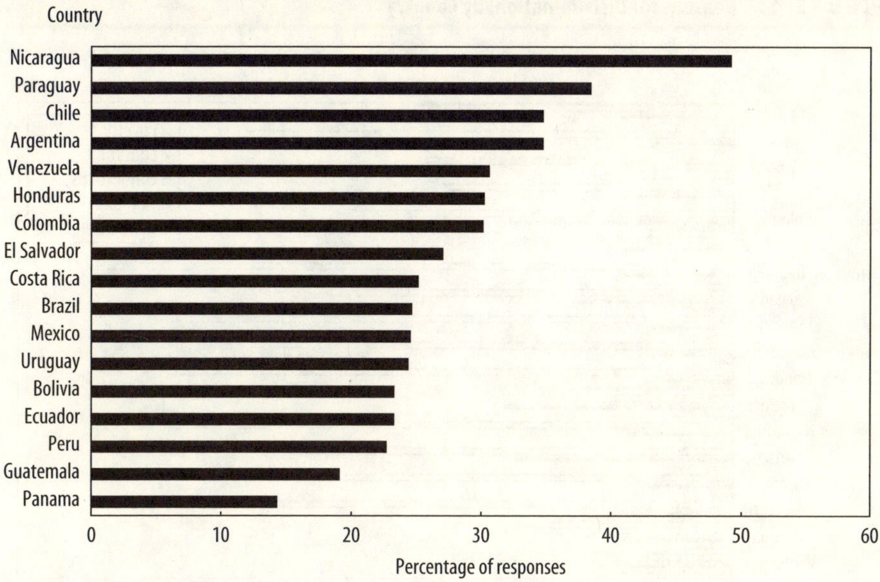


Source: Latinobarómetro (2001).

a. For each country, the figure reports that percentage of Latinobarómetro respondents in 2001 who think that poverty is the main reason that people are not treated equally.

**FIGURE 3. Reasons for Discrimination in Latin America, 2004 and 2005[a]**

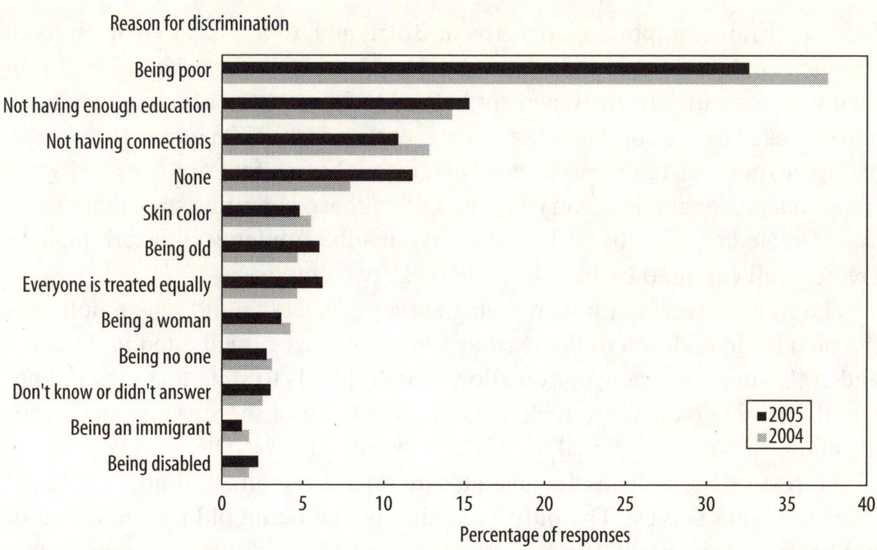


Source: Latinobarómetro (2004, 2005).

a. The figure reports responses in 2004 and 2005 to the following Latinobarómetro survey question: "Of all the reasons for which people are not treated equally, which one affects you the most?"

**FIGURE 4. Reasons for Discrimination, by Country**[a]

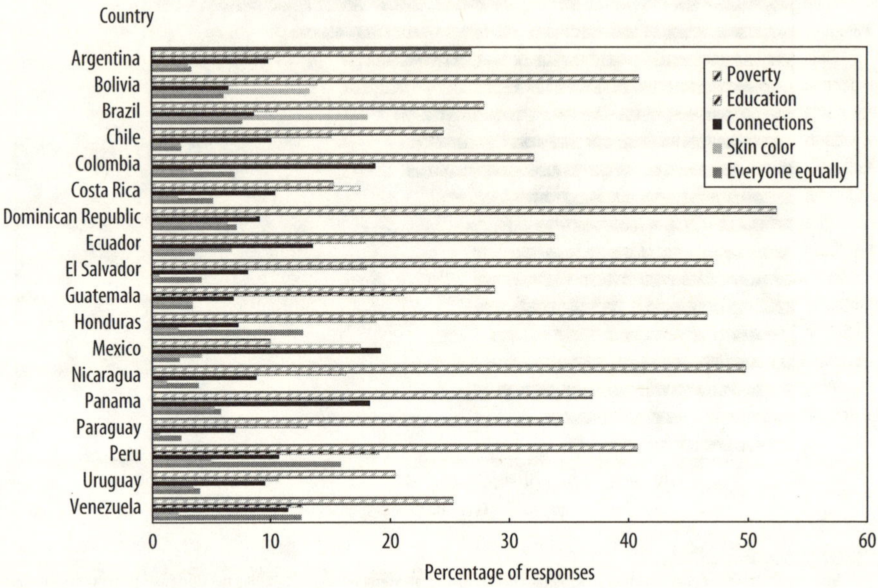


Source: Latinobarómetro (2005).

a.–For each country, the figure reports responses to the following 2005 Latinobarómetro survey question: "Of all the reasons for which people are not treated equally, which one affects you the most?"

Skin color raises important concerns in Brazil and, to a lesser extent, Bolivia. The percentages of respondents who felt that everyone is treated equally in their country varies from 16 percent in Peru to 2 percent in Mexico, Paraguay, and Chile. The cases of Paraguay (35 percent) and Chile (25 percent) are interesting, as none of the reasons cited for unequal treatment are assigned great importance. Nonetheless, very few people in these countries state that everyone is treated equally there. This suggests that the subtleties of discrimination are not well captured by the survey in these two countries.

The most recent Latinobarómetro survey, for 2006, further complicates the picture. In addition to the reasons for unequal treatment cited in the 2004 and 2005 surveys, a new option allowed individuals to state that they did not feel discriminated against at all. Nearly 24 percent of the surveyed individuals chose this response, making it the new top answer. The relative ranking of the rest of the reasons for unequal treatment remained almost unaltered since the 2005 survey. The only exception is that being old ranked ahead of not having connections for the first time. As before, skin color, gender, and

**FIGURE 5. Reasons for Discrimination in Latin America, 2006[a]**

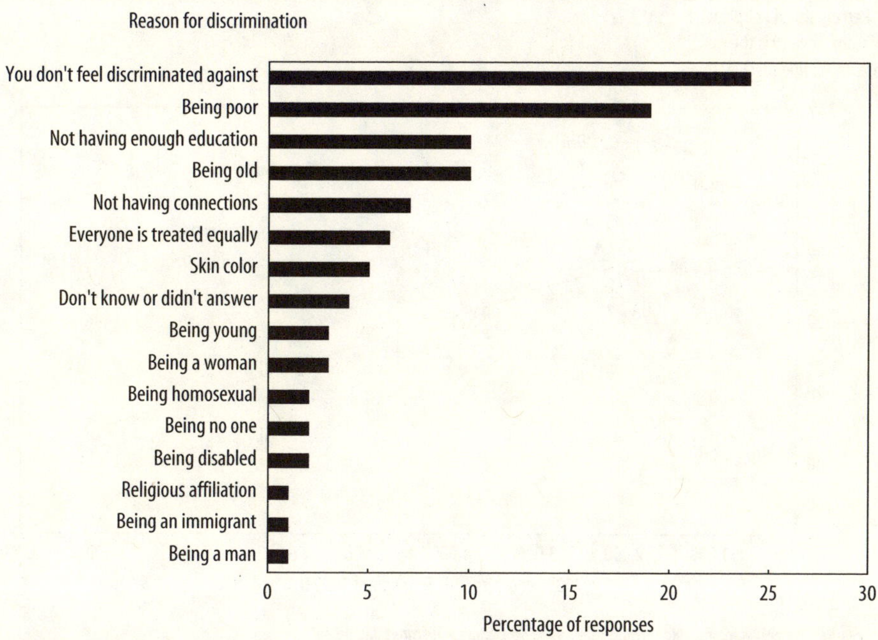


Source: Latinobarómetro (2006).

a. The figure reports responses to the following 2006 Latinobarómetro survey question: "Of all the reasons for which people are not treated equally, which one affects you the most?"

disabilities were not ranked high as characteristics triggering discriminatory behaviors. These results are shown in figure 5.[2]

The fact that the social characteristics typically linked to discrimination register low on the opinion surveys in most countries in Latin America is, in itself, quite remarkable. Perhaps societies in the region do not discriminate on the basis of ethnicity, race, or gender as much as conventional wisdom would

2. In Europe, the characteristics that the population perceives as being the drivers of discrimination (or disadvantaged treatment) are more social than economic in nature. Eurobarometer, the European opinion survey, dedicated a recent special issue (European Commission 2007) to exploring discriminatory perceptions in the twenty-five member countries of the European Union. The four groups ranked by surveyed respondents as the most disadvantaged were the disabled, the Roma (gypsies), people over fifty years of age, and people of a different ethnic group than the rest of the population. These characteristics come closer to what conventional wisdom would dictate in terms of groups that experience discrimination.

**FIGURE 6. Size of the Economy and Perceptions of Discrimination by Poverty**

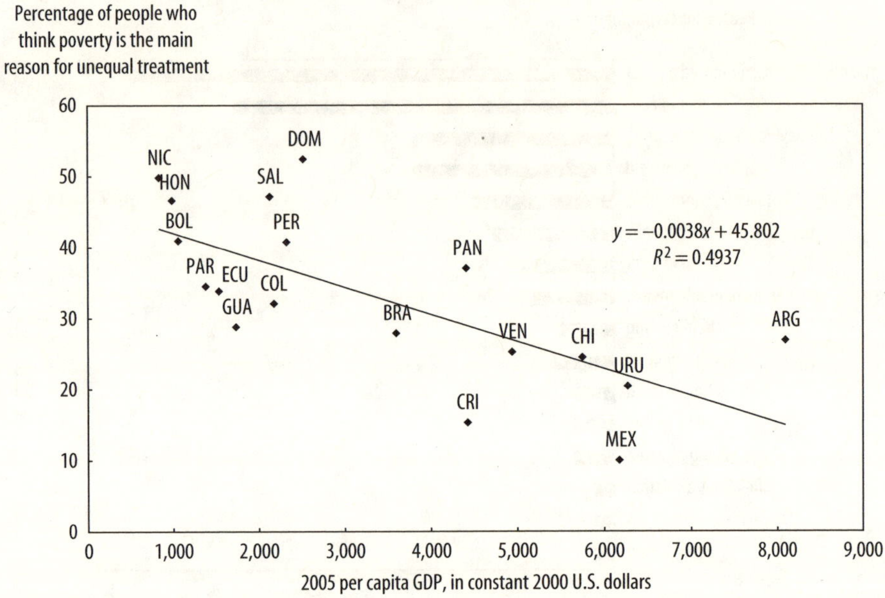


Source: Latinobarómetro (2005); World Bank, *World Development Indicators* database.

suggest. Alternatively, perhaps the individuals surveyed are reluctant to reveal their true beliefs for fear of retaliation or for concerns about being perceived as politically incorrect. Another problem may be that the factors indicated in opinion polls as being the most common reasons for discrimination are categories that do not capture poverty per se, but characteristics that respondents associate with it. In fact, the perception of discrimination by poverty may be highly correlated with other variables such as the general economic condition of the population or social characteristics that are more traditionally linked to discriminatory practices. The perception of poverty as a key discriminatory problem is fairly low in countries that are relatively homogeneous in terms of race. For instance, only about 20 percent of respondents link discrimination with poverty in Uruguay. By the same token, respondents in countries that are more racially diverse indicate that poverty is a crucial discriminatory issue. In Peru, for example, nearly 41 percent of respondents cite poverty as the most important reason for unequal treatment. Figures 6 and 7 present scatter plots and simple correlations between basic economic variables and perceptions of discrimination. Figure 6 shows that the perception of discrimination by

**FIGURE 7. Inequality and Perceptions of Nondiscrimination**

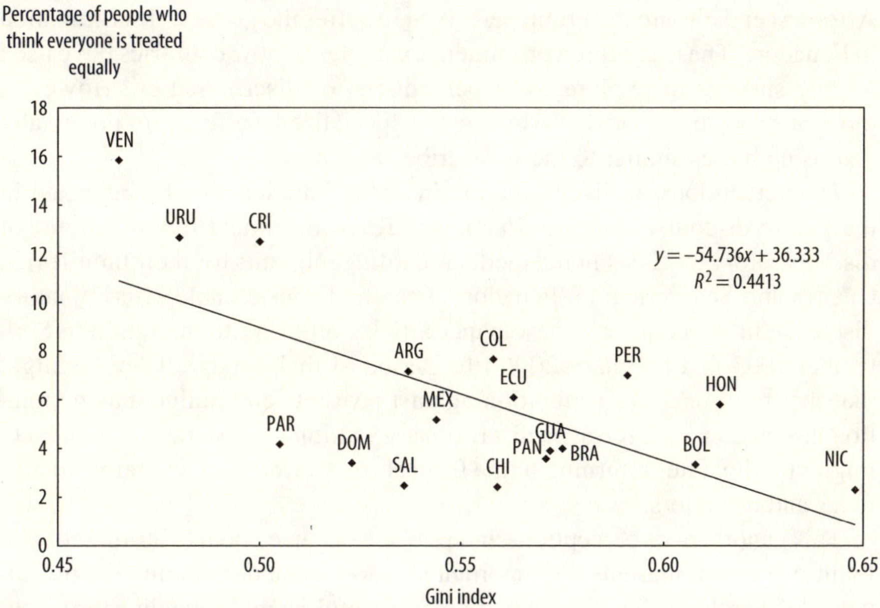


Source: Latinobarómetro (2005); World Bank, *World Development Indicators* database.

poverty is accentuated in smaller economies. Conversely, figure 7 suggests that people in more equal societies are more apt to view their environment as nondiscriminatory.

Given the above, some countries in the region have recently undertaken efforts to gain more precise knowledge about the perception of discrimination. For example, researchers in Peru have adapted the discrimination scales of the 1995 Detroit Area Study; they find that 88 percent of a representative sample of Peruvians report having experienced at least one situation of discrimination.[3] In Mexico, the results of the First National Survey of Discrimination show that nine out of every ten individuals with certain characteristics (such as disabilities, an indigenous background, homosexual orientation, advanced age, or membership in religious minorities) think discrimination exists in their country.[4] The Survey of Perceptions of Racism and Discrimination in Ecuador

3. The National Survey of Exclusion and Social Discrimination; see DEMUS (2005).
4. SEDESOL (2005).

reveals that while 62 percent of Ecuadoreans agree that there is racial discrimination in their country, only 10 percent admit to being openly racist; Afro-descendants are the group perceived to suffer the greatest discrimination in Ecuador.[5] These are three prominent examples of how countries have used ad hoc surveys to explore local perceptions of discrimination. However, most of these and related surveys, while specialized, suffer from potentially confusing biases similar to those described above.[6]

The perceptions of discrimination in Latin America are also reflected in the public discourse. Soruco, Piani, and Rossi document the intricacies of discriminatory attitudes in the media regarding migrants (or their families) in Cuenca and San Fernando, Ecuador.[7] They find considerable discriminatory discourse in the content of newspaper articles referring to migration in September 2005 and February 2006 (the period of their study). They highlight that the traditional discrimination against peasants and indigenous population has taken a new form, as discriminatory attitudes have been extended to migrants who, after returning home from abroad, bring back westernized attitudes and behaviors.

This panorama of perceptions and public discourse about discrimination in Latin America represents an important step toward understanding the magnitude of the problem, but it is not particularly useful for understanding the mechanisms through which discrimination occurs and the associated welfare costs. Nonetheless, as figures 6 and 7 suggest, the perception of discrimination (or the lack thereof) may be associated with economic outcomes such as the size of the economy and income distribution. An economic analysis of discrimination that moves beyond perceptions is greatly needed. A thorough understanding of the mechanisms through which discrimination occurs and the economic implications of related processes is essential for effective policy design.

## Beyond Opinion Polls

Analyzing discrimination from an economic perspective requires more than information on individual perceptions. These data are informative only to the extent that they influence individuals' economic decisions, actions, and outcomes. It is precisely in relation to outcomes that the economic literature sheds

5. Secretaría Técnica del Frente Social (2004).
6. Bertrand and Mullainathan (2001).
7. Soruco, Piani, and Rossi (2007).

light on discrimination, so we start by outlining a few working definitions of discrimination from the international economic literature for purposes of clarity and providing perspective on the studies described in this and subsequent sections.

Discrimination can take place under different circumstances or in different markets, and it can be based on different discriminatory characteristics such as race, ethnicity, gender, disability, and migratory condition, to name a few. Altonji and Blank define discrimination in labor markets as "a situation in which persons who provide labor market services and who are equally productive in a physical or material sense are treated unequally in a way that is related to an observable characteristic such as race, ethnicity, or gender. By 'unequal' we mean these persons receive different wages or face different demands for their services at a given wage."[8] This definition can be summarized as unequal treatment for the same productivity, which outside of labor markets would read unequal treatment for the same characteristics. As mentioned earlier, some characteristics are harder to observe than others. One avenue to better understanding discrimination along these lines would be to design studies aimed at uncovering the unobservables as much as possible. Before delving into this further, it is useful to distinguish between preference-based discrimination (people treating members of certain groups differently simply because they do not like them) and statistical discrimination (people using group membership as a proxy measure for unobserved characteristics). The latter corresponds to the popularly held notions of stigmatization or stereotyping. For instance, employers who assume that Afro-descendants have the ability to perform certain manual tasks but are not necessarily capable of fulfilling more intellectual responsibilities may not offer many opportunities for white-collar jobs to Afro-descendants. Consequently, an Afro-descendant might not even get in the door for an equal assessment of observable human capital characteristics. Stigmatization in this sense constitutes a form of discrimination that complements the notion of unequal treatment for the same characteristics.

The literature in the region tries to quantify discriminatory outcomes by means other than opinion polls. The topics of interest range from income differences to limited participation in labor markets (including limited access to human capital, segregation, differences in returns to human capital characteristics, limited access to jobs, and informality), limited access to health care services, education, and physical infrastructure and housing, and lack of political

8. Altonji and Blank (1999).

representation, social protection, and security (victimization). Gandelman, Ñopo, and Ripani, for example, document the literature on Latin America, addressing differences in the topics mentioned above with respect to race, ethnicity, migratory condition, disabilities, and gender.[9]

In this paper we focus on a particular family of studies, namely, wage gaps decompositions. Numerous efforts have focused on documenting earnings differentials between females and males, indigenous and nonindigenous people, or Afro-descendants and whites. As the pieces of the literature that we survey in this section show, comparisons of hourly labor earnings (wages or self-employment income) suggest the existence of notorious gaps. However, nonindigenous (or male) workers exhibit human capital characteristics that are, on average, more desirable than those of indigenous (or female) workers. Examples of those characteristics include education, labor market experience, and field of specialization. To attribute the whole earnings gap to the existence of labor market discrimination would therefore be misleading. At least a component of the gap can be attributed to differences in observable human capital characteristics that the labor market rewards and, hence, is not attributable to the existence of discrimination. Blinder and Oaxaca were the first to explore this avenue of research, in which the profession has been able to identify, to some extent, the magnitude of this component.[10]

To summarize the basic idea behind this approach, we denote the two comparison groups as A and B. We can then estimate a Mincer equation for each group:

$$y_i^A = \boldsymbol{\beta}^A \mathbf{x}_i^A + \varepsilon_i^A$$

and

$$y_i^B = \boldsymbol{\beta}^B \mathbf{x}_i^B + \varepsilon_i^B,$$

where $y$ is the logarithm of hourly wages, $\mathbf{x}$ the vector of observable characteristics, $\boldsymbol{\beta}$ the vector of their corresponding rewards, and $\varepsilon$ the residuals. The wage gap, which is the difference between the average logarithms of hourly wages of the comparison groups, can be computed as

$$\text{Gap} = \overline{y}^A - \overline{y}^B = \hat{\boldsymbol{\beta}}^A \overline{\mathbf{x}}^A - \hat{\boldsymbol{\beta}}^B \overline{\mathbf{x}}^B,$$

9. Gandelman, Ñopo, and Ripani (2007).
10. Blinder (1973); Oaxaca (1973).

which, in turn, after some algebraic manipulation can be expressed as

$$\text{Gap} = \hat{\boldsymbol{\beta}}^{A}\left(\overline{\mathbf{x}}^{A} - \overline{\mathbf{x}}^{B}\right) + \left(\hat{\boldsymbol{\beta}}^{A} - \hat{\boldsymbol{\beta}}^{B}\right)\overline{\mathbf{x}}^{B}.$$

We next denote the first component as $\Delta_{\mathbf{x}}$ and the second as $\Delta_0$, so we can write the equation as a two-component sum:

$$\text{Gap} = \Delta_{\mathbf{x}} + \Delta_0.$$

The first component, $\Delta_{\mathbf{x}}$, captures the part of the wage gap that can be attributed to the existence of differences in average observable characteristics between the two comparsion groups. The second component, $\Delta_0$, is what remains unexplained and can be attributed to the existence of elements that play a role in the determination of wages in labor markets but that the econometrician cannot observe (one of those elements being discrimination). The literature includes various extensions of this basic setup, including correction for selection into active labor market participation, the use of quantile regressions instead of ordinary least squares (OLS), additional explorations of the distribution of the gaps, microsimulations, and matching comparisons. Tables 1 and 2 summarize some of the literature for the region that applies the Blinder-Oaxaca approach (and its extensions) to the analysis of racial and gender wage gaps, respectively.

The unexplained gaps reported in the tables are those that remain after controlling for different sets of observable characteristics (presented in the last columns).[11] They are computed as percentages of the average hourly wages of the groups with lower earnings (namely, females, Afro-descendants, and indigenous). The results summarized in the tables suggest more similarities than differences in the literature, especially for gender gaps. The discrepancies in the literature on racial gaps mostly depend on the differences of the racial groups that each paper compares and the methods employed. Work in this area is lacking for many Latin American nations, however.[12]

For this study, we use the most recent surveys available, together with the Harmonized National Household Surveys assembled by the Inter-American Development Bank's Research Department, to perform comparable wage gap decompositions by race for five countries and by gender for seventeen of them. Table 3 presents information on the surveys used for each country.

11. That is, they correspond to $\Delta_0$, according to the notation introduced above.

12. Tables 1 and 2 do not represent exhaustive lists of the research on wage gaps in the region, but they are as comprehensive as possible within the context of the present study.

**TABLE 1. Decompositions, by Race**

| *Study* | *Data source*[a] | *Coverage* | *Comparison groups* | *Unexplained wage gap (percent)* | *Methodology and control variables* |
|---|---|---|---|---|---|
| Arcand and d'Hombres (2004) | PNAD (1998) | Brazil | Whites vs. browns | 17 | Blinder-Oaxaca with quantile regressions; sample selection corrected with controls for experience, schooling, self-evaluation of health, family status, region of residence, location (urban or rural), signature of a formal labor contract, and occupation |
| | | | Whites vs. blacks | 27 | |
| Arias, Yamada, and Tejerina (2002) | PNAD (1996) | Brazil | Whites vs. blacks | 33 | Blinder-Oaxaca with quantile regressions adjusting for differences in education and work experience |
| Barrón (2005) | ENAHO (May 2003–April 2004) | Lima, Peru | Born in Lima vs. born in other provinces | 5–9 | Propensity score matching with controls for gender, mother's education, age, schooling, private and public education, formal and informal employment, and potable water |
| Campante, Crespo, and Leite (2004) | PNAD (1996) | Brazil | Whites vs. blacks and browns | 14 | Blinder-Oaxaca with controls for education, experience, formal employment, sector, public and private job, regional characteristics, and mother's education |
| De Ferranti and others (2004) | Household surveys: Brazil (1996); | Bolivia | White vs. nonwhite men | 37 | Blinder-Oaxaca with controls for education, area, age, and other individual and labor market characteristics |
| | Bolivia (1999); | Brazil | | 15 | |
| | Guatemala (2000); | Guatemala | | 28 | |
| | Guyana (1999) | Guyana | | 5 | |
| Gallardo (2006) | EMEDINHO and ENEMDUR (2000) | Ecuador | White vs. mestizo men[b] | 17 | Blinder-Oaxaca with 2SLS using as controls: experience, education, area, and formal occupation |
| | | | White vs. mestizo women[b] | 44 | |
| | | | White vs. mestizo men[c] | 18 | |
| | | | White vs. mestizo women[c] | 40 | |

| | | | | | |
|---|---|---|---|---|---|
| Garcia-Aracil and Winter (2006) | ECV (1999) | Ecuador (excl. Amazon) | Nonindigenous vs. indigenous | 59 | Blinder-Oaxaca with controls for education and residence |
| Guimarães (2006) | PNAD (2002) | Brazil | Whites vs. blacks and browns | 16 | Blinder-Oaxaca with controls for education, experience, sex, household chief, sector, type of contract, and region |
| Larrea and Montenegro (2006) | ECV (1998) | Ecuador (excl. Amazon) | Nonindigenous vs. indigenous | 57 | Blinder-Oaxaca with controls for education and labor market |
| Leite (2005) | PNAD (1996) | Brazil | Whites vs. blacks and browns | 19 | 2SLS with IV for ability bias and controls for mother's and father's education; quantile regression for schooling |
| Ñopo and others (2007) | LSMS (2000) and an additional racial module | Peru | Whites vs. indig. (self-employed) | 13–19 | Blinder-Oaxaca with controls for education and experience, personal and family characteristics, and labor market |
| | | | Whites vs. mestizos (self-empl.) | 5–8 | |
| | | | Mestizos vs. indig. (self-empl.) | 3–7 | |
| | | | Whites vs. indigenous (waged) | 11–14 | |
| | | | Whites vs. mestizos (waged) | 0–12 | |
| | | | Mestizos vs. indig. (waged) | 6–13 | |
| Soares (2000) | PNAD (1998) | Brazil | White vs. black and brown men | 116 | Blinder-Oaxaca with controls for experience, education, sector, type of labor contract, and region |

a. ECV: *Encuesta de Condiciones de Vida;* EMEDINHO: *Encuesta de Medición de Indicadores de la Niñez y los Hogares;* ENAHO: *Encuesta Nacional de Hogares;* ENEMDUR: *Encuesta de Empleo, Desempleo y Subempleo en el Area Urbana y Rural;* LSMS: Living Standards Measurement Study (World Bank); PNAD: *Pesquisa Nacional por Amostra de Domicílios.*

b. Mestizos are self-identified.

c. Mestizos are identified by primary language.

**TABLE 2. Decompositions, by Gender**

| Study | Data source[a] | Coverage | Unexplained wage gap (percent) | Methodology and control variables |
|---|---|---|---|---|
| Aguilar and Dresdner (2000) | CASEN (1987, 1990, 1992, 1994, 1996, 1998) | Chile | 9–21 | Blinder-Oaxaca with correction for selection bias |
| Brown, Pagan, and Rodríguez-Oreggia (1999) | ENEU (1987, 1993) | Mexico 1987 | 18 | Blinder-Oaxaca with controls for age, education, experience, occupation, and other individual characteristics |
| | | 1993 | 17 | |
| Contreras and Puentes (2000) | EOD (1966–96) | Chile | 10–20 | Blinder-Oaxaca with correction for selection bias |
| De Ferranti and others (2004) | Household surveys: Brazil (1996); Bolivia (1999); Guatemala (2000); Guyana (1999) | Bolivia | 36 | Blinder-Oaxaca with controls for education, area, age, and other individual and labor market characteristics |
| | | Brazil | 53 | |
| | | Guatemala | 78 | |
| | | Guyana | 55 | |
| Deutsch and others (2005) | EHPM (1989, 1993, 1997) | Costa Rica 1989 | 24 | Blinder-Oaxaca with Fluckiger and Silber methodology (occupational segregation) and controls for education, experience, number of children, occupation, and other labor market characteristics |
| | | 1993 | 12 | |
| | | 1997 | 20 | |
| | EPED (1997) | Ecuador | 20 | |
| | ECH (1989, 1992, 1997) | Uruguay 1989 | 26 | |
| | | 1982 | 20 | |
| | | 1997 | 20 | |
| Fuentes, Palma, and Montero (2005) | CASEN (1990, 1992, 1994, 1996, 1998, 2000, 2003) | Chile 1990 | 59 | Blinder-Oaxaca and Ransom with controls for education |
| | | 1992 | 49 | |
| | | 1994 | 25 | |
| | | 1996 | 29 | |
| | | 1998 | 25 | |
| | | 2000 | 22 | |
| | | 2003 | 28 | |
| Gonzales and Rossi (2002) | ECH (1986, 1990, 1994, and 1997) | Uruguay 1986 | 25 | Blinder-Oaxaca and Ransom with correction of selection bias and controls for age, education, marital status, and labor market |
| | | 1990 | 26 | |
| | | 1994 | 18 | |
| | | 1997 | 13 | |
| Khandker (1990) | ENNIV (1984) | Peru | 17 | Blinder-Oaxaca with correction for selection bias |

| | | | | |
|---|---|---|---|---|
| Montenegro (2001) | CASEN (1990, 1992, 1994, 1996, 1998) | Chile 1990 | 24 | Blinder-Oaxaca with quantile regressions and controls for education and experience |
| | | 1992 | 24 | |
| | | 1994 | 21 | |
| | | 1996 | 22 | |
| | | 1998 | 19 | |
| Ñopo (2008) | ENAHO (1999) | Lima, Peru | 23 | Matching (nonparametric decomposition) with controls for age, schooling, work experience, and formality |
| | Encuesta Especializada de Empleo (1986, 1987, 1989–95); ENAHO (1996–2000) | Lima, Peru | 29 | Matching (nonparametric decomposition) with controls for age, schooling, marital status, and migratory condition |
| Ñopo (2007) | CASEN (1992–2003) | Chile | 10–20 at the bottom of the wage distribution; 40–80 at the top of the wage distribution | Matching (nonparametric decomposition) with controls for education, age, marital status, occupation, and other labor market characteristics |
| Psacharopoulos and Tzannatos (1992) | Household surveys of each country | Colombia 1979 | 15–20 | Blinder-Oaxaca with and without correction for selection bias |
| | | Mexico 1984 | 15–20 | |
| | | Peru 1990 | 15–20 | |
| | | Argentina 1985 | 40–50 | |
| | | Bolivia 1989 | 40–50 | |
| | | Ecuador 1987 | 40–50 | |
| | | Jamaica 1989 | 40–50 | |
| Santos and Saba (2005) | PNAD (1982–90 and 1992–99) | Brazil 1982–90 | 30 | Blinder-Oaxaca and Ransom, with controls for education, age, race, household head, formal labor relation, urban region, and metropolitan area |
| | | 1992–99 | 28 | |
| Tenjo, Ribero, and Bernat (2005) | Household surveys of each country (1998) | Argentina | 9 | Blinder-Oaxaca with selectivity correction and controls for education and experience |
| | | Brazil | 32 | |
| | | Colombia | 8 | |
| | | Costa Rica | 10 | |
| | | Honduras | 19 | |
| | | Uruguay | 22 | |

a. CASEN: *Encuesta de Caracterización Socioeconómico Nacional;* ECH: *Encuesta Continua de Hogares;* EHPM: *Encuesta de Hogares de Propósitos Múltiples;* ENAHO: *Encuesta Nacional de Hogares;* ENEU: *Encuesta Nacional de Empleo Urbano;* ENNIV: *Encuesta Nacional de Hogares sobre Medición de Niveles de Vida;* EOD: *Encuesta de Ocupación y Desocupación de la Universidad de Chile;* EPED: *Encuesta Periódica sobre Empleo y Desempleo;* PNAD: *Pesquisa Nacional por Amostra de Domicílios.*

**TABLE 3. Countries Used and Their Surveys**

| *Country* | *Survey* | *Year* | *No. observations* |
|---|---|---|---|
| Argentina | Encuesta Permanente de Hogares Continua (EPHC) | 2005 | 29,336 |
| Bolivia | Encuesta de Hogares—Programa MECOVI | 2002 | 6,884 |
| Brazil | Pesquisa Nacional por Amostra de Domicilios (PNAD) | 2003 | 140,042 |
| Chile | Encuesta de Caracterización Socioeconómica Nacional (CASEN) | 2003 | 79,261 |
| Colombia | Encuesta Continua de Hogares (ECH) | 2003 | 40,468 |
| Costa Rica | Encuesta de Hogares de Propósitos Múltiples | 2004 | 13,891 |
| Dominican Rep. | Encuesta Nacional de Fuerza de Trabajo (ENFT) | 2003 | 9,864 |
| Guatemala | Encuesta Nacional sobre Condiciones de Vida | 2002 | 3,900 |
| Honduras | Encuesta Permanente de Hogares de Propósitos Múltiples | 2003 | 9,591 |
| Mexico | Encuesta Nacional de Ingresos y Gastos de los Hogares (ENIGH) | 2002 | 23,694 |
| Nicaragua | Encuesta Nacional de Hogares sobre Medición de Nivel de Vida | 2001 | 5,808 |
| Panama | Encuesta de Hogares | 2003 | 17,636 |
| Peru | Encuesta Nacional de Hogares (ENAHO)—Condiciones de Vida y Pobreza | 2003 | 23,536 |
| Paraguay | Encuesta Permanente de Hogares (EIH) | 2003 | 10,571 |
| El Salvador | Encuesta de Hogares de Propósitos Múltiples del Programa MECOVI | 2002 | 18,547 |
| Uruguay | Encuesta Continua de Hogares (ECH) | 2005 | 20,557 |
| Venezuela | Encuesta de Hogares por Muestreo | 2004 | 47,888 |

The wage gap decompositions presented here follow the approach developed by Ñopo using matching comparison techniques instead of Mincer equations.[13] The introduction of matching to the analysis of wage gaps raises a point that is commonplace in the impact evaluation literature (which developed matching), but has been absent from the gap decomposition discussion. Namely, a proper account of the differences in characteristics must take into consideration that the supports of the comparison groups' observable characteristics do not overlap completely. Matching naturally moves the analysis toward such a comparison of supports, as well as toward the distribution (and not just the average) of the comparison groups' observable characteristics. As a result, the matching estimators deliver more accurate measures of the decompositions of wage gaps than Mincer equations. Empirical comparisons of decompositions made with matching techniques and with traditional OLS reveal that the latter tends to overestimate the unexplained component of the gap by 2 to 8 percent points. Additionally, decompositions based on matching deliver estimators for two components of the wage gaps that are attributable to the existence of uncommon supports and provide interesting insights for the analysis of the gaps. One of those components, denoted $\Delta_M$ in the appendix, accounts for the fact that males attain combinations of observable characteris-

13. Ñopo (2004). See the appendix for a brief discussion of the decomposition method.

**TABLE 4. Racial Wage Gaps after Controlling for Observable Characteristics[a]**
Percent

| | Relative racial gaps and controlled differences | | | |
|---|---|---|---|---|
| | | Controls | | |
| *Country* | *Hourly wage gap of whites relative to natives* | *Gender, age, and education* | *Gender, age, education, and marital status* | *Gender, age, education, marital status, and residence in the capital city* |
| Bolivia | 38.2 | 22.5 | 24.3 | 24.3 |
| Brazil | 88.1 | 31.1 | n.a. | n.a. |
| Chile | 51.8 | 16.1 | 15.3 | 11.3 |
| Guatemala | 98.9 | 36.2 | 40.0 | 16.5 |
| Paraguay | 84.3 | 42.7 | 38.6 | 38.9 |

n.a. Not available.

a. Wage is equal to the hourly monetary labor income from the main occupation. The sample only includes people with incomes higher than zero.

tics that females do not. For the case of gender wage gap decompositions, this corresponds to individuals in their mid-40s, with a college degree or more, married, with kids, and working in managerial occupations. That is, this corresponds to the typical profile of corporate middle and upper managers, a clearly male-dominated segment of the labor markets. The second component, denoted $\Delta_F$ in the appendix, accounts for the reverse situation, in which females in labor markets attain certain combinations of characteristics that males do not. This corresponds to cases of working individuals in their early 30s, with a high school diploma or less, single, with kids, and born outside the capital city. That is, this corresponds to the typical profile of domestic servants, a clearly female-dominated segment of the labor markets.

We were able to compute racial wage gaps only in the five countries where we found a variable for racial self-identification. This corresponds to quechuas, aymaras, guaraníes, chiquitaños, and mojeños in Bolivia; pretos and pardos in Brazil; people who state that they belong to an indigenous group in Chile; people from around fifteen different indigenous groups in Guatemala; and guaraníes in Paraguay. We are aware of the limitations of the self-identification approach to determining racial groups in the region, but it allows us to compare the most number of countries under the same basis.[14]

Table 4 shows racial wage gaps in hourly wages with and without controls for different sets of observable characteristics. That is, according to the nota-

14. Telles and Lim (1998) and Ñopo, Saavedra, and Torero (2007) discuss the limitations of the self-identification approach.

**TABLE 5. Components of the Racial Wage Gap Stemming from Uncommon Supports**
Percent

| | *Controls* | | | | | |
|---|---|---|---|---|---|---|
| | *Gender, age, and education* | | *Gender, age, education, and marital status* | | *Gender, age, education, marital status, and residence in the capital city* | |
| *Country* | *Whites* | *Natives* | *Whites* | *Natives* | *Whites* | *Natives* |
| Bolivia | 0.4 | 0.2 | −2.2 | 2.4 | 2.6 | −2.0 |
| Brazil | 0.0 | 0.0 | n.a. | n.a. | n.a. | n.a. |
| Chile | 5.5 | 0.0 | 9.7 | 0.1 | 22.5 | 0.2 |
| Guatemala | 51.9 | 1.0 | 50.1 | 5.0 | 68.8 | 2.5 |
| Paraguay | 28.1 | 0.8 | 28.4 | 2.6 | 33.7 | 2.3 |

n.a. Not available.

tion introduced above, we report the values of the gap and $\Delta_0$ for different sets of control characteristics. The gaps have been computed using information only from individuals who reported positive labor earnings in their main occupation in the surveys. The gaps are reported as percentages of the average hourly wages in the main occupation of the group with lower wages.

The highest racial wage gaps, between 90 and 100 percent, are found in Brazil and Guatemala. However, after we control for gender, age, education, marital status, and residence in the capital city (in three different sets of variables), the remaining gaps are less than half the original values. Two of the decompositions could not be performed for Brazil because their survey did not include information on marital status. In the other countries, we obtain similar results when we control for gender, age, and education and when we control for these three characteristics plus marital status and residence in the capital city.

Table 5 shows the components of the wage gaps that are attributable to the lack of common support on the distribution of observable characteristics of whites and natives, for the three sets of control characteristics. The results show that the existence of unmatched whites (or whites out of the common support) contributes notably to the total racial wage gaps, especially in Guatemala and, to a lesser degree, Paraguay and Chile. This is the result of two factors: a sizable share of the working population of whites and natives differs in their observable characteristics, and whites with characteristics out of the common support earn hourly wages in the top percentiles of the wage distribution.

We computed gender wage gap decompositions for seventeen countries. Following a similar approach to that used in the racial decompositions, we also computed unexplained wage gaps for three sets of controlling characteristics:

**TABLE 6. Gender Wage Gaps after Controlling for Observable Characteristics[a]**
Percent

| | | *Relative gender gaps and controlled differences* | | |
|---|---|---|---|---|
| | | *Controls* | | |
| *Country* | *Hourly wage gap of males relative to females* | *Age and education* | *Age, education, and marital status* | *Age, education, marital status, and residence in the capital city* |
| Argentina | 2.0 | 15.3 | 15.2 | 14.8 |
| Bolivia | 6.7 | 4.4 | 5.3 | 7.3 |
| Brazil | 19.6 | 46.3 | n.a. | n.a. |
| Chile | 12.9 | 32.7 | 28.3 | 27.5 |
| Colombia | 8.0 | 14.6 | 10.9 | 11.3 |
| Costa Rica | −6.2 | 13.1 | 11.2 | 10.0 |
| Dominican Republic | 12.0 | 29.5 | 29.0 | n.a. |
| Guatemala | 27.3 | 17.4 | 16.2 | 22.5 |
| Honduras | −6.2 | 3.4 | 1.9 | 2.1 |
| Mexico | 9.9 | 12.8 | 11.3 | 13.4 |
| Nicaragua | 3.8 | 21.0 | 17.9 | 16.4 |
| Panama | −2.8 | 25.1 | 22.4 | 23.4 |
| Peru | 31.1 | 27.6 | 28.9 | 31.9 |
| Paraguay | 17.9 | 23.5 | 18.5 | 20.4 |
| El Salvador | 18.1 | 19.8 | 18.0 | 16.7 |
| Uruguay | 13.2 | 37.2 | 34.3 | 34.0 |
| Venezuela | −1.5 | 13.2 | 12.0 | 11.9 |

n.a. Not available.

a. Wage is equal to the hourly monetary labor income from the main occupation. The sample only includes people with incomes higher than zero.

originally controlling for age and education only; adding marital status to the previous two; and adding residence in the capital city to the previous three. We report the unexplained components of the gender wage gaps in table 6 and the components attributable to the lack of common support in table 7.

The wage gap is negative in Costa Rica, Honduras, Panama, and Venezuela. That is, females earn more per hour than males, on average, in these four countries. However, when we control for the sets of characteristics mentioned above—in other words, when we compare males and females with the same characteristics—males earn more than their female counterparts. Other countries in the region similarly present higher controlled gaps than original gaps, which reflects the fact that females have surpassed males in schooling attainment in the region.[15] Regarding the components of the wage gap stemming

15. See Duryea and others (2007).

**TABLE 7. Components of the Gender Wage Gap Stemming from Uncommon Supports**
Percent

| | *Controls* | | | | | |
|---|---|---|---|---|---|---|
| | *Age and education* | | *Age, education, and marital status* | | *Age, education, marital status and residence in the capital city* | |
| *Country* | *Males* | *Females* | *Males* | *Females* | *Males* | *Females* |
| Argentina | 0.0 | 0.0 | 0.1 | –0.5 | 0.7 | –0.9 |
| Bolivia | 1.3 | 0.2 | 1.8 | 0.3 | 4.7 | –1.3 |
| Brazil | 0.0 | 0.0 | n.a. | n.a. | n.a. | n.a. |
| Chile | 0.0 | 0.0 | 0.1 | –0.5 | 0.2 | –0.7 |
| Colombia | 0.2 | 0.0 | 0.4 | –0.4 | 1.0 | –1.0 |
| Costa Rica | –0.1 | 0.1 | –0.3 | –2.1 | 0.9 | –2.4 |
| Dominican Republic | –0.2 | –0.1 | 0.5 | –2.2 | n.a. | n.a. |
| Guatemala | 9.9 | –2.6 | 13.4 | –2.9 | 17.7 | –8.4 |
| Honduras | 2.7 | –0.3 | 3.2 | –6.2 | 6.6 | –8.2 |
| Mexico | 0.4 | 0.0 | 1.1 | –2.7 | 2.1 | –2.1 |
| Nicaragua | 3.0 | –0.6 | 4.0 | 0.3 | 9.5 | –3.0 |
| Panama | 0.2 | 0.0 | –0.4 | –1.8 | 1.1 | –3.0 |
| Peru | 0.2 | 0.1 | 0.1 | 0.8 | 1.2 | –0.1 |
| Paraguay | 0.8 | –0.4 | 2.0 | –2.2 | 5.1 | –3.2 |
| El Salvador | 0.4 | 0.0 | 1.2 | –1.5 | 2.1 | –1.9 |
| Uruguay | –0.3 | 0.1 | –0.7 | –0.1 | –1.5 | –0.6 |
| Venezuela | 0.0 | 0.0 | 0.0 | –0.5 | 0.2 | –0.9 |

n.a. Not available.

from uncommon supports, the estimators suggest a sizable "upper management effect" only in Guatemala and, to a lesser degree, in Bolivia, Honduras, Nicaragua, and Paraguay.

The failure to explain the existent wage gaps on the basis of observable differences in human capital characteristics may lead to claims of discrimination in Latin American labor markets. This avenue for quantifying unexplained wage gaps, however, is subject to criticism. The most common involves the failure to truly identify discriminatory behaviors based on the presence of unobservable characteristics. That is, these studies typically can only analyze human capital characteristics that are easily observable (such as schooling, labor market experience, field of specialization, and sector choice), while other, less easily observed characteristics also help explain earnings gaps. Good examples of these unobservable characteristics include entrepreneurial attitudes, motivation, work ethic, commitment, and assertiveness. Researchers cannot capture such characteristics in a survey, but an employer or, more generally, the relevant actors in the labor market can observe them and act accordingly. If indigenous and nonindigenous workers (or females and males) demonstrate regular differences in some of these "unobservable characteristics," then the components of the earnings gap attributable to discrimination would be overestimated. The literature has moved toward incorporating different attempts to observe the unobservable, that is, to capture, with research methods, the richest possible information that the relevant actors in the markets face in making their decisions.

## Observing the Unobservable

Very recent research, sponsored by the Inter-American Development Bank through its Latin American and Caribbean Research Network, finds mixed evidence for the unequal treatment definition of discrimination.[16] Further attempts to disentangle preference-based and statistical discrimination suggest that Latin Americans do not practice the former type of discrimination. Gutiérrez and Núñez assess social class discrimination based on the administrative records of alumni of a Chilean university, which provided school performance variables in addition to the traditional human capital variables that most studies use.[17] This allowed them to uncover some of the traditional unobservable elements of individual productivity. To assess class differences, they asked a pool of individuals to rate the extent to which they associated a surname with the upper or lower classes. Their results point to the existence of some sort of "classism" in Chile. Individuals with surnames perceived as belonging to the upper class earned significantly more than individuals with surnames perceived as being from the lower class, even after the authors controlled for human capital characteristics such as school-performance indicators. Bravo, Sanhueza, and Urzua similarly interviewed college alumni to study gender differences in labor market earnings among graduates of the business, law, and medicine schools of a single university; they find evidence

16. See Inter-American Development Bank's website "Network Study: Discrimination and Economic Outcomes" (www.iadb.org/res/network_study.cfm?st_id=86). See also Marquez and others (2007) for a comprehensive summary of the research network's results.

17. Gutiérrez and Núñez (2004).

of unjustified gender differences in earnings only in the legal profession.[18] The gender differences found in business and economics vanished after they controlled for family conditions. The gender differences among alumni of the medical school vanished when they controlled for hours worked, firm size, and geographic region.

In a separate study, Bravo, Sanhueza, and Urzúa replicated the standard hiring audit study in Santiago, Chile.[19] They mailed resumes of fictitious applicants to job postings that appeared in the largest Santiago newspapers. The "synthetic" resumes were created such that for each job posting they sent responses from female and male applicants, with upper- and lower-class surnames, and from wealthy and poor municipalities (neighborhoods). With these variations by gender, surname, and municipality, they randomly created human capital characteristics and labor market histories for their fictitious applicants. From March to August 2006, they sent out 6,300 resumes and recorded the callbacks received by their fictitious applicants. They found no systematic differences in callback rates by gender or surname or municipality. This surprising result contrasts with the findings of Bertrand and Mullainathan, who originally applied this methodological approach in Chicago and Boston and found substantial differences in callback rates for fictitious applicants with black-sounding and white-sounding names.[20] The result suggests that Chilean employers—or at least those who advertise their job vacancies in the newspapers—do not actively discriminate in the first rounds of their hiring process.

Moreno and others designed a field experiment to detect discrimination in hiring in Lima, Peru.[21] Instead of creating a sample of synthetic resumes to be sent in response to job postings, they monitored the functioning of the Ministry of Labor's job intermediation service. The enriched design improved on the traditional audit studies in that it measured actual job offers and not only callbacks. The authors detected no significant differences in job hiring by race or gender. Males and females, as well as white-looking and indigenous-looking applicants, were equally likely to receive job offers in the three occupations covered in the study: salesperson, secretary, and administrative or accounting assistant. The study design included interviewing the applicants

18. Bravo, Sanhueza, and Urzúa (2007b).
19. Bravo, Sanhueza, and Urzúa (2007a); see also Riach and Rich (2002).
20. Bertrand and Mullainathan (2004).
21. Moreno and others (2004).

before their job interview. In these interviews, the authors were able to capture a rich set of human capital characteristics that were used to control the study results. One of the aspects explored in the interview was expectations and motivations. When they asked individuals how much they wanted to earn at the job in question, they found no race differences but significant gender differences. Females asked for wages between 6 and 9 percent lower than their male competitors, even after the authors controlled for a rich set of observable characteristics. This reveals some sort of self-discrimination or self-punishment in labor markets.[22]

Another experimental approach to understanding discrimination was developed by Cárdenas and others, who applied a battery of games (such as dictator, distributive dictator, ultimatum, trust, and third-party punishment) to a sample of people involved in the provision of social services in Bogotá, Colombia, including both beneficiaries and public officials.[23] To properly measure the behavior of public officials, they also gathered information on nonpublic officials to generate counterfactuals. They used this setup to measure the extent to which individuals who provide social services to the poor discriminate against the beneficiaries of those services. Across the board, they found an interesting prosocial behavior on the part of the average player. Public officials stated having more prosocial norms than their nonpublic official counterparts, but when facing real economic incentives in the field, public officials showed lower levels of fairness—in the form of altruism, trust, and social punishment—than nonpublic officials. Both public officials and their control group favored women and households with lower education and more dependents (especially if the dependents were children), whereas former combatants in Colombia's political conflict, street recyclers, street vendors, and people living in common-law unions received less favorable treatment.

Castillo, Petrie, and Torero, in another experimental setup, uncover some stereotyping among a representative sample of young Lima residents, but the attitudes vanished after information about performance was publicly revealed.[24] Using a repeated linear public goods game, they measured the extent to which people trust each other and engage in reciprocal behavior. In the game, each subject was given an endowment of twenty-five tokens and asked to divide it between a private and a public investment, which had

22. For similar evidence in the United States, see Babcock and Laschever (2003).
23. Cárdenas and others (2007).
24. Castillo, Petrie, and Torero (2007).

different returns depending not only on the individual's decision, but also on the decisions of their peers. They found that people used personal characteristics to choose partners, showing evidence of stereotyping in favor of women, tall people, and white-looking people. However, when the individuals were given information about the past performance of other players, that information overrode the previously held stereotypical beliefs. In the presence of an information shortage, performance-optimizing individuals relied on observable characteristics as a proxy measure of performance, thereby stereotyping their peers. They stopped doing so whenever the stereotyping proved to be suboptimal for their performance-maximizing objectives.

Elías, Elías, and Ronconi performed a similar study, within a simplified setup, of group formation and popularity among adolescents in Argentina.[25] They asked students in a sample of classrooms in Buenos Aires and Tucumán to rank their classmates according to their preferences for forming a team. The students were also asked to assess the beauty of their classmates. This subjective information about students was complemented with administrative records on grades, disciplinary actions, participation in scholarship programs, and tenure at the school. The authors interpret the aggregate ranking of the students as a measure of popularity. The only factor that was important in determining popularity was academic performance, whereas ethnicity, skin color, and parental wealth and nationality played no role as explanatory factors. Beauty was only important in mixed schools. The authors also find preferences for assortative mating, in that the students' academic performance was strongly correlated with their corresponding top choice in the rankings. They find similar results for beauty, parents' education, and gender.

Finally, Gandelman, Gandelman, and Rothschild test the hypothesis of differential treatment in the courts on the basis of gender, using housing-related cases in Uruguay.[26] They analyze data for 2,437 cases involving foreclosure proceedings, annulment of purchase agreements, actions in rem (that is, proceedings against property), annulments of promissory purchase agreements, and evictions, to assess the effect of the gender composition of the defendant household on the duration of the process. They find a strong correlation between the presence of women and the granting of time extensions in the processes, after controlling for a set of covariates. Judges were more lenient with women across the board.

25. Elías, Elías, and Ronconi (2007).
26. Gandelman, Gandelman, and Rothschild (2007).

## Conclusions

Discrimination is well-rooted in the Latin American collective mind. Most individuals in the region firmly believe that there is some sort of discrimination in the marketplace. When asked about the basis for this discrimination, however, most people in the region do not believe that it operates against the groups traditionally discriminated against (indigenous groups, Afro-descendants, and women, to cite the most prominent historical examples). Rather, they state that the poor suffer the worst discrimination, followed by the uneducated and those with weak social connections. These perceptions of the identity of the discriminated groups pose interesting and challenging questions for the research agenda, pointing toward the existence of discrimination on the basis of economic characteristics, rather than biological or sociological characteristics.

An economic analysis of discrimination requires not only information on perceptions, but also an exploration of economic decisions and their outcomes. The economic literature in the region has advanced toward an understanding of discrimination by analyzing outcomes. We have presented examples centered on the labor market (including, wages, occupations, and formality), access to public goods and services (such as education, health, and security), and political representation, among other areas, which provide well-documented outcomes by gender, race, and ethnicity. In this survey, we have provided comparative measures of gender and racial wage gaps, after controlling for observable characteristics, following the matching comparisons approach developed by Ñopo.[27] We have stressed the unfavorable situation of females and minority groups with respect to males and whites regarding wages. Additionally, the racial wage gap decompositions carried out with the matching comparisons approach uncover important differences not only in wages for comparable characteristics, but also in the access to those comparable characteristics (as revealed by the sizable components of the wage gap explained by the lack of common support). However, the documentation of differentiated outcomes is not necessarily proof of discrimination, as the presence of unobservable factors limits the possibility of assessing gender, racial, or ethnic discrimination. It is very difficult to properly identify discrimination, given the existence of innumerable unobservable elements; it is even more problematic to quantify its economic impact.

27. Ñopo (2008).

This paper also reviews very recent experimental research performed in the region, using tools to observe the unobservable. Many of the results obtained from controlled experimental setups seem to contradict the idea that Latin Americans act discriminatorily. The evidence points to the existence of stereotyping that vanishes when information is revealed. To some extent, there is also evidence that self-discrimination partially explains discriminatory outcomes. Both stereotyping and self-discrimination are behaviors that may simply result from equilibrium situations in which market agents present substantial differences in endowments. Under these circumstances, labor markets (or the other markets analyzed in this paper) simply amplify differences that exist in other spheres. These avenues merit further research to explore the mechanisms underlying these behaviors.

How can these generalized perceptions of discrimination coexist with the lack of evidence of discriminatory behavior? We close the paper by proposing two explanations to the apparent puzzle. First, many other transaction points or markets, not yet analyzed by the experimental literature, may present evidence of discriminatory behavior. The experimental literature has made great strides in obtaining a deeper understanding of the functioning of discriminatory behavior and increasing the ability to observe the unobservable, but the gains in specificity come at the cost of limiting the possibility of generalizing the results (that is, reduced external validity). The sample of studies outlined here does not exhaust either the set of relevant transaction points or the intergroup interactions. More research is needed, not only to analyze processes of discrimination in other markets or transaction points, but also to improve the external validity of the situations already analyzed.

Second, in their daily activities most Latin Americans observe substantial differences in human, physical, financial, and social assets that are associated with gender, racial, ethnic, and class distinctions. These differentiated outcomes do not necessarily emerge as a result of the discriminatory practices of Latin Americans today. Unfortunately, the confusion between differentiated outcomes and discrimination is commonplace in the academic and political discussion. This, in turn, has automatically translated to public discourse and collective memories, and the extremely unequal distribution of wealth and assets reinforces the generalized notion that there is discrimination in Latin America. An important step toward understanding the issues and designing good policies is to recognize the differences between these facts, as they require different responses from governments, states, and societies. It is important to clarify the discussion in order to move forward.

## Appendix: A Simplified Version of the Decomposition of Wage Gaps Based on Matching

We start by defining the gap as the difference of expected values of earnings between males and females:[28]

$$\text{Gap} = E(Y|M) - E(Y|F).$$

More specifically, we use a subindex on the expectation symbol to clarify the distribution of characteristics under which the expected values are computed. Thus,

$$\text{Gap} = E_M(Y|M) - E_F(Y|F).$$

One of the constituent points of this decomposition is the explicit recognition that the supports for the distributions of characteristics for *F* and *M* do not overlap completely. Matching allows us to recognize the common support directly. Those observations that fall within the common support can be matched, and those that fall outside the common support cannot. To take this into account, we separate the expected values into two elements (using some properties of expected values and probabilities):

$$E_M(Y|M) = \mu_M(\text{matched}) * E_M(Y|M,\text{matched}) + \mu_M(\text{unmatched}) * E_M(Y|M,\text{unmatched}).$$

and

$$E_F(Y|F) = \mu_F(\text{matched}) * E_F(Y|F,\text{matched}) + \mu_F(\text{unmatched}) * E_F(Y|F,\text{unmatched}),$$

where $\mu_F$ and $\mu_M$ denote the probability distributions of characteristics under *F* and *M*, respectively. Using the fact that μ (unmatched) = 1 − μ (matched)

28. Detailed discussions of the implicit assumptions made within this appendix are presented in Ñopo (2008). For expositional clarity, we present the setup for gender wage gap decompositions only. Applying the approach to racial gap decompositions simply requires relabeling the compared groups.

under both probability distributions ($F$ and $M$), the Gap can be rewritten, after some rearrangements, as

$$\begin{aligned}\text{Gap} = {} & \mu_M(\text{unmatched}) * \left[E_M(Y|M,\text{unmatched}) - E_M(Y|M,\text{matched})\right] \\ & + E_M(Y|M,\text{matched}) - E_F(Y|F,\text{matched}) \\ & + \mu_F(\text{unmatched}) * \left[E_F(Y|F,\text{matched}) - E_F(Y|F,\text{unmatched})\right].\end{aligned}$$

Using the Blinder-Oaxaca approach of adding and subtracting a counterfactual element, we add and subtract $E_F(Y|M, \text{matched})$:

$$\begin{aligned}\text{Gap} = {} & \mu_M(\text{unmatched}) * \left[E_M(Y|M,\text{unmatched}) - E_M(Y|M,\text{matched})\right] \\ & + E_M(Y|M,\text{matched}) - E_F(Y|M,\text{matched}) + E_F(Y|M,\text{matched}) \\ & - E_F(Y|F,\text{matched}) + \mu_F(\text{unmatched}) * \Big[E_F(Y|F,\text{matched}) \\ & - E_F(Y|F,\text{unmatched})\Big],\end{aligned}$$

or simply Gap $= \Delta_M + \Delta_X + \Delta_0 + \Delta_F$, where

$$\begin{aligned}\Delta_M &= \mu_M(\text{unmatched}) * \left[E_M(Y|M,\text{unmatched}) - E_M(Y|M,\text{matched})\right]; \\ \Delta_x &= E_M(Y|M,\text{matched}) - E_F(Y|M,\text{matched}); \\ \Delta_0 &= E_F(Y|M,\text{matched}) - E_F(Y|F,\text{matched}); \\ \Delta_F &= \mu_F(\text{unmatched}) * \left[E_F(Y|F,\text{matched}) - E_F(Y|F,\text{unmatched})\right].\end{aligned}$$

With this notation, $\Delta_M$ and $\Delta_F$ are the components of the wage gap that account for differences in the support of the distributions of observable characteristics. $\Delta_M$ measures the contribution to the wage gap of the fact that there are some combinations of observable characteristics that males reach and females do not (for instance, middle-aged individuals who are corporate managers and have many years of occupational experience). $\Delta_M$ is then the expected increase in the average female wage if females achieve those individual male characteristics that remain unattained by females. Analogously, $\Delta_F$ measures the contribution to the wage gap of the existence of certain human capital profiles that are exclusively female (for instance, recent migrants who are single, with children, with low schooling attainment and who work as domestic servants). Thus $\Delta_F$ measures the expected increase in average female wages if all females achieve characteristics that are comparable to those of males.

As in the traditional Blinder-Oaxaca decomposition, $\Delta_X$ measures the extent to which the wage gap can be explained by differences in observable characteristics between the comparison groups. In our setup, however, this refers not only to the difference in average characteristics, but also to differences in their distributions. Thus $\Delta_X$ accounts for the expected decrease in male wages when their individual characteristics follow the distribution of their female counterparts.

Finally, $\Delta_0$ is left as the component of the wage gap that cannot be explained on the basis of differences in observable characteristics of the comparison groups. This can be explained as either discrimination in pay or the existence of gender differences in unobservable characteristics that are related to productivity (or a combination of both). The results reported in tables 4 and 5 in the paper refer to this component.

# Comments

**Lucas Ronconi:** Alberto Chong and Hugo Ñopo present a very interesting paper in which they accomplish a number of things. First, they present findings from Latinobarómetro, showing that most Latin Americans think that there is discrimination in the region and that the poor and those with low education suffer the most. Second, they review the evidence on wage differentials by gender and race and present their own estimates using a matching comparison technique. The authors find wage differentials not explained by the usual covariates, although they argue that this is not sufficient evidence of discrimination because of unobservables. Third, they review recent experimental studies, which usually find little or no evidence of discrimination.

The most interesting contribution of the paper is to posit how the generalized perception about discrimination captured in the Latinobarómetro surveys can coexist with the lack of evidence of discriminatory behavior in the experimental studies. The question is well captured in the title: "The Mystery of Discrimination in Latin America." Regrettably, the paper does little to answer the apparent contradiction. The authors propose two explanations. First, there is discrimination, but it is not captured by the few experimental studies. Second, there is stereotyping based on the large differences in endowments across groups, but it vanishes when information is revealed.

The answer may actually be much simpler. Opinion polls reflect the views of citizens, while the experimental evidence is analyzed by social scientists (mostly economists). The two groups may define discrimination differently. Economists usually think of discrimination in terms of unequal wages for the same productivity, but for many people, discrimination is unequal treatment. The following example is illustrative. My colleagues and I asked about 1,000 high school students in Argentina if they think there is discrimination in the labor market: 88 percent answered affirmatively.[1] We then asked them which

1. Elías, Elías, and Ronconi (2007).

characteristics matter for labor market success: 93 percent of those who said that there is discrimination in the labor market mentioned education as a very important factor, while only 4 percent said skin color is a very important factor, 5 percent parental wealth, 7 percent beauty, and 9 percent other factors. This suggests that most teenagers in Argentina think that employers discriminate when they treat job applicants with different education levels differently. Furthermore, this may help explain why Latin Americans think that the two groups that experience the most discrimination are the poor and those with low levels of education.

**Miguel Urquiola:** This paper provides a summary of emerging economic research on discrimination in Latin America and also presents some new results. The gist of the paper is that the region presents a puzzle. On the one hand, there seems to be a widespread perception that Latin America is rife with different forms of discrimination that affect everyday life and perhaps the possibility of achieving social and political stability. This would be consistent, for instance, with explicit pronouncements by leaders such as Bolivia's president, Evo Morales, and with a general perception that exclusion along many dimensions matters in the region. On the other hand, the paper makes the case that these perceptions are contradicted by two pieces of evidence. First, opinion surveys suggest that a surprisingly high proportion of Latin Americans feel that people receive unequal treatment because of observable "reasonable" traits like the fact that they have less education, rather than because of, say, their ethnicity. Second, studies that would seem to credibly isolate discrimination, essentially by emulating research designs used previously in the United States, find little evidence of it (in some cases even in contrast to U.S.-based findings). As the authors state, this raises the following question: "How can these generalized perceptions of discrimination coexist with the lack of evidence of discriminatory behavior?"

While these are interesting and provocative results, it may be premature to call this a full-blown puzzle, for a series of reasons. To start, it is unclear that the comparisons the paper makes are based on a single definition of discrimination. Economists generally use a relatively tidy definition of discrimination, according to which discrimination exists if two individuals who are equally productive are paid different wages for the same job due to differences in their ethnicity, for example; this is essentially the concept underlying the paper's use of Oaxaca-type decompositions. The Latinobarómetro opinion surveys that the paper uses, however, do not make this definition clear to respondents. The 2004 version, for instance, asks, "Of all the reasons for which people are not treated equally, which one affects you more?" The possible answers include being poor, not having enough education, not having enough connections, and "the color of my skin." The authors emphasize that given these choices, people in many countries and survey rounds attach a substantially greater weight to factors like education or poverty, as opposed to factors like race. They argue that this points to "the existence of discrimination on the basis of economic characteristics, rather than biological or sociological characteristics."

This is an interesting finding, but it does not necessarily mean that people believe there is no discrimination. It might be consistent, for instance, with the bulk of respondents' believing that their race per se affects their wages, but that education affects them more. In other words, an Aymara man in Argentina or Bolivia might believe that one reason he is not treated equally is that he has less schooling, but he might also believe that he would receive lower wages even if he had the same schooling and productivity as a non-Aymara individual. Furthermore, in answering education, people may be expressing that they believe there is some type of exclusion in terms of who can get a quality education, even if it is simply in terms of who can get admitted into a "good" school. For instance, people of certain backgrounds might simply feel unwelcome in certain schools in a highly stratified school system like Chile's, and choosing education as an answer might be a way to express frustration with that. Additionally, a large number of people cite poverty as a reason for discrimination, which has perhaps even greater potential for different interpretations than education.

A final related issue is that the paper uses some of the Latinobarómetro rounds to track changes in attitudes over time. For instance, the authors mention that the results of the 2001 survey "are not entirely consistent with the answers to a similarly worded question asked only a few years later." Yet the wording of the questions in the two surveys used for comparison varies in ways that could affect responses. In 2001 the relevant question was as follows: "From what you have heard, which groups do you think suffer the most discrimination, or do you think that there is no discrimination?" In 2004 the question was reworded: "Of all the reasons for which people are not treated equally, which one affects you more?" The simple fact that one of these questions is about "people" while the other is about "you" could affect the way people respond. The interpretation of the survey evidence is thus somewhat delicate, although the patterns the authors present are surprising and certainly merit further work.

The paper also presents evidence on wage gaps for multiple countries. The authors' main innovation is to use matching methods rather than the standard OLS Mincer and Oaxaca decompositions. This presumably introduces greater flexibility in the specifications, allowing observables to better explain gaps, and is an interesting and innovative exercise. I only have two comments in this regard. First, the exercise does not necessarily move any closer to estimating underlying discrimination, since it still does not account for unobservables. Second, it would be useful to see OLS results as well, for comparison with multiple earlier studies in the countries covered. This would help maximize the usefulness of these results (which already contribute quite a bit by bringing data on so many countries together). I hope these estimates can be made available, if only online.

Finally, I have less to say on the discussion of studies that use quasi-experimental designs, to some extent emulating methodologies developed in the United States. These studies represent an interesting body of work, and taken together they further the authors' claim that the region seems to produce less evidence of discrimination than one might expect. By their very nature, however, these analyses are implemented in very specific settings, which at least partially limits their usefulness for formulating more general statements.

In short, Chong and Ñopo are onto an interesting area of work, and I hope they and others will continue to contribute to it.

## References


Aguilar, Renato, and Jorge Dresdner. 2000. "La evolución de la discriminación salarial por género en Chile: 1987–1998." University of Gothenburg.

Altonji, Joseph G., and Rebecca M. Blank. 1999. "Race and Gender in the Labor Market." In *Handbook of Labor Economics,* vol. 3, edited by Orley Ashenfelter and David E. Card, pp. 3143–259. Amsterdam: North-Holland.

Arcand, Jean Louis, and Beatrice d'Hombres. 2004. "Racial Discrimination in the Brazilian Labor Market: Wage, Employment and Segregation Effects." *Journal of International Development* 16(8): 1053–066.

Arias, Omar, Gustavo Yamada, and Luis Tejerina. 2002. "Education, Family Background, and Racial Earnings Inequality in Brazil." Washington: Inter-American Development Bank, Sustainable Development Department.

Babcock, Linda C., and Sara Laschever. 2003. *Women Don't Ask: Negotiation and the Gender Divide.* Princeton University Press.

Barrón, Manuel. 2005. "Cuánto cuesta ser provinciano a un empleado de Lima Metropolitana: una aproximación mediante Propensity Score Matching." *Observatorio de la Economía Latinoamericana* 47 (August).

Bertrand, Marianne, and Sendhil Mullainathan. 2001. "Do People Mean What They Say? Implications for Subjective Survey Data." *American Economic Review* 91(2): 67–72.

———. 2004. "Are Emily and Greg More Employable than Lakisha and Jamal? A Field Experiment on Labor Market Discrimination." *American Economic Review* 94(4): 991–1013.

Blinder, Alan S. 1973. "Wage Discrimination: Reduced Form and Structural Estimates." *Journal of Human Resources* 7(4): 436–55.

Bravo, David, Claudia Sanhueza, and Sergio Urzúa. 2007a. "An Experimental Study about Labor Market Discrimination: Gender, Social Class, and Neighborhood." Washington: Inter-American Development Bank.

———. 2007b. "Is There Labor Market Discrimination among Professionals in Chile? Lawyers, Doctors, and Business-People." Washington: Inter-American Development Bank.

Brown, Cynthia J., José A. Pagan, and Eduardo Rodríguez-Oreggia. 1999. "Occupational Attainment and Gender Earnings Differentials in Mexico." *Industrial and Labor Relations Review* 53(1): 123–35.

Campante, Filipe R., Anna R. V. Crespo, and Phillippe G. Leite. 2004. "Desigualdade salarial entre raças no mercado de trabalho urbano brasileiro: aspectos regionais." *Revista Brasileira de Economia* 58(2): 185–210.

Cárdenas, Juan Camilo, and others. 2007. "Discrimination in the Provision of Social Services to the Poor: A Field Experimental Study." Working Paper 003885. Universidad de Los Andes-CEDE.

Castillo, Marco, Ragan Petrie, and Máximo Torero. 2007. "Ethnic and Social Barriers to Cooperation: Experiments Studying the Extent and Nature of Discrimination in Urban Peru." Washington: Inter-American Development Bank, Latin American Research Network.

Contreras, Dante, and Esteban Puentes. 2000. "Is the Gender Wage Discrimination Decreasing in Chile? Thirty Years of 'Robust' Evidence." Santiago: University of Chile, Department of Economics.

De Ferranti, David M., and others. 2004. *Inequality in Latin America and the Caribbean: Breaking with History.* Washington: World Bank.

DEMUS (Estudio para la Defensa y los Derechos de la Mujer). 2005. *Encuesta nacional sobre exclusión y discriminación social, 2005.* Lima.

Deutsch, Ruthanne, and others. 2005. "Working within Confines: Occupational Segregation by Gender in Costa Rica, Ecuador, and Uruguay." In *Women at Work: Challenges for Latin America,* edited by Claudia Piras. Washington: Inter-American Development Bank.

Duryea, Suzanne, and others. 2007. "The Educational Gender Gap in Latin America and the Caribbean." Working Paper 600. Washington: Inter-American Development Bank, Research Department.

Elías, Julio, Víctor Elías, and Lucas Ronconi. 2007. "Discrimination and Social Networks: Popularity among High School Students in Argentina." Research Network Working Paper R-539. Washington: Inter-American Development Bank.

European Commission. 2007. "Discrimination in the European Union." Special Eurobarometer 263. Brussels.

Fuentes, Jeannette, Amalia Palma, and Rodrigo Montero. 2005. "Discriminación salarial por género en Chile: una mirada global." *Estudios de Economía* 32(2): 133–57.

Gallardo, María Lourdes. 2006. "Ethnicity-Based Wage Differentials in Ecuador's Labor Market." Master's thesis, Cornell University.

Gandelman, Eduardo, Nestor Gandelman, and Julie Rothschild. 2007. "Gender Differentials in Judicial Proceedings: Field Evidence from Housing-Related Cases in Uruguay." Washington: Inter-American Development Bank.

Gandelman, Nestor, Hugo Ñopo, and Laura Ripani. 2007. "Traditional Excluding Forces: A Review of the Quantitative Literature on the Economic Situation of Indigenous Peoples, Afro-Descendants, and People Living with Disability." Working Paper 619. Washington: Inter-American Development Bank, Research Department.

García-Aracil, Adela, and Carolyn Winter. 2006. "Gender and Ethnicity Differentials in School Attainment and Labor Market Earnings in Ecuador." *World Development* 34(2): 289–307.

González, Cecilia, and Máximo Rossi. 2002. "Discriminación salarial por género y efectos de la feminización de las ocupaciones en Uruguay (1986–1997)." Montevideo: University of the Republic, Department of Economics.

Guimarães, Roberta de Oliveira. 2006. "Desigualdade salarial entre negros e brancos no Brasil: discriminacao o exclusao?" *Economica* 8(2): 227–51. Rio de Janeiro.

Gutiérrez, Roberto, and Javier Núñez. 2004. "Classism, Discrimination and Meritocracy in the Labor Market: The Case of Chile." Working Paper 308. Santiago: University of Chile, Department of Economics.

Khandker, Shahidur R. 1990. "Labor Market Participation, Returns to Education, and Male-Female Wage Differences in Peru." Working Paper WPS 461. Washington: World Bank, Population and Human Resources Department.

Larrea, Carlos, and Fernando Montenegro. 2006. "Ecuador." In *Indigenous Peoples, Poverty, and Human Development in Latin America: 1994–2004,* edited by Gillette Hall and Harry A. Patrinos. Washington: World Bank.

Latinobarómetro. Various years. *Latinobarómetro.* Santiago: Latinobarómetro Corporation. Available online at www.latinobarometro.org.

Leite, Phillippe G. 2005. "Race Discrimination or Inequality of Opportunities: The Brazilian Case." Discussion Paper 118. Georg-August-Universität, Ibero-America Institute for Economic Research.

Marquez, Gustavo, and others, eds. 2007. *Outsiders? The Changing Patterns of Exclusion in Latin America and the Caribbean.* Harvard University Press.

Montenegro, Claudio E. 2001. "Wage Distribution in Chile: Does Gender Matter? A Quantile Regression Approach." *Policy Research Report on Gender and Development.* Working Paper 20. Washington: World Bank. Development Research Group.

Moreno, M., and others. 2004. "Gender and Racial Discrimination in Hiring: A Pseudo Audit Study for Three Selected Occupations in Metropolitan Lima." Discussion Paper 979. Bonn: Institute for the Study of Labor (IZA).

Ñopo, Hugo. 2004. "The Gender Wage Gap in Peru, 1986–2000: Evidence from a Matching Comparisons Approach." *Económica* 50(1–2). La Plata.

———. 2007. "The Gender Wage Gap in Chile, 1992–2003, from a Matching Comparisons Perspective." Discussion Paper 2698. Bonn: Institute for the Study of Labor (IZA).

———. 2008. "Matching as a Tool to Decompose Wage Gaps." *Review of Economics and Statistics* 90(2).

Ñopo, Hugo, Jaime Saavedra, and Máximo Torero. 2007. "Ethnicity and Earnings in a Mixed-Race Labor Market." *Economic Development and Cultural Change* 55(4): 709–34.

Oaxaca, Ronald. 1973. "Male-Female Wage Differentials in Urban Labor Market." *International Economic Review* 14 (3): 693–709.

Psacharopoulos, George, and Zafiris Tzannatos, eds. 1992. *Case Studies on Women's Employment and Pay in Latin America.* Washington: World Bank.

Riach, Peter A., and Judith Rich. 2002. "Field Experiments of Discrimination in the Market Place." *Economic Journal* 112(483): 480–518.

Santos, Marina, and Jorge Saba. 2005. "Trade Openness and Gender Discrimination." Washington: World Bank.

Secretaría Técnica del Frente Social. 2004. *Encuesta nacional sobre racismo y discriminación racial en el Ecuador, 2004.* Quito.

SEDESOL (Secretaría de Desarrollo Social). 2005. *Primera encuesta nacional sobre discriminación en México, 2005.* Mexico City.

Soares, Serguei Suarez Dillon. 2000. "O perfil da discriminação no mercado de trabalho: homens negros, mulheres brancas e mulheres negras." Discusión Paper 769. Brasília: Instituto de Pesquisa Econômica Aplicada.

Soruco, Ximena, Giorgina Piani, and Máximo Rossi. 2007. "What Emigration Leaves Behind: The Situation of Emigrants and Their Families in Ecuador." Cuenca, Ecuador: Fundación Sur.

Telles, Edward E., and Nelson Lim. 1998. "Does It Matter Who Answers the Race Question? Racial Classification and Income Inequality in Brazil." *Demography* 35(4): 465–74.

Tenjo, Jaime, Rocio Ribero, and Luisa Bernat. 2005. "Evolution of Salary Differences between Men and Women in Six Latin American Countries." In *Women at Work: Challenges for Latin America,* edited by Claudia Piras. Washington: Inter-American Development Bank.

ERNESTO LÓPEZ-CÓRDOVA
ALEJANDRO MICCO
DANIELKEN MOLINA

# How Sensitive Are Latin American Exports to Chinese Competition in the U.S. Market?

Chinese exports increasingly compete with Latin American and Caribbean products in world markets.[1] Competition in the U.S. market is particularly relevant. The United States has been Latin America's most important trade partner throughout the postwar era. Trade with the United States stood at 60 percent of the region's total world trade in 2000, up from less than 47 percent in 1960 and a low of 37 percent in 1978.[2] Latin America has also been an important trade partner for the United States, although the region's share has fluctuated over the last three decades. Trade with Latin America as a share of total trade fell in the 1980s, but it has picked up since then. U.S.-China trade has also increased its share, growing from basically zero in the 1960s to more than 5 percent currently.

The remarkable growth of U.S. trade with China and the challenges it portends for Latin American countries are evident in U.S. import data (see table 1). From 1990 to 2003, Latin American exports to the United States increased from $58 billion to $196 billion, growing at an annual rate of 6.9 percent in real terms. Since U.S. imports from the world as a whole grew at 4.8 percent over the same period, Latin America's share of the U.S. market rose from 13.5 in 1990 to 17.5 in 2003. Chinese sales to the United States, however, grew at a breakneck 16.6 percent annually, reaching $147 billion in 2003. China's dynamic export performance led to a fourfold increase in the country's share of U.S. imports to 13.2 percent in 2003.

Although Latin America as a whole had a fair export performance over the last decade, aggregate figures mask important differences among countries

López-Córdova is with the Inter-American Development Bank; Micco is with the Ministry of Finance of Chile; Molina is a third-year doctoral student at the University of California–San Diego.

1. See Devlin, Estevadeordal, and Rodríguez (2006).
2. By trade, we mean here the sum of exports and imports.

**TABLE 1. U.S. Imports and Average Tariffs, by Origin[a]**

| | Volume (millions of dollars) | | | Distribution (percent) | | | Annual real growth rate (percent) | | | Average tariff (percent) | | |
|---|---|---|---|---|---|---|---|---|---|---|---|---|
| Region of origin | 1990 | 2000 | 2003 | 1990 | 2000 | 2003 | 1990–2000 | 1990–2003 | 2000–03 | 1990 | 2000 | 2003 |
| *Total trade* | | | | | | | | | | | | |
| World | 431,318 | 1,152,203 | 1,116,347 | 100.0 | 100.0 | 100.0 | 7.3 | 4.8 | −3.2 | 4.6 | 2.5 | 2.1 |
| Latin America and the Caribbean | 58,286 | 198,906 | 195,848 | 13.5 | 17.3 | 17.5 | 10.0 | 6.9 | −2.7 | 3.0 | 1.3 | 0.8 |
| Mexico | 25,872 | 128,408 | 128,430 | 6.0 | 11.1 | 11.5 | 14.2 | 10.2 | −2.2 | 2.8 | 0.8 | 0.4 |
| Central America | 2,704 | 11,824 | 11,654 | 0.6 | 1.0 | 1.0 | 12.7 | 9.0 | −2.7 | 5.0 | 5.2 | 4.4 |
| Caribbean | 4,494 | 9,770 | 9,193 | 1.0 | 0.8 | 0.8 | 5.1 | 2.9 | −4.1 | 4.9 | 3.3 | 2.2 |
| Andean | 14,670 | 29,295 | 25,011 | 3.4 | 2.5 | 2.2 | 4.2 | 1.5 | −7.2 | 1.4 | 0.7 | 0.5 |
| South America | 10,546 | 19,609 | 21,560 | 2.4 | 1.7 | 1.9 | 3.5 | 2.9 | 1.0 | 4.3 | 2.4 | 1.6 |
| China | 14,254 | 98,267 | 146,989 | 3.3 | 8.5 | 13.2 | 18.0 | 16.6 | 11.9 | 7.8 | 4.7 | 3.6 |
| Rest of the world | 358,778 | 855,030 | 773,510 | 83.2 | 74.2 | 69.3 | 6.1 | 3.3 | −5.4 | 4.7 | 2.6 | 2.2 |

Source: Authors' calculations, based on U.S. Customs import data.

a. Annual real growth rates calculated using U.S. consumer price index (CPI) as a deflator. Average tariffs are calculated as duties divided by the value of imports. The regions are defined as follows: South America is composed of Argentina, Brazil, Chile, French Guiana, Guyana, Paraguay, Suriname, and Uruguay. The Andean countries are Bolivia, Colombia, Ecuador, Peru, and Venezuela. The set of Central American countries includes Belize, Costa Rica, El Salvador, Guatemala, Honduras, Nicaragua, and Panama. The Caribbean subgroup is made up of Antigua and Barbuda, Aruba, Barbados, Bermuda, Cuba, Dominica, Dominican Republic, Grenada, Haiti, Jamaica, Netherlands Antilles, Saint Kitts and Nevis, Saint Lucia, Saint Vincent and the Grenadines, the Bahamas, Trinidad and Tobago, Montserrat, and the British Virgin Islands. Last, Mexico is listed individually.

in the region. The lion's share of the growth in exports from Latin America, more than 80 percent, came from Mexico, which increased its share of the U.S. market from 6.0 to 11.5 percent from 1990 to 2003. Over the same period, exports from Caribbean, Andean, and other South American countries grew more slowly than world exports to the United States; only Central America, along with Mexico, performed better than the world as a whole. Moreover, even Mexico has not been able to keep up with China's dynamic export performance, despite being bound to the United States by geography and the North American Free Trade Agreement. By 2003, China had surpassed Mexico as the United States' second most important import supplier, after Canada.

Aggregate trade figures also hide differences in the sectoral composition of Chinese and Latin American exports to the United States (table 2). Latin America is an important supplier of agricultural and mining products (including oil) to the United States, with respective shares of around 50 and 30 percent of U.S. import demand. Close to a quarter of all Latin American exports consists of nonmanufacturing goods; this figure is as high as three-quarters in the case of the Andean countries. At the opposite extreme, Mexico has the highest share of manufacturing exports to the United States (86 percent), followed by Central America and South America excluding the Andean countries (84 percent in both cases).[3] Central American countries saw a particularly significant change in the composition of their exports, with a twenty percentage points drop in the share of agricultural exports compensated by an equal rise in manufacturing. In contrast to Latin America, China is a relatively insignificant supplier of agricultural and mining exports, while manufactures represent over 99 percent of exports to the United States.

We find important differences within the manufacturing sector, as well (table 3). In 2003, approximately a fifth of all Chinese exports to the U.S. market was in leather goods (including footwear), textiles, and apparel, compared

3. The Latin American data are disaggregated into five subgroups, with the Andean countries classified separately from the rest of South America. Throughout the paper, we use the term *South America* to cover the following set of countries: Argentina, Brazil, Chile, French Guiana, Guyana, Paraguay, Suriname, and Uruguay. The *Andean countries* are Bolivia, Colombia, Ecuador, Peru, and Venezuela. The set of *Central American* countries includes Belize, Costa Rica, El Salvador, Guatemala, Honduras, Nicaragua, and Panama. The *Caribbean* subgroup is composed of Antigua and Barbuda, Aruba, Barbados, Bermuda, Cuba, Dominica, Dominican Republic, Grenada, Haiti, Jamaica, Netherlands Antilles, Saint Kitts and Nevis, Saint Lucia, Saint Vincent and the Grenadines, the Bahamas, Trinidad and Tobago, Montserrat, and the British Virgin Islands. Last, Mexico is listed individually, owing to its strong trade relations with the United States.

**TABLE 2. U.S. Imports and Average Tariffs, by Sector and Origin[a]**

| Sector and region | Volume (millions of dollars) | | | Regional distribution (percent) | | | As percentage of manufacturing imports | | | Annual real growth rate (percent) | | | Average tariff (percent) | | |
|---|---|---|---|---|---|---|---|---|---|---|---|---|---|---|---|
| of origin | 1990 | 2000 | 2003 | 1990 | 2000 | 2003 | 1990 | 2000 | 2003 | 1990–2000 | 1990–2003 | 2000–03 | 1990 | 2000 | 2003 |
| *Agriculture* | | | | | | | | | | | | | | | |
| World | 10,350 | 17,621 | 18,266 | 100.0 | 100.0 | 100.0 | 2.4 | 1.5 | 1.6 | 2.6 | 1.8 | –1.0 | 3.6 | 1.4 | 0.7 |
| Latin America and the Caribbean | 5,243 | 8,499 | 8,848 | 50.7 | 48.2 | 48.4 | 9.0 | 4.3 | 4.5 | 2.1 | 1.4 | –0.9 | 2.9 | 0.6 | 0.3 |
| Mexico | 1,873 | 3,152 | 3,491 | 18.1 | 17.9 | 19.1 | 7.2 | 2.5 | 2.7 | 2.5 | 2.2 | 1.2 | 5.2 | 0.6 | 0.2 |
| Central America | 988 | 1,820 | 1,706 | 9.6 | 10.3 | 9.3 | 36.6 | 15.4 | 14.6 | 3.4 | 1.6 | –4.3 | 0.7 | 0.1 | 0.1 |
| Caribbean | 142 | 163 | 170 | 1.4 | 0.9 | 0.9 | 3.2 | 1.7 | 1.8 | –1.4 | –1.3 | –0.9 | 0.6 | 0.0 | 0.0 |
| Andean | 1,188 | 1,611 | 1,622 | 11.5 | 9.1 | 8.9 | 8.1 | 5.5 | 6.5 | 0.3 | –0.2 | –2.0 | 2.2 | 0.2 | 0.1 |
| South America | 1,052 | 1,753 | 1,860 | 10.2 | 9.9 | 10.2 | 10.0 | 8.9 | 8.6 | 2.4 | 1.8 | –0.2 | 2.1 | 1.6 | 0.7 |
| China | 105 | 298 | 401 | 1.0 | 1.7 | 2.2 | 0.7 | 0.3 | 0.3 | 8.0 | 8.0 | 8.0 | 2.4 | 28.5 | 1.8 |
| Rest of the world | 5,003 | 8,824 | 9,017 | 48.3 | 50.1 | 49.4 | 1.4 | 1.0 | 1.2 | 3.0 | 1.9 | –1.5 | 4.3 | 1.2 | 1.0 |
| *Mining* | | | | | | | | | | | | | | | |
| World | 49,326 | 104,516 | 126,384 | 100.0 | 100.0 | 100.0 | 11.4 | 9.1 | 11.3 | 4.9 | 4.7 | 4.2 | 0.3 | 1.2 | 0.0 |
| Latin America and the Caribbean | 13,100 | 31,523 | 36,311 | 26.6 | 30.2 | 28.7 | 22.5 | 15.8 | 18.5 | 6.2 | 5.3 | 2.5 | 0.2 | 0.1 | 0.0 |
| Mexico | 5,064 | 12,116 | 14,589 | 10.3 | 11.6 | 11.5 | 19.6 | 9.4 | 11.4 | 6.1 | 5.7 | 4.1 | 0.2 | 0.0 | 0.0 |
| Central America | 25 | 154 | 181 | 0.1 | 0.1 | 0.1 | 0.9 | 1.3 | 1.6 | 16.6 | 13.3 | 3.2 | 0.3 | 0.3 | 0.0 |

| | | | | | | | | | | | | | | | |
|---|---|---|---|---|---|---|---|---|---|---|---|---|---|---|---|
| Caribbean | 782 | 980 | 2,735 | 1.6 | 0.9 | 2.2 | 17.4 | 10.0 | 29.8 | –0.5 | 7.3 | 37.7 | 0.2 | 0.0 | 0.0 |
| Andean | 6,912 | 17,325 | 17,110 | 14.0 | 16.6 | 13.5 | 47.1 | 59.1 | 68.4 | 6.6 | 4.4 | –2.6 | 0.3 | 0.2 | 0.0 |
| South America | 318 | 948 | 1,696 | 0.6 | 0.9 | 1.3 | 3.0 | 4.8 | 7.9 | 8.5 | 10.8 | 18.8 | 0.4 | 0.1 | 0.1 |
| China | 725 | 608 | 329 | 1.5 | 0.6 | 0.3 | 5.1 | 0.6 | 0.2 | –4.4 | –8.3 | –20.2 | 0.7 | 0.2 | 0.3 |
| Rest of the world | 35,501 | 72,385 | 89,743 | 72.0 | 69.3 | 71.0 | 9.9 | 8.5 | 11.6 | 4.5 | 4.6 | 5.1 | 0.3 | 1.7 | 0.0 |
| *Manufacturing* | | | | | | | | | | | | | | | |
| World | 371,642 | 1,030,066 | 971,697 | 100.0 | 100.0 | 100.0 | 86.2 | 89.4 | 87.0 | 7.7 | 4.9 | –4.1 | 5.2 | 2.7 | 2.4 |
| Latin America and the Caribbean | 39,943 | 158,884 | 150,689 | 10.7 | 15.4 | 15.5 | 68.5 | 79.9 | 76.9 | 11.7 | 7.9 | –3.9 | 3.9 | 1.6 | 1.1 |
| Mexico | 18,935 | 113,140 | 110,351 | 5.1 | 11.0 | 11.4 | 73.2 | 88.1 | 85.9 | 16.3 | 11.5 | –3.0 | 3.3 | 0.9 | 0.4 |
| Central America | 1,690 | 9,849 | 9,767 | 0.5 | 1.0 | 1.0 | 62.5 | 83.3 | 83.8 | 16.0 | 11.5 | –2.5 | 7.6 | 6.2 | 5.2 |
| Caribbean | 3,570 | 8,627 | 6,288 | 1.0 | 0.8 | 0.6 | 79.4 | 88.3 | 68.4 | 6.2 | 1.7 | –12.0 | 6.1 | 3.7 | 3.2 |
| Andean | 6,571 | 10,359 | 6,279 | 1.8 | 1.0 | 0.6 | 44.8 | 35.4 | 25.1 | 1.8 | –2.9 | –17.2 | 2.5 | 1.7 | 1.8 |
| South America | 9,177 | 16,908 | 18,004 | 2.5 | 1.6 | 1.9 | 87.0 | 86.2 | 83.5 | 3.4 | 2.6 | –0.1 | 4.6 | 2.6 | 1.8 |
| China | 13,424 | 97,361 | 146,259 | 3.6 | 9.5 | 15.1 | 94.2 | 99.1 | 99.5 | 18.6 | 17.0 | 12.0 | 8.2 | 4.6 | 3.6 |
| Rest of the world | 318,274 | 773,822 | 674,749 | 85.6 | 75.1 | 69.4 | 88.7 | 90.5 | 87.2 | 6.3 | 3.2 | –6.5 | 5.2 | 2.7 | 2.5 |

Source: Authors' calculations, based on U.S. Customs import data.

a. Annual real growth rates calculated using U.S. consumer price index as a deflator. Average tariffs are calculated as duties divided by the value of imports. Regions defined as in table 1.

**TABLE 3. U.S. Manufacturing Imports and Average Tariffs, by Industry and Origin[a]**

| Industry and region | Volume (millions of dollars) | | | Regional distribution (percent) | | | As percentage of manufacturing imports | | | Annual real growth rate (percent) | | | Average tariff (percent) | | |
|---|---|---|---|---|---|---|---|---|---|---|---|---|---|---|---|
| of origin | 1990 | 2000 | 2003 | 1990 | 2000 | 2003 | 1990 | 2000 | 2003 | 1990–2000 | 1990–2003 | 2000–03 | 1990 | 2000 | 2003 |
| *Apparel and textiles* | | | | | | | | | | | | | | | |
| World | 43,417 | 97,872 | 102,332 | 100.0 | 100.0 | 100.0 | 11.7 | 9.5 | 10.5 | 5.5 | 4.0 | −0.7 | 12.9 | 10.3 | 8.7 |
| Latin America and the Caribbean | 5,678 | 23,742 | 21,662 | 13.1 | 24.3 | 21.2 | 14.2 | 14.9 | 14.4 | 12.2 | 8.0 | −5.1 | 13.0 | 6.0 | 4.6 |
| Mexico | 1,211 | 10,810 | 8,907 | 2.8 | 11.0 | 8.7 | 6.4 | 9.6 | 8.1 | 21.1 | 13.6 | −8.3 | 12.0 | 2.4 | 0.8 |
| Central America | 876 | 6,806 | 7,241 | 2.0 | 7.0 | 7.1 | 51.8 | 69.1 | 74.1 | 19.4 | 14.6 | −0.1 | 14.0 | 8.7 | 6.8 |
| Caribbean | 1,362 | 3,249 | 2,769 | 3.1 | 3.3 | 2.7 | 38.1 | 37.7 | 44.0 | 6.1 | 2.9 | −7.3 | 13.8 | 8.5 | 6.5 |
| Andean | 375 | 952 | 1,147 | 0.9 | 1.0 | 1.1 | 5.7 | 9.2 | 18.3 | 6.8 | 6.1 | 4.1 | 14.5 | 10.6 | 6.8 |
| South America | 1,854 | 1,925 | 1,598 | 4.3 | 2.0 | 1.6 | 20.2 | 11.4 | 8.9 | −2.4 | −3.7 | −8.1 | 12.1 | 10.6 | 10.0 |
| China | 6,319 | 21,710 | 28,680 | 14.6 | 22.2 | 28.0 | 47.1 | 22.3 | 19.6 | 10.1 | 9.4 | 7.3 | 11.6 | 11.8 | 9.4 |
| Rest of the world | 31,420 | 52,420 | 51,990 | 72.4 | 53.6 | 50.8 | 9.9 | 6.8 | 7.7 | 2.4 | 1.2 | −2.4 | 13.1 | 11.5 | 10.1 |
| *Machinery and equipment* | | | | | | | | | | | | | | | |
| World | 193,344 | 611,125 | 563,178 | 100.0 | 100.0 | 100.0 | 52.0 | 59.3 | 58.0 | 9.1 | 5.8 | −4.8 | 4.2 | 1.6 | 1.3 |
| Latin America and the Caribbean | 15,227 | 93,195 | 92,528 | 7.9 | 15.2 | 16.4 | 38.1 | 58.7 | 61.4 | 16.6 | 11.9 | −2.4 | 2.6 | 0.7 | 0.4 |
| Mexico | 12,470 | 85,640 | 83,570 | 6.4 | 14.0 | 14.8 | 65.9 | 75.7 | 75.7 | 17.9 | 12.8 | −3.0 | 2.7 | 0.7 | 0.4 |
| Central America | 90 | 1,602 | 954 | 0.0 | 0.3 | 0.2 | 5.3 | 16.3 | 9.8 | 29.8 | 16.8 | −17.7 | 1.9 | 0.4 | 0.5 |

| | | | | | | | | | | | | | | | |
|---|---|---|---|---|---|---|---|---|---|---|---|---|---|---|---|
| Caribbean | 283 | 881 | 970 | 0.1 | 0.1 | 0.2 | 7.9 | 10.2 | 15.4 | 9.0 | 7.1 | 1.0 | 2.0 | 0.5 | 0.5 |
| Andean | 189 | 345 | 315 | 0.1 | 0.1 | 0.1 | 2.9 | 3.3 | 5.0 | 3.3 | 1.3 | −5.0 | 1.6 | 0.5 | 0.4 |
| South America | 2,196 | 4,728 | 6,719 | 1.1 | 0.8 | 1.2 | 23.9 | 28.0 | 37.3 | 5.0 | 6.2 | 10.0 | 1.8 | 0.6 | 0.6 |
| China | 2,517 | 44,330 | 71,850 | 1.3 | 7.3 | 12.8 | 18.7 | 45.5 | 49.1 | 29.6 | 26.0 | 14.9 | 5.1 | 2.3 | 1.9 |
| Rest of the world | 175,600 | 473,600 | 398,800 | 90.8 | 77.5 | 70.8 | 55.2 | 61.2 | 59.1 | 7.4 | 3.7 | −7.6 | 4.3 | 1.7 | 1.5 |
| *Other manufacturing* | | | | | | | | | | | | | | | |
| World | 134,881 | 321,069 | 306,187 | 100.0 | 100.0 | 100.0 | 36.3 | 31.2 | 31.5 | 6.1 | 3.7 | −3.7 | 4.1 | 2.4 | 2.3 |
| Latin America and the Caribbean | 19,039 | 41,946 | 36,499 | 14.1 | 13.1 | 11.9 | 47.7 | 26.4 | 24.2 | 5.3 | 2.4 | −6.6 | 2.3 | 1.2 | 0.7 |
| Mexico | 5,254 | 16,690 | 17,874 | 3.9 | 5.2 | 5.8 | 27.7 | 14.8 | 16.2 | 9.2 | 7.0 | 0.1 | 2.7 | 0.9 | 0.3 |
| Central America | 725 | 1,441 | 1,572 | 0.5 | 0.4 | 0.5 | 42.9 | 14.6 | 16.1 | 4.2 | 3.4 | 0.7 | 0.6 | 1.1 | 0.7 |
| Caribbean | 1,925 | 4,497 | 2,549 | 1.4 | 1.4 | 0.8 | 53.9 | 52.1 | 40.5 | 5.9 | −0.5 | −19.0 | 1.2 | 0.9 | 0.6 |
| Andean | 6,007 | 9,062 | 4,817 | 4.5 | 2.8 | 1.6 | 91.4 | 87.5 | 76.7 | 1.4 | −4.2 | −20.8 | 1.8 | 0.8 | 0.6 |
| South America | 5,127 | 10,255 | 9,687 | 3.8 | 3.2 | 3.2 | 55.9 | 60.7 | 53.8 | 4.3 | 2.3 | −4.0 | 3.1 | 2.1 | 1.4 |
| China | 4,588 | 31,321 | 45,729 | 3.4 | 9.8 | 14.9 | 34.2 | 32.2 | 31.3 | 17.9 | 16.2 | 11.0 | 5.3 | 2.9 | 2.8 |
| Rest of the world | 111,254 | 247,802 | 223,959 | 82.5 | 77.2 | 73.1 | 35.0 | 32.0 | 33.2 | 5.4 | 2.8 | −5.4 | 4.4 | 2.6 | 2.5 |

Source: Authors' calculations, based on U.S. Customs import data.

a. Annual real growth rates calculated using U.S. consumer price index as a deflator. Average tariffs are calculated as duties divided by the value of imports. Regions defined as in table 1.

with around 8 to 9 percent in the case of Mexico or South America (excluding the Andean countries) and 75 percent for Central America. Machinery and equipment exports amounted to almost a half of all Chinese sales to the United States, compared with 5 percent for the Andean countries, 10 percent for Central America, and 76 percent for Mexico.

China's strong export performance and Latin America's relative weakness have been made patently manifest since 2000. During the 2000–03 period, the U.S. demand for world goods declined at a rate of 3.2 percent per year, while demand for Latin American goods fell 2.7 percent. In contrast, Chinese exports to the United States expanded at a rate of 11.9 percent per year in the period. Figures for the manufacturing sector are even more dismal: Latin American exports in general recorded a yearly decline of 3.9 percent, while Caribbean exports fell 12 percent annually and Andean exports 17 percent. Chinese exports of leather goods, textiles, and apparel expanded at an annual rate of 7.3 percent, compared with an annual contraction of more than 8 percent for Mexico and South America and more than 5 percent for Latin America as a whole. China's machinery and equipment exports grew by 15 percent annually, while exports from Central America contracted by almost 18 percent per year. The region as a whole performed slightly better in this area.

China's export performance has been undeterred by higher tariffs, relative to Latin America, levied in the United States. In 2003, average tariffs on manufacturing imports were more than three times higher on Chinese than on Latin American goods. Mexican exports of leather goods, textiles, and apparel paid 0.8 percent ad valorem, on average, compared with 9.4 percent in the case of Chinese exports. Although averages hide differences in the composition of exports coming from each country and should be read with caution, tariff provisions under the North American Free Trade Agreement (NAFTA), the Andean Trade Preference Act (ATPA), or the Caribbean Basin Initiative (CBI) clearly give a preferential edge to some Latin American nations over China. While several studies demonstrate that tariff preferences (such as those under NAFTA) have indeed led to increased exports to the United States, China appears to have a comparative advantage that is difficult to compensate through low tariffs on Latin American exports.[4]

The picture that emerges from the trade statistics reveals that China has become a direct competitor with Latin American countries in their prime export destination, and this competition is rapidly eroding Latin America's share of the U.S. market. This is particularly the case for manufacturing exporters, such

4. On increased exports to the United States, see Moreira (2007); Nordas (2004).

as Mexico, Central America, and the Caribbean, and low-wage industries, like leather goods, textiles, and apparel. A key issue in this context is how changes in the policy environment would alter the current situation. Some of the countries that are most vulnerable to Chinese competition have recently established trade agreements granting them preferential access to the U.S. market (for example, the Central America Free Trade Agreement, or CAFTA). The region as a whole has similarly contemplated establishing a hemispheric Free Trade Area of the Americas (FTAA). Such initiatives might help the region compete more effectively with China in the United States. At the same time, the January 2005 removal of quotas in place under the Multi-Fiber Agreement has increased China's presence in U.S. apparel and textile consumption. An additional factor that would affect Latin American exports to the United States is the possibility of a steep appreciation of the Chinese currency, the renminbi.

How much would hemispheric free trade improve the competitiveness of Latin American exports to the United States? How has the elimination of apparel and textile import quotas in place under the Multi-Fiber Agreement (MFA) affected the region's exports of these products? How much would a revaluation of the renminbi translate into increased Latin American and Caribbean exports? To shed light on these questions, we use detailed U.S. import data (specifically, at the six-digit level of the Harmonized System, disaggregated by partner country, over the 1990–2003 period) to measure the elasticity of substitution between Latin American and Chinese exports to the United States. We assume that the preferences for domestic and imported varieties of a representative consumer in the U.S. market are represented by a utility function with constant elasticity of substitution. We then derive an expression for U.S. demand for imports from each country, which is a function of the price of imports from the given country, a sectoral price index, the elasticity of substitution, and U.S. income allocated to the consumption of the product in question.

To correctly estimate the elasticity of substitution in the demand equation, we need to deal with the endogeneity bias that arises between the demand equation and the price level of the good. We therefore instrument the price of the final good with three sets of instruments: transport costs, import tariffs, and input prices (that is, wages, cost of inputs, and cost of capital). Given the level of desegregation of our data, we are able to estimate the elasticity of substitution per economic sector, which is in line with the results obtained by recent studies. We use the estimated elasticities to forecast how alternative policy scenarios that affect the relative price of Latin American and Chinese goods would change U.S. import patterns. We consider three scenarios: a revaluation of the renminbi; the elimination of tariffs on Latin American and Caribbean exports to the United States as a result of a hemispheric free trade agreement; and the elimination of apparel and textile import quotas in the U.S. market.

The rest of the paper proceeds as follows. The next section outlines the empirical strategy followed to correctly estimate the elasticity of substitution per economic sector. The paper then describes the data and presents the estimation results. We use these estimation results to simulate the impact of the policy scenarios described above on Latin American exports to the U.S. market, and the final section concludes.

## Empirical Framework

In this section, we present our empirical framework for estimating U.S. import elasticities. We assume that there is a set of goods and that each country can produce a different variety of each good. For goods produced in a given sector, U.S. imports are characterized by a constant elasticity of substitutions (CES) demand function. Therefore, U.S. expenditures ($p^c q_{jsct}$) on good $j$ in sector $s$ from country $c$ in year $t$ are given by the following equation (in logs):

$$p^c q_{jsct} = d_{jsct} + (1 - \sigma_s)(p^c_{jsct} - p^c_{.s.t}) + y_{st}, \quad (1)$$

where $p^c_{.s.t}$ is the log U.S. aggregate price for goods in sector $s$ in year $t$. The term $d_{jsct}$ is a demand shifter (in logs), $\sigma_s$ represents the elasticity of substitution among goods in sector $s$, $p^c_{jsct}$ is the CIF price of good $j$ from country $c$ paid by consumers in the United States, and $y_{st}$ is U.S. expenditure on goods classified in sector $s$ (in logs). We assume that the demand shifter could be decomposed into a country-good component ($d_{jsc}$) plus a country-year component ($d_{ct}$). This is a flexible specification that allows us to have different preferences for each good and variety. It also allows preferences for goods from a given country, as well as the U.S. expenditure share in each sector, to vary over time.

A standard simultaneity bias arises when we try to estimate the demand elasticity ($\sigma$) in equation 1 using ordinary least squares (OLS). We therefore proceed to instrument the CIF price variable ($p^c_{jsct}$) with a set of three instrumental variables: transport costs, tariffs, and input prices. Once we have instrumented the price of the good, we proceed to estimate equation 1 with country-good fixed effects ($d_{jsc}$), country-year dummies ($d_{ct}$), and sector-year fixed effects. The latter controls aggregate prices ($p^c_{.s.t}$) and U.S. expenditure in a given sector ($y_{st}$).

We assume that firms produce $q_{jsct}$ with labor and capital using a Cobb-Douglas technology. Under this assumption, the producer's price in a given country is given by

$$(2) \quad p^{s}_{jsct} = \ln\left(\mu_{jsc}\right) - a_{jsct} + \alpha^{l}_{jsc} w_{ct} + \alpha^{k}_{jsc} r_{ct} + \left(1 - \alpha^{l}_{jsc} - \alpha^{k}_{jsc} - \alpha^{m}_{jsc}\right) q_{jsct},$$

where $\mu$ is the markup (price divided by marginal costs) and $\alpha_S$ are input elasticities, all of them fixed overtime. The term $a_{jsct}$ represents log total factor productivity (TFP), and $w_{ct}$ and $r_{ct}$ are the factor prices of employment and capital required to produce *j* in country *c*, respectively. We assume that TFP could be decomposed into a country-good component ($q_{jsc}$) and a country-year component ($a_{ct}$). In equilibrium, the price per unit of consumption that a consumer pays in the U.S. market (in logs) is equal to the producer price ($p^{s}_{jsct}$) of the good, plus the tariff level ($\tau_{jsct}$) and transport costs ($tc_{jsct}$):

$$(3) \quad p^{c}_{jsct} = p^{s}_{jsct} + \ln\left(1 + \tau_{jsct} + tc_{jsct}\right) \approx p^{s}_{jsct} + \tau_{jsct} + tc_{jsct}.$$

Substituting equation 2 into equation 3, we obtain the following equation:

$$(4) \quad p^{c}_{jsct} = \ln\left(\mu_{jsc}\right) - a_{jsc} - a_{ct} + \alpha^{l}_{jsc} w_{ct} + \alpha^{k}_{jsc} r_{ct} + \left(1 - \alpha^{l}_{jsc} - \alpha^{k}_{jsc} - \alpha^{m}_{jsc}\right) q_{jsct} + \tau_{jsct} + tc_{jsct}.$$

Equation 4 suggests the set of instruments required to correctly estimate the demand elasticity in equation 1. The first set of instruments is given by the interaction between the input requirement and the price of the input used in the production of good *j* in sector *s* of country *c* (one instrument per type of input); a second set of instruments is given by the U.S. tariff on good *j* from country *c* in year *t;* and the final instrument is given by the transport costs of importing good *j* from country *c*. On the one hand, an increase in U.S. demand for goods from country *c* will increase input prices in country *c*. The comovement between exports and input prices does not invalidate our instrument because equations 1 and 4 include a country-year dummy that captures any aggregate movement. More precisely, our first set of instruments is the differential effect of input prices across goods with different input requirements per economic sector. On the other hand, as pointed out by Clark, Dollar, and Micco, transport costs are increasing in the value of the transported good.[5] Our third instrument should therefore be the component of transport costs

5. Clark, Dollar, and Micco (2004).

that is orthogonal to the price of good *j*. For this reason, we regress transport costs against the good price and use the residual as our third instrument.[6]

To compute our proxies for sector input elasticities, we consider the direct and indirect labor and capital requirements.[7] Total input requirements are as follows:[8]

$$\left[\alpha^{l}_{jsc}, \alpha^{k}_{jsc}, \alpha^{m}_{jsc}\right] = \mathrm{inv}\left(I - \mathbf{A}'\right) \times \left[Sh^{l}_{jsc}, Sh^{k}_{jsc}\right], \tag{5}$$

where $Sh^{l}_{jsc}$ and $Sh^{k}_{jsc}$ are sector expenditures on labor and capital over sector output.[9] When we compute prices using these input requirements (equation 4), we are implicitly assuming that imported and domestic intermediate goods have the same price path.[10]

## Data

As mentioned above, equations 1 and 4 determine the set of variables needed to estimate the intersectoral elasticities of substitution. In general, our variables are given by the set of instruments required to estimate equation 4, with a

6. We also include country-year and product fixed effects in this regression.

7. For each of the ten countries in our analysis (besides the United States), we use the country's own input-output matrix (**A**) to compute these requirements.

8. The input-output matrix has the following format: $\begin{bmatrix} \mathbf{A}_{dom} + \mathbf{A}_{imp} \\ VA \end{bmatrix}[D]$, where $\mathbf{A}_{dom}$ and $\mathbf{A}_{imp}$ are the $N \times N$ matrices of required domestic and imported intermediate goods, respectively ($N$ is the number of sectors); $D$ is final demand; and $VA$ is value added, which is made up of labor compensation ($WL$) and others. Therefore,

$$\left[\alpha^{l}_{jsc}, \alpha^{k}_{jsc}, \alpha^{m}_{jsc}\right] = \left[\overline{\mathbf{VA}}', A'_{imp} \times \mathbf{ones}\,(1, N)\right],$$

where $\overline{\mathbf{VA}}$ is the matrix of sectoral value added as a share of sector output and **ones** $(1, N)$ is a vector of ones with dimension $1 \times N$.

9. The input-output matrix has the following format: $\begin{bmatrix} \mathbf{A} \\ VA \end{bmatrix}[D]$, where **A** is the $N \times N$ matrix of required intermediate goods (N is the number of sectors); $D$ is final demand; and $VA$ is value added, which is made up of labor compensation ($WL$) and others (which we assume as capital). Therefore,

$$\left[Sh^{l}_{jsc}, Sh^{k}_{jsc}\right] = \left[\overline{\mathbf{VA}'}\right],$$

where $\overline{\mathbf{VA}}$ is the matrix of sectoral value added as a fraction of sector output.

10. If we assume that imported and domestic intermediate goods have different prices over time, we need to decompose the input-output matrix into its domestic and imported component. See appendix A.

second set of variables required to estimate equation 1. We performed the estimations using the information available for the period 1990–2003 for the following countries: Brazil, Canada, China, Colombia, Germany, India, Indonesia, Japan, Mexico, Turkey, and the United Kingdom. The country selection is based on the relative importance of trade with the United States and regional representation.

We obtain the data from three sources. First, data related to the value of imports, tariffs levied at the product level in the United States, the price of the product, and transport costs of the product per country of origin are obtained from the U.S. Import Database. These import data are reported at the ten-digit level of the Harmonized System, but we use the information at the six-digit level, which allows us to classify the products within industrial sectors, given by the four-digit International Standard Industrial Classification (ISIC) revision 2.

Second, input requirements calculated by equation 5 are obtained using the information available in the input-output tables in the Global Trade Analysis Project (GTAP) database. As expected, input requirements are calculated at the two-digit GTAP industrial classification, which happens to almost exactly match the ISIC revision 2, industrial classification.

Third, GDP per capita, which we use as a proxy for wages, is taken from the World Bank's *World Development Indicators*. We use this proxy when we interact the factor requirement with wages, following equation 4. We also interact the capital requirement with a time trend and country fixed effects.

The availability of input-output tables limits the number of countries that can be used to estimate the first stage implied by equation 4. A second constraint is given by the lack of time variation in the input-output tables, which are compiled infrequently.[11] Despite these two limitations, we expect that the variation across sectors and countries will enable us to correctly identify equation 4.

## Empirical Results

We now turn to our estimates of U.S. import elasticities. Table 4 reports the mean elasticity of substitution estimated from equation 1, setting $\sigma_s = \sigma$ for all sectors, but allowing for changes in U.S. sector expenditures over time

11. For specific information on the year of each input-output table, see the GTAP manual, version 5.

**TABLE 4. Mean Sector Elasticity: Second Stage**

| *Explanatory variable* | *(1)* | *(2)* | *(3)* |
|---|---|---|---|
| CIF price (1 – σ) | –3.954 | –3.952 | –3.933 |
| | (0.085)*** | (0.085)*** | (0.037)*** |
| *Summary statistic* | | | |
| No. observations | 375,302 | 375,302 | 375,302 |
| $R^2$ | 0.833 | 0.833 | 0.833 |
| Country year dummies | Yes | Yes | Yes |
| Product–country year dummies | Yes | Yes | Yes |
| No. sector-year dummies | 56 | 70 | 210 |

Source: Authors' calculations.

***Statistically significant at the 10 percent level.

a. The dependent variable is CIF import value (in logs). The regressions are estimated using instrumental variables (IV) with fixed effects. Our instruments for CIF price are as follows: sectoral labor share × GDP per capita; transport costs (orthogonal component of the FOB commodity price); U.S. tariff; and sector capital share × country trend. The reported *R* squared includes the variance of CIF import value explained by the fixed effects. Robust standard errors are in parentheses.

(sector-year dummies). In other words, all sectors have the same within-sector constant elasticity of substitution, but the elasticities between sectors could be different.[12] To recapitulate, CIF import value is the (log) CIF value of U.S. imports of commodity *j* in sector *s* from country *c* at time *t;* CIF price is the (log) instrumented CIF price paid by U.S. consumers on imported commodity *j.* All regressions include unreported country-product, country-year and sector-year fixed effects.[13] Column 1 assumes there are only four sectors (agriculture and mining; textiles; fabricated metal products, machinery, and equipment; and other manufacturing products), which have the same within-sector elasticity, σ, although their expenditure share may change over time. In column 2 we split agriculture and mining, and in column 3 we assume the full range of sectors at two digits of the ISIC revision 2 (fifteen sectors in total). The CIF price coefficient (1 – σ) is of interest because σ is the key determinant of the effect of trade impediments on the bilateral volume of trade. Our estimates suggest that the within-sector U.S. import demand elasticity (σ) is around 4. The coefficient σ is estimated precisely, and it does not vary when we change the number of sectors we use to control for changes on

12. If the constant elasticity of substitution within sectors ($\sigma_w$) differs between sectors ($\sigma_b$), then the expenditure for a given commodity *j* in sector *s* from country *c* is

$$\begin{aligned} p^c q_{jsct} &= d_{jsct} + (1-\sigma_w)(p^c_{jsct} - p^c_{.s.t}) + (1-\sigma_b)(p^c_{.s.t} - p^c_{...t}) + y_{.t} \\ &= d_{jsct} + (1-\sigma_w)(p^c_{jsct} - p^c_{...t}) + (\sigma_w - \sigma_b)(p^c_{.s.t} - p^c_{...t}) + y_{.t}. \end{aligned}$$

The last two terms on the right-hand side are captured by the sector-year dummies.

13. Commodities are defined at the six-digit level of the Harmonized System classification.

**TABLE 5. Mean Sector Elasticity: First Stage**

| *Explanatory variable* | *(1)* | *(2)* | *(3)* |
|---|---|---|---|
| Sector labor share × GDP per capita (a) | 0.532 | 0.416 | 0.800 |
| | (0.186)*** | (0.185)** | (0.199)*** |
| Transport costs (b) | 0.728 | 0.728 | 0.726 |
| | (0.028)*** | (0.028)*** | (0.020)*** |
| U.S. tariff (c) | 0.401 | 0.405 | 0.397 |
| | (0.059)*** | (0.059)*** | (0.061)*** |
| *Summary statistic* | | | |
| No. observations | 375,302 | 375,302 | 375,302 |
| $R^2$ | 0.820 | 0.820 | 0.820 |
| *F* test, instruments | 253.42 | 252.36 | 479.66 |
| Joint significance test for (a), (b), and (c) (Prob > *F*) | 0.00 | 0.00 | 0.00 |
| Country year dummies | Yes | Yes | Yes |
| Product–country year dummies | Yes | Yes | Yes |
| Sector capital share × country trend | Yes | Yes | Yes |
| No. sector-year dummies | 56 | 70 | 210 |

Source: Authors' calculations.

**Statistically significant at the 5 percent level.

***Statistically significant at the 10 percent level.

a. The dependent variable is the CIF price (in logs). The regressions are estimated using ordinary least squares (OLS) with fixed effects. The reported *R* squared includes the variance of CIF import value explained by the fixed effects. Robust standard errors are in parentheses.

sector expenditure over time (columns 1 to 3). Our estimates are in the range of previous studies; in particular, our results for Mexico are in the lower bound of Romalis.[14]

As already mentioned, we need to use two-stage least squares (2SLS) to compute table 4. Table 5 presents the first stage of our previous estimations (equation 4). As in the previous case, columns 1 through 3 assume there are four, five, and fifteen sectors, respectively. All regressions include country-product, country-year, and sector-year fixed effects. Our first instrument is the interaction of the sector's labor share and GDP per capita, which we use as a proxy for wages. As expected, the coefficient is positive and highly significant: a fall in wages reduces prices. Given country-product and country-year fixed effects, all the identification comes from the fact that changes in wages have a stronger effect on labor-intensive sectors than on capital-intensive sectors. In all cases, this coefficient is statistically different from zero. Our second instrument is transport costs (the orthogonal component with respect to the value of the commodity). As expected, this coefficient is positive and significant at one percent. In this case, the coefficient is close to its theoretical

14. Romalis (2005). The estimates are also similar in magnitude to elasticities estimated by Clausing (2001) and Head and Ries (2001).

**TABLE 6. Different Sector Elasticities: Second Stage**

| *Explanatory variable* | *(1)* | *(2)* |
|---|---|---|
| CIF price (1 – σ), sector 10–20 | −1.501<br>(0.119)*** | |
| CIF price (1 – σ), sector 10 | | −1.969<br>(0.147)*** |
| CIF price (1 – σ), sector 20 | | −0.587<br>(0.195)*** |
| CIF price (1 – σ), sector 32 | −3.525<br>(0.109)*** | −5.770<br>(0.099)*** |
| CIF price (1 – σ), sector 38 | −5.749<br>(0.099)*** | −4.172<br>(0.099)*** |
| CIF price (1 – σ), sector 3, other manufacturing | −4.153<br>(0.098)*** | −3.521<br>(0.109)*** |
| *Summary statistic* | | |
| No. observations | 375,302 | 375,302 |
| $R^2$ | 0.834 | 0.834 |
| Country year dummies | Yes | Yes |
| Product–country year dummies | Yes | Yes |
| No. sector-year dummies | 56 | 70 |

Source: Authors' calculations.

***Statistically significant at the 10 percent level.

a. The dependent variable is the CIF import value (in logs). The regressions are estimated using IV with fixed effects. The reported *R* squared includes the variance of CIF import value explained by the fixed effects. Robust standard errors are in parentheses.

value (one). The third instrument is the tariff level. This variable has a positive effect on consumer prices, and it is significant at the 1 percent level. To control for the evolution of the cost of capital, we also include the interaction of the sector's capital share and a country-trend, which we use as a proxy for the different evolution of capital costs per country through time. In sum, our instruments all have the expected signs and are highly significant.

In the previous exercise, we assume that all sectors have the same within-sector demand elasticity. This is a strong assumption that we can relax with our methodology, contrary to previous papers.[15] Table 6 presents our estimates for different within-sector elasticities. In column 1 we compute four different within-sector elasticities (agriculture and mining; textiles; fabricated metal products, machinery, and equipment; and other manufacturing products). Within manufacturing, textile products have significantly larger within-sector elasticity (6.74) with respect to the other sectors. The combined agriculture and mining sector has a surprisingly low elasticity (2.5). When we split

15. Romalis (2005) states that "there is insufficient tariff variation to obtain meaningful substitution elasticity estimates for detailed industries."

agriculture and mining (column 2), the within-sector elasticities increase significantly in both subsectors, to 2.99 for agriculture and almost 1.50 for mining. These results are consistent with what we would expect for a commodity sector like mining. As the results in table 6 show, within-sector elasticities vary significantly across sectors. This sector heterogeneity needs to be taken into account when one estimates the potential effect of any change in trade policies on bilateral trade.

## Policy Scenarios

Based on our within-sector elasticity results, this section considers alternative policy scenarios and forecasts their potential implications on exports to the United States from Latin America and the Caribbean, China, and the rest of the world. First, we consider the change in exports to the United States resulting from a 1 percent reduction in the price of all Chinese goods (what we call the Chinese export-price elasticity of U.S. imports in table 7). Our estimates in this regard are relevant for considering, in turn, alternative scenarios such as a revaluation of the Chinese renminbi. Second, we consider the extent to which U.S. trade policy, such as eliminating tariffs on imports from Latin America or quotas on textile imports from China, would affect U.S. import patterns. The methodology for computing the forecasts is described in appendix B.

### *Elasticity of U.S. Imports to Changes in Chinese Prices*

Table 7 presents estimates of the Chinese export-price elasticity of U.S. imports in table 6. A price drop leads to a 3.7 percent expansion of Chinese exports to the United States, according to our results, while exports from other regions fall. In particular, sales from Latin America and the rest of the world decline by nearly 0.1 percent each. Total U.S. imports increase by a mere 0.4 percent. As expected, the biggest impact is in the manufacturing sector, where China's export offer is concentrated. Chinese exports of leather goods, textiles, and apparel rise by 4.6 percent, drastically displacing exports from Mexico (0.3 percent) and South America (0.8 percent). Machinery and equipment sales from Central America decline by nearly 0.2 percent as they are displaced by the 3.7 percent increase in Chinese exports.

Next we apply the export-price elasticities in table 7 to assess how a revaluation of the Chinese renminbi would affect U.S. imports from China and, in turn, help the rest of the world increase exports to the United States. The

**TABLE 7. Chinese Export-Price Elasticity of U.S. Imports, by Region, 2003[a]**

| | | | | *Manufacturing* | | | |
|---|---|---|---|---|---|---|---|
| *Region* | *Total trade* | *Agriculture* | *Mining* | *Total manufacturing* | *Leather, apparel, and textiles* | *Machinery and equipment* | *Other* |
| World | 0.427 | 0.039 | 0.001 | 0.488 | 1.029 | 0.409 | 0.453 |
| Latin America and the Caribbean | –0.080 | –0.002 | –0.001 | –0.094 | –0.245 | –0.084 | –0.032 |
| Mexico | –0.084 | –0.002 | –0.001 | –0.092 | –0.247 | –0.085 | –0.049 |
| Central America | –0.105 | –0.001 | –0.001 | –0.130 | –0.143 | –0.182 | –0.037 |
| Caribbean | –0.099 | –0.003 | –0.002 | –0.112 | –0.208 | –0.106 | –0.009 |
| Andean | –0.011 | 0.000 | –0.001 | –0.046 | –0.186 | –0.081 | –0.010 |
| South America | –0.111 | –0.004 | –0.002 | –0.098 | –0.800 | –0.049 | –0.016 |
| China | 3.737 | 1.921 | 0.546 | 3.719 | 4.553 | 3.716 | 3.200 |
| Rest of the world | –0.074 | –0.004 | –0.001 | –0.082 | –0.385 | –0.072 | –0.029 |

Source: Authors' calculations.

a. The table reports the change in U.S. imports from each region in response to a 1 percent reduction in the price of Chinese goods. Regions defined as in table 1.

analysis is admittedly crude, as we assume that the exchange rate appreciation leads only to changes in the price of Chinese goods and that there are no general equilibrium effects on either the Chinese economy or the rest of the world. We also ignore potential adverse effects of the revaluation on the Chinese economy, such as any disruptions in the financial sector.

The scenario we consider involves a 20 percent revaluation of the renminbi. In such an event, the price of Chinese exports would not increase by the same percentage. Chinese exports embody a large fraction of inputs imported from other countries—as much as 70 percent of the value of exports, according to some authors. We take that figure as valid and thus assume that a revaluation only increases the price of Chinese inputs, including labor, embodied in exports, or 30 percent of their value. Under that assumption, a 20 percent revaluation implies a 6 percent increase in the price of Chinese exports. Table 8 shows our forecasts for U.S. imports under the scenario described.

The revaluation of the renminbi reduces Chinese exports to the United States by more than 22 percent ($43 billion based on 2004 trade figures), although total U.S. imports decline by only 2.6 percent ($24 billion). Chinese sales of leather goods, textiles, and apparel are the most sensitive, falling over 27 percent. The decline in U.S. imports from China is partly offset by increased exports from the rest of the world. Latin American sales grow by 0.5 percent, with South America benefiting the most. Exports of leather goods, textiles, and apparel from the region grow by 1.5 percent, or 4.8 percent in the case of South America.

### *U.S. Trade Policy*

This subsection assesses how changes in U.S. trade policy would affect imports from Latin America and China. We consider, first, the potential impact of preferential tariff access to the United States for Latin American exports resulting from free trade agreements and, second, the expected effects of the elimination of the Multi-Fiber Agreement quotas in January 2005.

**ELIMINATION OF U.S. TARIFFS ON LATIN AMERICAN GOODS.** We first look at reductions in U.S. tariffs on Latin American goods. Since the United States adopted NAFTA in 1994, the country has engaged in negotiations with other countries in the region to establish similar free trade agreements. In 2002 the United States approved a free trade agreement with Chile; it recently finished negotiating the CAFTA and is holding negotiations with Andean nations to establish a similar agreement. Ultimately, the United States would eliminate tariffs on all Latin American countries under an FTAA.

**TABLE 8. Chinese Revaluation and U.S. Imports, by Region, 2003[a]**

| Region | Total trade | Agriculture | Mining | Manufacturing | | | |
|---|---|---|---|---|---|---|---|
| | | | | Total manufacturing | Leather, apparel, and textiles | Machinery and equipment | Other |
| World | −2.560 | −0.237 | −0.003 | −2.930 | −6.172 | −2.455 | −2.718 |
| Latin America and the Caribbean | 0.479 | 0.011 | 0.006 | 0.566 | 1.468 | 0.502 | 0.191 |
| Mexico | 0.506 | 0.011 | 0.006 | 0.554 | 1.481 | 0.511 | 0.295 |
| Central America | 0.628 | 0.003 | 0.005 | 0.777 | 0.856 | 1.094 | 0.221 |
| Caribbean | 0.595 | 0.015 | 0.012 | 0.669 | 1.248 | 0.634 | 0.053 |
| Andean | 0.068 | 0.002 | 0.005 | 0.274 | 1.116 | 0.488 | 0.060 |
| South America | 0.665 | 0.025 | 0.013 | 0.587 | 4.802 | 0.292 | 0.097 |
| China | −22.421 | −11.525 | −3.277 | −22.311 | −27.319 | −22.294 | −19.198 |
| Rest of the world | 0.444 | 0.023 | 0.005 | 0.491 | 2.311 | 0.433 | 0.172 |

Source: Authors' calculations.

a. The table reports the change in U.S. imports from each region in response to a 20 percent currency revaluation. Regions defined as in table 1.

We consider the elimination of U.S. tariffs on imports from Latin America from their 2003 level; results are in table 9. In the aggregate, the region's exports increase by 3 percent, although there is a wide variation among the different subregions. The biggest growth would take place in Central America, which would experience a 21 percent increase in goods shipped to the United States, driven largely by sales of leather goods, textiles, and apparel (36 percent). Exports in this category record the fastest growth for all the Latin American subregions: 21 percent for the Caribbean, 29 percent for Andean countries, and 36 percent for the rest of South America. The smallest increase in exports would come from Mexico, given that tariffs on Mexican exports to the United States were already drastically reduced by 2003 as a result of NAFTA.

Our forecasts are in line with other studies. For example, a United States International Trade Commission (USITC) report analyzing the potential impact of CAFTA on trade patterns estimates that U.S. imports from the five Central American counterparties to the agreement (namely, Costa Rica, El Salvador, Guatemala, Honduras, and Nicaragua) and from the Dominican Republic would increase by 21 percent, which falls within our range of forecast for the Caribbean and Central America.[16] With regard to the FTAA, Hertel and others estimate that total U.S. imports worldwide would rise by around 2.2 percent, whereas Watanuki and Monteagudo put that figure at 1.1 percent; in contrast, we estimate an increase of only 0.4 percent in aggregate U.S. imports.[17]

Our results highlight the importance of preferential trade between the United States and Latin America for boosting exports from the region. The flip side is a small reduction in exports from China and the rest of the world to the United States of around 0.3 and 0.1 percent, respectively. The largest declines, as expected, would occur in exports of leather goods, textiles, and apparel.

**ELIMINATION OF TEXTILE QUOTAS.** Table 10 presents a breakdown of U.S. apparel imports by region. China's share of U.S. apparel imports rose from 13.2 to 18.6 percent from 2000 to 2004. In the same period, Latin America's share of the U.S. market fell from 30.8 to 26.3 percent. China's increasing market share, and Latin America's loss, came despite the fact that tariffs on Latin American imports declined more than those on Chinese goods. One potential explanation for the rising presence of Chinese apparel was the elimination, in 2002, of a number of import quotas on textile and apparel imports originally adopted under the Multi-Fiber Agreement (MFA). MFA quotas

16. USITC (2004, table 4-4).
17. Hertel and others (2007); Watanuki and Monteagudo (2002).

**TABLE 9. Tariff Elimination on Latin American Goods and U.S. Imports, by Region, 2003[a]**

| | | | | Manufacturing | | | |
|---|---|---|---|---|---|---|---|
| *Region* | *Total trade* | *Agriculture* | *Mining* | *Total manufacturing* | *Leather, apparel, and textiles* | *Machinery and equipment* | *Other* |
| World | 0.407 | 0.363 | 0.005 | 0.432 | 3.113 | 0.103 | 0.142 |
| Latin America and the Caribbean | 3.078 | 0.772 | 0.030 | 3.718 | 20.254 | 0.781 | 1.350 |
| Mexico | 0.802 | 0.952 | 0.000 | 0.837 | 2.809 | 0.670 | 0.634 |
| Central America | 20.960 | 0.000 | −0.007 | 27.085 | 36.453 | 0.600 | 0.000 |
| Caribbean | 8.995 | −0.125 | 0.000 | 9.752 | 21.210 | 0.989 | 0.638 |
| Andean | 1.335 | −0.015 | 0.063 | 5.984 | 28.973 | 2.232 | 0.755 |
| South America | 6.463 | 1.911 | 0.013 | 5.807 | 36.180 | 2.091 | 3.374 |
| China | −0.305 | −0.031 | −0.004 | −0.240 | −1.103 | −0.044 | −0.007 |
| Rest of the world | −0.134 | −0.020 | −0.005 | −0.156 | −1.703 | −0.029 | −0.025 |

Source: Authors' calculations.

a. The table reports the change in U.S. imports from each region in response to a tariff reduction on Latin American imports to the level of Mexico in 2001. Regions defined as in table 1.

**TABLE 10. U.S. Apparel Imports and Average Tariffs, by Origin**[a]

| Region | Volume (millions of dollars) | | | | Regional distribution (percent) | | | | Average tariffs (percent) | | | |
|---|---|---|---|---|---|---|---|---|---|---|---|---|
| | 1997 | 2000 | 2003 | 2004 | 1997 | 2000 | 2003 | 2004 | 1997 | 2000 | 2003 | 2004 |
| World | 47,084 | 62,928 | 66,499 | 70,533 | 100.0 | 100.0 | 100.0 | 100.0 | 12.6 | 12.1 | 11.2 | 10.9 |
| Latin America and the Caribbean | 13,669 | 19,376 | 18,150 | 18,517 | 29.0 | 30.8 | 27.3 | 26.3 | 5.6 | 5.5 | 3.4 | 3.3 |
| Mexico | 5,317 | 8,704 | 7,178 | 6,930 | 11.3 | 13.8 | 10.8 | 9.8 | 1.0 | 0.4 | 0.7 | 0.7 |
| Central America | 4,781 | 6,702 | 7,159 | 7,560 | 10.2 | 10.7 | 10.8 | 10.7 | 8.9 | 9.9 | 6.0 | 6.0 |
| Caribbean | 2,871 | 2,987 | 2,540 | 2,481 | 6.1 | 4.7 | 3.8 | 3.5 | 6.9 | 7.5 | 2.5 | 2.3 |
| Andean | 575 | 844 | 1,062 | 1,331 | 1.2 | 1.3 | 1.6 | 1.9 | 13.1 | 14.7 | 4.1 | 1.8 |
| South America | 125 | 140 | 211 | 215 | 0.3 | 0.2 | 0.3 | 0.3 | 10.3 | 12.9 | 14.1 | 12.3 |
| China | 7,279 | 8,307 | 10,997 | 13,106 | 15.5 | 13.2 | 16.5 | 18.6 | 11.8 | 10.5 | 10.0 | 9.5 |
| Rest of the world | 26,136 | 35,245 | 37,352 | 38,909 | 55.5 | 56.0 | 56.2 | 55.2 | 16.6 | 16.1 | 15.3 | 14.9 |

Source: Authors' calculations.

a. Regions defined as in table 1.

were binding for China and other Asian nations, which limited market access for apparel exports from those countries. During the Uruguay Round, countries agreed to dismantle such quotas gradually, removing them altogether by January 2005. The implementation of the final stage in the elimination of textile quotas in the United States and elsewhere created widespread apprehension in Latin America that unfettered Chinese exports to the United States would continue to erode the region's exports to the U.S. market.

We apply our framework to the analysis of the potential impact of eliminating MFA quotas on exports to the United States. We use available estimates of the export tariff equivalent of the quotas and our estimated elasticities of substitution to explore the implications of the ensuing relative price changes. According to the USITC, the export tariff equivalent of the quota on Chinese apparel sales to the United States was approximately 21 percent.[18] In estimating elasticities in section 4, we assumed that all Chinese apparel exports were subject to the export tariff equivalent rate, in addition to the usual duties applied in the United States. Here we use these elasticities to assess the impact of eliminating the export tariff equivalent.

Columns 1 and 2 of table 11 present our estimations of the impact of quota elimination on U.S. imports. Chinese exports increase by an impressive 40.3 percent, paralleled by drops everywhere else. As a result, U.S. imports grow by a modest 3.6 percent. Latin America is undeniably affected, but our estimations are smaller than the common perception seems to be—between 2 and 3 percent, with a much smaller decline for South America (0.5 percent). Table 11 also reports our estimations of the change in each region's share of the U.S. market (in percentage points). China's share rises by 5.8 points, Latin America's falls by 1.7, and the rest of the world accounts for the balance.

To assess whether our estimates are reasonable, we adopt an alternative strategy to measure the impact of removing quotas on each region's market participation. We employ a difference-in-differences approach in which we compare the change in market shares from 2000 to 2003 in tariff lines that had import quotas removed in 2002 (the treatment group), with those in tariff lines that had quotas eliminated in 2005 (the control group). Specifically, let $Share_{irt}$ stand for region $r$'s share of U.S. imports of good $i$ (measured at the ten-digit Harmonized System tariff line level) in period $t \in \{2000, 20003\}$. All goods $i$ that had quotas removed in January 2002 are defined as belonging to the treatment group. The control group consists of all $i$ that had quotas removed in January 2005. We believe the latter provides a better control group than the

18. USITC (2002).

**TABLE 11. Elimination of MFA Quotas and U.S. Apparel Imports, by Region, 2003[a]**

| Region | *Using elasticities of substitution*: *Imports (percent change)* | *Using elasticities of substitution*: *Market share participation (change in percentage points)* | *Based on difference-in-differences results*: *Market share participation (change in percentage points)* | *Based on difference-in-differences results*: *P value of point estimate* |
|---|---|---|---|---|
| World | 3.6 | 0.0 | . . . | . . . |
| Latin America and the Caribbean | −2.8 | −1.7 | −2.5 | 0.3 |
| Mexico | −2.7 | −0.7 | −2.2 | 0.3 |
| Central America | −2.9 | −0.7 | −1.8 | 0.3 |
| Caribbean | −2.9 | −0.2 | −0.3 | 0.8 |
| Andean | −2.7 | −0.1 | 0.4 | 0.4 |
| South America | −0.5 | 0.0 | −0.6 | 0.4 |
| China | 40.3 | 5.8 | 25.3 | 0.0 |
| Rest of the world | −4.0 | −4.1 | −24.4 | 0.0 |

Source: Authors' calculations.
. . . Not applicable.
a. Regions defined as in table 1.

set of all apparel goods regardless of when their quotas were removed, if they were ever subject to any. We then estimate the following equation separately for each region, *r*:[19]

$$(6)\qquad Share_{irt} = \beta_0 + \beta^{\tau}_{irt} + \beta_2 1(i \in Treatment) + \beta_3 1(t = 2003) + \beta_4 1(t = 2003) \times 1(i \in Treatment) + \varepsilon_{it}.$$

The U.S. tariff on imports of *i* from *r* is represented by $\tau$. Coefficient $\beta_2$ captures time-invariant differences in the import share of goods in the treatment group. Coefficient $\beta_3$ reflects shocks after 2002, other than the quota elimination, on the market share of all goods. The coefficient of interest, $\beta_4$, is equal to the change in the market share of goods that had quotas removed in 2002. Our identifying assumption is that there are no unobserved shocks that affect the market share of goods in the treatment group that are contemporaneous with the elimination of the quotas.

We summarize our findings in columns 3 and 4 of table 11, alongside our previous elasticity-based results. For Latin America and the Caribbean, the difference-in-differences point estimates are remarkably similar to our previous

19. We also estimated a variant of this equation in which we pool all regions together and incorporate regional dummies and their interaction with all other regressors, except for the tariff $\tau$. The results were qualitatively the same.

findings—namely, a market-share loss of around 2.5 percentage points—although we cannot reject the null hypothesis that the impact on market share is zero for all subregions of Latin America. In contrast, the difference-in-differences estimates for China and the rest of the world are substantially higher (in absolute terms). Overall, the difference-in-differences approach suggests that Chinese market-share gains have come at the expense not of Latin America, but of the rest of the world.

Finally, as a robustness exercise, we calculated the same policy scenarios using elasticities of substitution estimated by Broda and Weinstein instead of our own estimates.[20] In particular we used their estimates at the four-digit level of industrial classification (ISIC revision 3). The results obtained at this higher level of desegregation are very similar to the results reported in tables 7 through 9.[21]

## Conclusions

In this paper we estimate the elasticity of substitution of exports to the United States using detailed trade data over the 1990–2003 period. We use a two-stage least squares framework to correctly identify the elasticity parameter of interest. Our elasticity estimates are in line with those of other recent studies.

We use those estimates to assess the extent to which Latin American and Chinese goods compete in the U.S. market by estimating how alternative policy scenarios could affect exports to the United States. We consider the following three scenarios: currency revaluation in China; the elimination of U.S. tariffs on Latin American exports under a free trade agreement among all countries of the Americas; and the elimination of quotas on apparel and textile exports under the Multi-Fiber Agreement.

We find that a 20 percent appreciation of the renminbi reduces Chinese exports to the United States by a fifth, although U.S. imports decline by only 1.7 percent since other regions increase sales to that market (0.5 percent for Latin America). With respect to productivity, we find that faster TFP growth in China explains about half of the gap in export growth between that country and Latin America. An FTAA would increase Latin America's exports to the United States by around three percent. The removal of MFA quotas would

20. See Broda and Weinstein (2006).

21. Results are available on request.

lead to a sharp increase in Chinese sales to the United States (40 percent), but Latin America would see its share of the U.S. market decline by only 2.5 percentage points. China's gains would come mainly at the expense of other world regions.

## Appendix A: Input Requirements

To compute input requirements in the main text, we assume that production only requires labor and capital. In this appendix, we assume that firms produce $q_{jsct}$ with labor, capital, and imported intermediate goods using a Cobb-Douglas technology. Under this assumption, the consumer's price is

$$p^s_{jsct} = \ln\left(\mu_{jsc}\right) - a_{jsc} - a_{ct} + \alpha^l_{jsc} w_{ct} + \alpha^k_{jsc} r_{ct} + \alpha^m_{jsc} p^m_{ct}$$
$$+\left(1 - \alpha^l_{jsc} - \alpha^k_{jsc} - \alpha^m_{jsc}\right) q_{jsct} \tau_{jsct} + tc_{jsct},$$

where $w_{ct}$, $r_{ct}$, and $p^m_{ct}$ are the factor prices for employment, capital, and the imported goods required to produce *j* in country *c*, respectively. To compute the proxies for input elasticities, we consider the direct and indirect requirements of labor, capital, and imported intermediate goods of each produced good. Direct and indirect input requirements ($\alpha$) are computed using each country's input-output matrix (**A**), which is decomposed into domestic and imported intermediate goods ($\mathbf{A} = A_{dom} + A_{imp}$). We compute the direct and indirect input requirements as follows:

$$\left[\alpha^l_{jsc}, \alpha^k_{jsc}, \alpha^m_{jsc}\right] = inv\left(I - A'_{dom}\right) \times \left[Sh^l_{jsc}, Sh^k_{jsc}, Sh^m_{jsc}\right],$$

where $Sh^l_{jsc}$, $Sh^k_{jsc}$ and $Sh^m_{jsc}$ are sector expenditures on labor, capital, and imported intermediated goods (direct) over sectoral output.[22]

22. The input-output matrix has the following format: $\begin{bmatrix} \mathbf{A}_{dom} + \mathbf{A}_{imp} \\ VA \end{bmatrix}[D]$, where $\mathbf{A}_{dom}$ and $\mathbf{A}_{imp}$ are the $N \times N$ matrices of required domestic and imported intermediate goods, respectively ($N$ is the number of sectors); $D$ is final demand; and $VA$ is value added, which is composed by labor compensation ($WL$) and others. Therefore,

$$\left[\alpha^l_{jsc}, \alpha^k_{jsc}, \alpha^m_{jsc}\right] = \left[\overline{\mathbf{VA}}', A'_{imp} \times \mathbf{ones}\ (1, N)\right],$$

where $\overline{\mathbf{VA}}$ is the matrix of sectoral value added as a fraction of sector output.

The implicit assumption in this setup is that all imported intermediate goods have the same price—or, more precisely, the same price path. In the main text, the implicit assumption is that imported and domestic intermediate goods have the same price path over time (product by product). In this case, everything collapses to labor and capital requirements. In unreported exercises, we estimate equation 5 under the assumption of different price trends for imported and domestic intermediate inputs, and the results remained statistically equal to the results obtained under the assumption of the same price pattern of domestic and imported intermediate goods.

## Appendix B: Policy Scenario Simulations

We assume that the consumer in the U.S. market has a constant elasticity of substitution utility function for goods classified in the same economic sector. The expenditure function of good $j$ imported from country $c$ at time $t$ is thus given by the following equation:

$$p^c q_{jsct} = \left( \frac{p^c_{jsct}}{p^c_{.s.t}} \right)^{(1-\sigma_x)} b_{st} Y_{st},$$

where $p^c_{.s.t} = \left( \sum_{j \in S} \sum_{c} p^c_{jsct}{}^{(1-\sigma_x)} \right)^{\frac{1}{(1-\sigma_x)}}$ and $b_{st} Y_{st} \equiv y_{st}$.

Therefore, the effect on the expenditure of a change in the price of the imported good is given by the following equation:

$$\frac{\partial \ln \left( p^c q_{jsct} \right)}{\partial p^c_{jsct}} = \left( 1 - \sigma_s \right) \left( \frac{\partial \ln p^c_{jsct}}{\partial p^c_{jsct}} - \frac{\partial \ln p^c_{.s.t}}{\partial p^c_{jsct}} \right) \Delta p^c_{jsct},$$

where the total effect on expenditure per good is explained by two effects: the own price effect and the indirect effect, which is in turn explained by the change in the sectoral price index. The indirect effect is given by the following expression:

$$\frac{\partial \ln p^c_{.s.t}}{\partial p^c_{jsct}} = \frac{p^c_{jsct}{}^{(1-\sigma_s)}}{\left( \sum_{j \in S} \sum_{c} p^c_{jsct}{}^{(1-\sigma_s)} \right)} = \varphi_{jsct}.$$

Therefore, the change in expenditure of a good is given by the following equation:

$$\frac{\partial \ln\left(p^c q_{jsct}\right)}{\partial p^c_{jsct}} = \left(1-\sigma_s\right)\left(1-\varphi_{jsct}\right)\frac{\Delta p^c_{jsct}}{p^c_{jsct}}.$$

Aggregating the effect per economic sector and region, we obtain the following expression:

$$E_{s,reg} = \sum_{c \in reg} \omega_c \sum_{j \in S} \frac{\partial \ln\left(p^c q_{jsct}\right)}{\partial p^c_{jsct}},$$

and

$$E_{s,reg} = \left(1-\sigma_s\right)\sum_{c \in reg} \omega_c \sum_{j \in S}\left(1-\varphi_{jsct}\right)\Delta \bar{p}^c_{jsct},$$

where $\omega_c = \dfrac{\sum_{j \in S}\left(p^c_{jsct} q^c_{jsct}\right)}{\sum_{c \in reg}\sum_{j \in S}\left(p^c_{jsct} q^c_{jsct}\right)}$ and $\Delta \bar{p}^c_{jsct} = \dfrac{\Delta p^c_{jsct}}{p^c_{jsct}}$.

The aggregate effect per region is then given by

$$E_{reg} = \sum_{S} \omega_{cs} \sum_{c \in reg} \omega_c \sum_{j \in S} \frac{\partial \ln\left(p^c q_{jsct}\right)}{\partial p^c_{jsct}}$$

and

$$E_{reg} = \sum_{S} \omega_{cs}\left(1-\sigma_s\right)\sum_{c \in reg} \omega_c \sum_{j \in S}\left(1-\varphi_{jsct}\right)\Delta \bar{p}^c_{jsct},$$

where $\omega_{cs} = \dfrac{\sum_{c \in reg}\sum_{j \in S}\left(p^c_{jsct} q^c_{jsct}\right)}{\sum_{S}\sum_{c \in reg}\sum_{j \in S}\left(p^c_{jsct} q^c_{jsct}\right)}$.

These two equations are the expressions used to estimate the effect of the policy scenarios analyzed in the paper. The simulations assume that any change produced by a policy scenario is reflected in a change in the price of the imported good. We only have to aggregate the effects per economic sector and per region to get the desired calculations.

# Comments

**Luis F. López-Calva:** In their paper, Ernesto López Córdova, Alejandro Micco, and Danielken Molina estimate elasticities of substitution for Chinese versus Latin American imports in the U.S. market, and simulate the effect of three different scenarios on the composition of U.S. imports. The scenarios are the revaluation of the Chinese currency, a total liberalization in U.S. trade flows (FTAA scenario), and the elimination of quotas on apparel and textile exports under the Multi-Fiber Agreement (MFA). The analysis is methodologically solid and adds to the literature, especially in terms of understanding the regionwide competitive position from the Latin American perspective. The key point of the paper is thus the study of trade competition between China and Latin America in the U.S. market, a crucial theme for the region in the medium term. Among the results, a very important finding has to do with the revaluation of the Chinese currency, given that several recent studies estimate the realignment to be around 40 percent. The paper suggests that a realignment would reduce Chinese imports to the U.S. by 20 percent.

The econometric estimation follows a well-established procedure, but the paper enhances solutions of the bias induced by the endogeneity of the price variable. Estimating the elasticity of substitution in the demand equation, which includes the demand for imports from each country, involves potential endogeneity related to the price level of the imported good. The authors employ an IV solution, using three instruments for robustness: transport costs, import tariffs, and input prices (that is, wages, cost of inputs, and cost of capital). The third instrument, however, requires detailed input-output (IO) data. This raises serious doubts regarding the quality of this information. In Mexico, for example, the data are updated from an IO matrix originally constructed in 1980. IO data have similar quality problems in several countries. Nevertheless, the authors correctly address some potential problems of the instruments given the existing data, and robustness checks are important in that respect.

A more general problem related to general equilibrium effects is that input prices could suffer from endogeneity, as well (that is, an increase in exports could increase input prices). The paper therefore includes a first-stage specification to ensure that the instruments reflect the differential effect of input prices across goods, with different input requirements per economic sector. Finally, the potential endogeneity of transport costs with respect to export volume is solved by regressing transport costs against the good price and using the residual as an instrument. The instruments generally seem to work well, suggesting that the exercise provides the best feasible analysis, given the existing data at hand.

The paper adds to the literature by carrying out first the standard exercise of allowing elasticities to vary across sectors while keeping within-sector elasticities constant, but then furthering the empirical analysis by allowing within-sector elasticities to vary. This within-sector variation is crucial for the accuracy and interpretation of the simulations.

The results are intuitive and compare fairly well with related work. An obvious caveat, however, relates to the general equilibrium implications of the hypothetic scenarios, which are not necessarily grasped in the structure of the analysis. In different contexts but based on similar assumptions, general equilibrium exercises have been shown to result in higher elasticities of substitution compared to previous literature; this tendency is related to the need to distinguish between short- versus long-run elasticities.[1] The bias in the magnitude of the elasticities stems from the fact that all the resource reallocations induced by demand shifts are taken as partial equilibrium adjustments.

The paper would be strengthened by a more careful analysis of some of the strong results. For example, the realignment of the renminbi (by 20 percent) reduces Chinese exports to the United States by a fifth, while increasing Latin American exports by only 0.5 percent. What could be driving the loss of competitiveness of Latin America with respect to the rest of the world? Moreover, the authors do not address the repositioning of countries within Latin America in terms of trade with the United States. For example, South America has the largest gains in some simulations, while Central America best enhances its relative position in others. Clearly, the different scenarios are not neutral in terms of the intersectoral composition of imports, thus reflecting relative changes consistent with patterns of specialization by subregion.

This type of exercise could shed light on intraregional gains and losses, to further our understanding of the coalitions formed around issues like

1. Wear (1990).

FTAA-related schemes. Although the purpose of the exercise is to examine Latin America as a whole, and the methodology is shaped accordingly, researchers and policymakers alike know that Latin America does not compete against China as a monolithic group. Rather, specific countries are looking to enhance their relative positions. Overall regional competitiveness is important analytically, but it has little relevance for those making decisions and discussing the use of specific policy instruments.

**Peter K. Schott:** China's penetration of world markets has been unprecedented since its opening to international trade in the 1980s. Between 1972 and 2005, for example, its share of U.S. manufacturing imports rose from essentially zero to 19 percent. Over the same period, the manufacturing market share of all of Latin America increased from 3 to 14 percent, while the share of OECD economies declined from 83 to 48 percent.[1] China has achieved this growth by extending the range of products it exports, as well as by increasing its exports per product. By 2005, China was present in 85 percent of all U.S. manufacturing product import markets. Latin America and the OECD, by contrast, were present in 69 and 97 percent, respectively.

López Córdova, Micco, and Molina explore the implications of Chinese export growth for Latin America by investigating the intensity with which Chinese and Latin American exports compete in the U.S. market. In particular, they estimate how Latin American export volumes would respond to four policy experiments: a 1 percent decline in the price of all Chinese exports; a 20 percent appreciation of the renminbi; an elimination of U.S. import tariffs on Latin American exports; and the elimination of quantitative export restrictions under the global Multi-Fiber Arrangement (MFA). The first three experiments do not (yet) have any real-world analogue; the results of the last experiment, however, can be compared to the actual response of Latin American and Chinese textile and apparel exports to the United States in 2005, the first year following the removal of the MFA restrictions.

In the first part of the paper, the authors use a standard approach to estimate the elasticity of substitution between exports from China and other countries, taking into account the techniques by which countries manufacture their exports. While the latter detail is a nice contribution to this literature, it necessarily restricts the range of countries for which data are available to just eleven. In the second part of the paper, the authors use their estimated elasticities to

1. Schott (2008).

**TABLE 12. Summary of López Córdova, Micco, and Molina's Results**
Percent

| *Experiment* | *China's exports* | *Latin America's exports* | *U.S. imports* |
|---|---|---|---|
| 1 percent decline in China's import prices | 3.7 | −0.1 | 0.3 |
| 20 percent appreciation of the RMB (6 percent price increase) | −22.1 | 0.5 | −1.7 |
| Elimination of Latin American import tariffs | −0.3 | 3.1 | 0.4 |
| Elimination of MFA quotas | 40.3 | −2.8 | 2.2 |

MFA = Multi-Fiber Arrangement; RMB = renminbi.

back out the change in Latin American and Chinese export volumes mandated by the price changes implied by the above experiments. The authors are careful to stress that their results ignore potentially important general equilibrium effects.

The basic results of the authors' experiments are summarized in table 12, which shows that the appreciation of the renminbi and the abolishment of the MFA induce the largest responses on the part of China and U.S. imports. As mentioned above, the results of the latter experiment provide a rough gauge of the usefulness of the authors' approach, since they can be compared to actual outcomes associated with the abolition of the MFA. The authors predict that the elimination of U.S. textile and apparel quotas will result in a 40 percent increase in Chinese textile and apparel exports and a concomitant 3 percent decline in Latin American exports of these products. In fact, total Chinese textile and apparel export volumes rose 39 percent in 2005, while Latin American exports fell 5.3 percent, as displayed in figure 1.[2] The actual U.S. import response was much stronger than predicted, growing 9 percent instead of the estimated 2 percent.

A key message of table 12 is that relatively large swings in Chinese export growth do not imply similarly large swings in Latin American export growth, and vice versa. This outcome is influenced, in part, by the fact that China and Latin America incompletely specialize in different sets of goods: as noted by the authors, China's exports lean toward manufactured products, while Latin American exports are relatively more resource based. An interesting avenue to explore in future research is how exports of raw materials from Latin America to China respond to the types of policy experiments noted in the

2. Brambilla, Khandelwal, and Schott (2007) These growth rates are for all textile and apparel exports, whether or not their quotas were already relaxed in prior rounds of the phase out of the MFA. Chinese exports of the textile and apparel products bound by quotas in 2004 grew in excess of 150 percent in 2005.

**FIGURE 1. U.S. Textile and Apparel Market**[a]

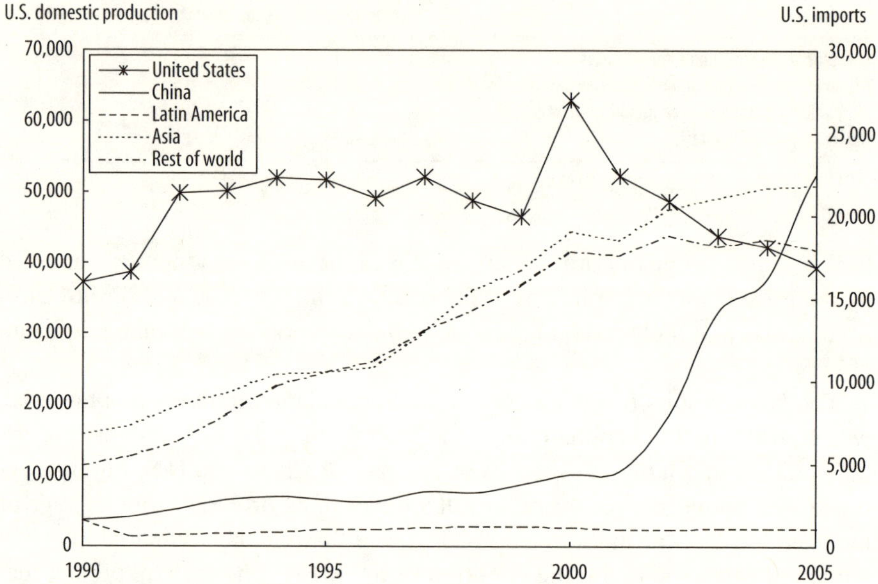


Source: Brambilla, Khandelwal, and Schott (2007).
a. In billions of square meter equivalents.

paper. Anecdotal evidence of Chinese firms' seeking to secure access to raw materials in Latin America and Africa abounds.

Another generalization worthy of exploration is vertical differentiation. Countries' export prices are correlated with their level of development.[3] This correlation has been interpreted as capturing vertical differentiation in terms of quality or other hedonic attributes: capital- and skill-abundant countries use their endowment advantage to produce vertically superior varieties that are relatively capital or skill intensive and possess added features or higher quality, thereby commanding a relatively high price. Chinese export products generally sell at a discount relative to Latin American products in the U.S. market.[4] It would be both useful and interesting to estimate elasticity parameters that allow for differential substitutability between high- and low-quality products, as well as to investigate the extent to which vertical differentiation

3. See Schott (2004); Hummels and Klenow (2005).
4. Schott (2003).

might rise or fall endogenously as a result of the types of policy experiments outlined above. Removal of U.S. import quotas, for example, might prompt changes in the quality of textiles and clothing China exports to the United States, which might prompt a reaction by Latin American firms.[5]

Finally, although the paper does a good job at highlighting the responsiveness of Latin American exports to changes in their own and other countries' export prices, it would be useful to relate those outcomes to changes in welfare. Such changes undoubtedly depend a great deal on the particular channels of trade that are modeled, but guiding the reader through these relationships would be quite instructive.

5. Aw and Roberts (1986); Feenstra (1988).

## References

Aw, Bee Yan, and Mark J. Roberts. 1986. "Measuring Quality Change in Quota-Constrained Import Markets: The Case of U.S. Footwear." *Journal of International Economics* 21 (1–2): 45–60.

Brambilla Irene, Amit Khandelwal, and Peter K. Schott. 2007. "China's Experience under the Multi-Fiber Arrangement (MFA) and the Agreement on Textiles and Clothing (ATC)." Working Paper 13346. Cambridge, Mass.: National Bureau of Economic Research.

Broda, Christian, and David E. Weinstein. 2006. "Globalization and the Gains from Variety." *Quarterly Journal of Economics* 121(2): 541–85.

Clark, Ximena, David Dollar, and Alejandro Micco. 2004. "Port Efficiency, Maritime Transport Costs, and Bilateral Trade." Working Paper 10353. Cambridge, Mass.: National Bureau of Economic Research.

Clausing, Kimberly. 2001. "Trade Creation and Trade Diversion in the Canada–United States Free Trade Agreement." *Canadian Journal of Economics* 34(3): 677–96.

Devlin, Robert, Antoni Estevadeordal, and Andrés Rodríguez, eds. 2006. *The Emergence of China: Opportunities and Challenges for Latin America and the Caribbean.* Harvard University Press for the Inter-American Development Bank and the David Rockefeller Center for Latin American Studies.

Feenstra, Robert C. 1988. "Quality Change under Trade Restraints in Japanese Autos." *Quarterly Journal of Economics* 103(1): 131–46.

Head, Keith, and John Ries. 2001. "Increasing Returns versus National Product Differentiation as an Explanation for the Pattern of U.S.-Canada Trade." *American Economic Review* 91(4): 858–76.

Hertel, Thomas, and others. 2007. "How Confident Can We Be in CGE-Based Assessments of Free Trade Agreements?" *Economic Modelling* 24(4): 611–35.

Hummels, David, and Peter Klenow. 2005. "The Variety and Quality of a Nation's Exports." *American Economic Review* 95(3): 704–23.

Moreira, Mauricio Mesquita. 2007. "Fear of China: Is There a Future for Manufacturing in Latin America?" *World Development* 35(3): 355–76.

Nordas, Hildegum Kyvik. 2004. "The Global Textile and Clothing Industry post the Agreement on Textiles and Clothing." Geneva: World Trade Organization.

Romalis, John. 2005. "NAFTA's and CUSFTA's Impact on North American Trade." Working Paper 11059. Cambridge, Mass.: National Bureau of Economic Research.

Schott, Peter K. 2003. "A Comparison of Latin American and Asian Product Exports to the United States, 1972 to 1999." *Cuadernos de Economía* 40(121): 414–22.

———. 2004. "Across-Product versus within-Product Specialization in International Trade." *Quarterly Journal of Economics* 119(2): 647–78.

———. 2008. "The Relative Sophistication of Chinese Exports." *Economic Policy* 23(1): 5–49.

[USITC] United States International Trade Commission. 2002. "The Economic Effects of Significant U.S. Import Restraints: Third Update." USITC Publication 3717. Washington.

———. 2004. "U.S.–Central America–Dominican Republic Free Trade Agreement: Potential Economywide and Selected Sectoral Effects." USITC Publication 3717. Washington.

Watanuki, Masakazu, and Josefina Monteagudo. 2002. "FTAA in Perspective: North-South and South-South Agreements in the Western Hemispheric Countries." Paper presented at the Fifth Annual Conference on Global Economic Analysis. Global Trade Analysis Project, Taipei, Taiwan, June 5–7.

Wear, S. L. 1990. "The Elasticity of Substitution between Imports from Different Sources: Estimates for New Zealand." SALTER Working Paper 7. Melbourne: Australian Government Productivity Commission.

RAFAEL DI TELLA
ALEXANDER DYCK

# Cost Reductions, Cost Padding, and Stock Market Prices: The Chilean Experience with Price-Cap Regulation

*Every four years, you feel you are going to war.*

*Alejandro Jadresic, former Minister of Energy of Chile*

The flaws of traditional rate-of-return regulation are well known. They include a lack of incentives to reduce costs, as well as a tendency for firms to choose the wrong mix of inputs and to misreport costs in order to inflate the revenues allowed by the regulator. Political discretion in implementing this regulatory regime may further discourage efficient investments by giving firms reason to fear holdup problems after investments are made, particularly when consumer groups are able to capture the regulator.[1]

The introduction of price-cap regulation was expected to correct some of these problems. By guaranteeing prices rather than returns and by using long regulatory lags, a price-cap system gives firms the incentive to cut their costs, since they get to keep the residual between prices and costs. Beesley and Littlechild, for example, argue that price-cap regulation "is less vulnerable to 'cost-plus' inefficiency and overcapitalization."[2] Moreover, price caps largely limit firms' incentives to game the system, both because adjustments within review periods are predetermined and because, in practice, review

Di Tella is with Harvard Business School; Dyck is with the Rotman School of Management, University of Toronto.

Mehmet Beceren and Jesus Serrano provided invaluable research assistance. We thank, without implicating, Bharat Anand, Alexander Galetovic, Bill Hogan, Fabio Kanczuk, Axel Christiansen, Mario Epelbaum, John Mayo, Hugh Rudnick, Carlos Rufin, and Federico Sturzenegger for helpful discussions.

1. See, for example, Posner (1969); Averch and Johnson (1962); Acton and Vogelsang (1989).

2. Beesley and Littlechild (1989, p. 456).

procedures often include an element of yardstick competition.[3] Limiting regulatory discretion is expected to be particularly useful in developing countries. Price caps can potentially enhance political commitment, reduce holdup problems and lobbying by regulated firms, and therefore encourage more efficient investment decisions.[4] Another advertised benefit of price-cap regimes is the reduced burden it places on the regulator. These theoretical advantages have encouraged the adoption of price-cap regimes across the developed and developing world.

Partly because of the system's relatively recent introduction, little empirical work has been carried out on industry performance under price-cap regulation. Some empirical work focuses on the U.S. telecommunications sector, which has used a price-cap system for several years. Mathios and Rogers provide evidence of significant price reductions (of up to 7 percent) in states that changed rate-of-return for price-cap regulation.[5] A number of issues naturally arise. Do price reductions measure the extent of efficiency gains? Was this a one-off gain, or will further efficiency gains materialize over time? Moreover, since states adopt regulatory changes voluntarily, one should also wonder if these reductions are simply capturing the fact that these states have very active regulators (that would have achieved similar reductions with rate-of-return systems), rather than reflecting a general property of price caps. Are these gains bound to occur in other countries that adopt price caps, or are they very dependent on having a judiciary system of U.S. levels of independence?

Another important open question is the distribution of efficiency gains between firms and consumers. It is often argued that to make price caps less vulnerable to capture by producers or consumers, the system should remove discretion and contain a high degree of commitment. But this could make the system more vulnerable to strategic behavior by firms. In other words, the cost of credibility is a set of inflexible rules that may not always serve the regulatory needs of the country.

3. A number of key papers on price-cap regulation appeared on the 1989 symposium in the *RAND Journal of Economics.* See also Cabral and Riordan (1989) on incentives for cost reductions; Sappington (1980) and Sappington and Sibley (1992) on the strategic behavior of the regulated firm; Baron and Besanko (1987), Salant and Woroch (1992), and Gilbert and Newbery (1994) on regulatory commitment.

4. Levy and Spiller (1996). Some of these features, like limited discretion, are not inevitable components of a price-cap regulatory regime, but the connection is often made in practice, particularly in developing countries.

5. Mathios and Rogers (1989). Later studies, surveyed in Kridel, Sappington, and Weisman (1996), find conflicting results. For example, Blank, Kaserman, and Mayo (1998) do not find that price-cap regulation has reduced toll prices.

In this paper, we collect data on the performance of firms in the Chilean electricity distribution industry from 1988–99. The sector is characterized by privately owned firms operating in a regulatory system that was designed to operate as a pure price cap based on a significant regulatory lag (four years), with the explicit intent of reducing political discretion. The regime adopted has the properties that characterize price-cap regimes.[6] The broader institutional setting allows for a meaningful test of the performance of regulatory institutions, since Chile's judicial system and administrative bureaucracy compare favorably to other countries.[7] Perhaps the most significant feature of the Chilean price-cap regime is the attempt to explicitly limit the regulator's discretion at regulatory reviews. This includes a request to construct a model efficient company from which to derive the rates that will apply to all companies of a certain type (defined on the basis of customer density). The regulatory regime describes a number of steps to be used in constructing the model company and limits the regulator to using only data generated during the review period (which is the year prior to the review year).[8] The regulator must combine the information provided by the companies with its own estimates based on prespecified weights. Although the law dates to 1982, the emphasis on limiting discretion originated in the attempt to insulate the regulator from political pressures in the transition to democracy following the Pinochet regime, when left-of-center parties were expected to wield considerable power.[9]

We find that a measure of efficiency (namely, the ratio of reported costs to revenues) improves by 1.2 percent a year, on average, from 1989 to 1999. This pronounced reduction in costs is all the more remarkable because it includes three test years of 1991, 1995, and 1999. Although these estimates cannot be

6. See Acton and Vogelsang (1989).

7. See, for example, Levy and Spiller (1996).

8. Fischer and Serra (2000, p. 183) state that "the hypothetical efficient firm is built on the basis of the real firm that the regulators believe to be the most efficient among existing firms, introducing an elementary type of yardstick competition."

9. Fischer and Serra (2000) point out that South American regulators in general "suffer from a credibility problem as a result of the perceived threat of regulatory takings." This has resulted in weak regulators that are subject to strong pressure from the electric utility lobbies. They also state that "Chile is remarkable for the weakness of its regulator, which has never been able to impose the compensations to consumers envisaged for energy shortages. The possibility of appealing regulatory decisions to the courts has weakened the regulator even further" (p. 193). Fischer, Gutiérrez, and Serra (2003) discuss the high profits of the distribution companies. Chilectra's return on equity, for example, went from 8 percent in 1988 to 32 percent in the period 1996–98. They argue that the profit levels of the distribution companies are much higher than those of the generating companies, despite the fact that the latter are subject to greater risk.

interpreted as causal (since other institutions and policies may be causing cost reductions), they do suggest that price-cap regulation has not stood in the way of cost efficiencies, even during a period of political transition.

More importantly, we find a U-shaped pattern in cost reductions. Trends in cost reductions are reversed every four years, with costs 1.4 percent greater than would be expected on the basis of time trends alone. This reversal corresponds to years prior to regulatory reviews, when a new price cap is set for the next four-year interval. This pattern is consistent with strategic behavior by firms. Although caps are supposed to ignore information from specific firms and follow the costs of an ideal efficient company, as in the yardstick models, in practice there is a limited number of firms from which to draw the information, so the probability of each firm's cost reports' influencing the future price caps is high. Furthermore, the Chilean regulatory regime was designed with the objective of removing as much discretion from the hands of the regulator as possible, so a regulator that is captured by the industry and that incorporates inflated costs into future price caps can always claim not to have had the discretion to act differently.

We complement these findings with evidence from the stock market. Following Schwert and Rose, a number of papers use stock market reactions to evaluate the effect of regulations.[10] We modify the approach to evaluate the performance of the price cap, particularly the extent to which firms engage in strategic behavior. We start by constructing a measure of naïve cost expectations that excludes any indicator of the occurrence of review periods. We then look at the stock market's responses to cost announcements by firms during review and nonreview periods, taking as a benchmark a situation with no regulatory reviews. The relatively recent introduction of the regulatory regime means that there is a considerable amount of uncertainty concerning the evolution of the industry and the position of the regulatory agency vis-à-vis consumers and firms. The fact that a left-of-center coalition succeeded General Pinochet's government contributes to this uncertainty, as does the fact that the different actors have had very little time to observe the system at work.

Our first finding is that the occurrence of regulatory review periods has a negative effect on cumulative abnormal returns. Although the effect is not always significant at conventional levels, it suggests that the new system may be characterized by considerable uncertainty that is not priced in by the stock market. We also find that the stock market responds differently to cost reve-

10. Schwert (1981); Rose (1985). See also Whinston and Collins (1992); Dnes and others (1998).

lations during review and nonreview periods. Generally, costs that exceed cost expectations tend to depress the returns to holding a firm's stock. In review periods, however, we find that high cost reports increase returns. This is consistent with the presence of strategic behavior by firms that is not priced in prior to regulatory reviews and with the incorporation of high cost revelations into future rates by the regulator. This suggests that the emerging price caps may allow the firms to capture most of the welfare gains from their improvements in efficiency. The estimated effects fall over time, suggesting either that some learning is taking place or that uncertainty is being priced in by the market (or both). More generally, this suggests that it may be worthwhile to incorporate information produced by the stock market into the design of the optimal regulatory regimes.[11]

This evidence from Chile should have broad applications. The literature to date has analyzed evidence mainly from price-cap regimes in developed countries (primarily the United States and the United Kingdom), with a focus on the telecommunications industry. Our study thus extends the analysis along two dimensions, focusing on the electricity sector in a Latin American country. Moreover, the Chilean approach to regulating electricity distribution is closer to many theoretical models of pure price cap than other regimes. As Gilbert, Kahn, and Newbery argue, "The privatization and competitive structure of the electricity industry in Chile was the first major reorganization in the world. Its success has been one of the primary motivations for experimentation in other countries."[12]

Our paper proceeds in four additional sections. The next section provides some institutional background and describes qualitative data from field research and interviews conducted in Chile in 1999. We then describe our empirical approach. A subsequent section presents our main empirical results, while the final one concludes.

## Institutional Background

The regulatory reforms implemented in Chile in 1982, which included the introduction of a price-cap regime for the electricity distribution sector, were largely motivated by the inefficiency and excessive political discretion of prior regulatory regimes. Some of the main issues are well described in the

11. For a start in this direction, see Di Tella and Kanczuk (2002); Faure-Grimaud (2002).
12. Gilbert, Kahn, and Newbery (1996, p. 19).

literature, and we provide a short discussion and further institutional detail in appendix B.[13] In this section, we report complementary evidence on the actual performance of the regulatory regime, some of which we obtained in interviews conducted during field research in Santiago, Chile, and New York in the summer of 1999.[14] This evidence suggests that some participants in the field study believe the price caps have promoted significant improvements in firm efficiency, but have had limited effects on consumer welfare, as prices have tended to remain high and firms have tended to act strategically.[15]

In general, most participants felt that the system had a limited effect on prices. Evidence consistent with this contention is illustrated in figure 1, which reports the results from the industry association's and the regulator's studies on the value-added of distribution (VAD), which is the maximum price that distribution companies can charge. The figure shows the VADs by area of density, with the highest-density area defined as area 1 and the lowest as area 3. Each panel displays three lines, identifying the VAD study commissioned by the industry association of companies (always the upper line), the VAD study commissioned by the electricity regulator (always the lower line), and the end result, which was based on an explicit weighting of two-thirds for the regulator and one-third for the company. A lower VAD level suggests more efficient companies, with gains passed on to consumers. This evidence on the primary input into price determination explains why some participants in the field argue that the Chilean price-cap regime in distribution has had a limited effect. For example, in the high-density distribution area, the VAD is almost unchanged between 1984 and 1996. Studies of specific companies are not entirely consistent with this characterization. Data from the Ministry of Economics, for example, indicate that the VAD for Chilectra (Chile's largest distribution company) fell by 18 percent in the rate-setting process of 1992 and by an additional 5 percent in the rate-setting process of 1996, which was below the company's efficiency gains since privatization.[16]

13. For a more complete description of the Chilean reforms, see Hachette and Lüders (1993); Spiller and Martorell (1996); Bernstein (1995); Fischer and Serra (2000); Bustos and Galetovic (2002); Pollit (2005); Rudnick and Mocarquer (2007). For a discussion of some outstanding issues, including aspects of cost padding and regulatory commitment, see Galetovic and Sanhueza (2002).

14. Those interviewed include a former minister of energy, the head of the National Energy Commission, a former executive director of the regulatory commission, executives from four distribution and generation companies (including the most prominent companies in the industry), equity analysts from Chilean brokerage houses and pension funds, and analysts of distribution companies headquartered in New York City.

15. For a formal discussion, see Galetovic and Sanhueza (2002).

16. Fischer, Gutierrez, and Serra (2003).

**FIGURE 1. High Voltage VAD Estimates by the Government Regulator and the Industry Association of Regulated Companies**[a]

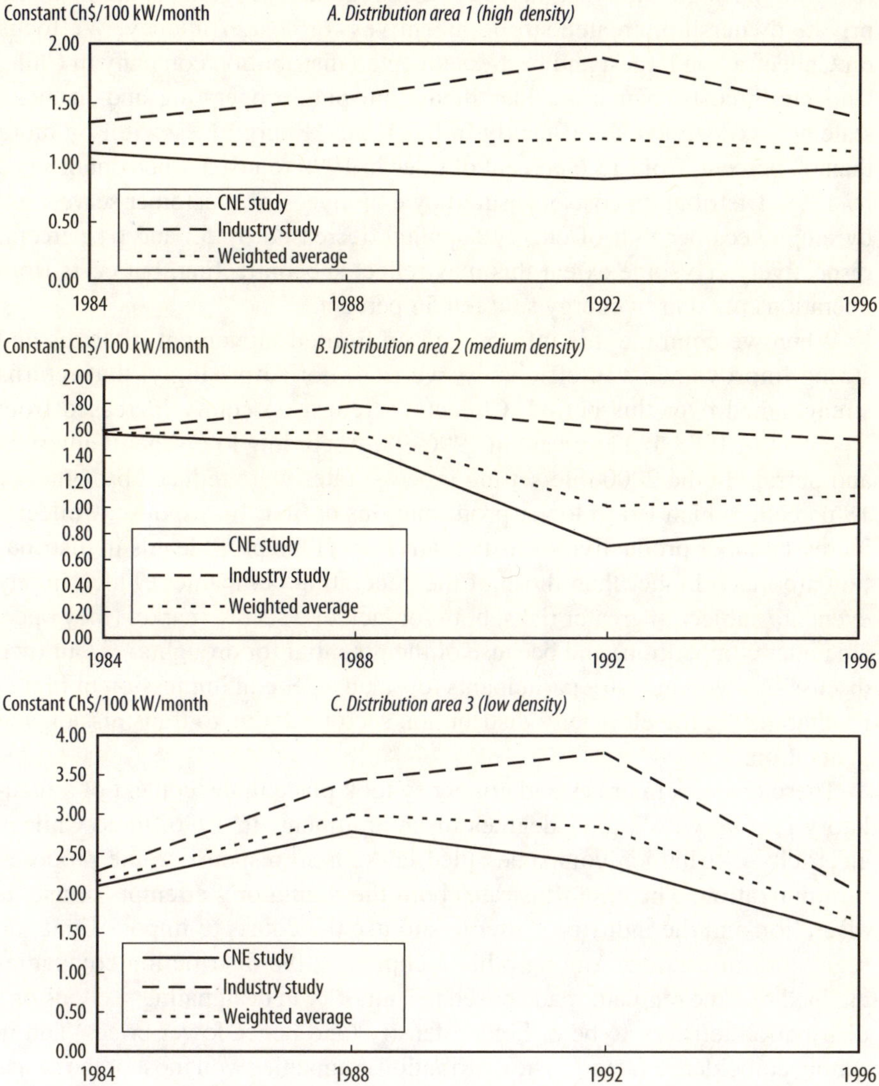


Source: Sebastián Bernstein, SYNEX Consulting Engineers.

a. The figure shows the value added of distribution (VAD) for high voltage electricity by area of density, with the highest density area defined as area 1 and the lowest as area 3. In each figure, the upper line represents the VAD study commissioned by the industry association of companies, the lower line represents the VAD study commissioned by the electricity regulator (CNE), and the middle line graphs an explicit weighting of two-thirds for the regulator and one-third for the industry association. A lower VAD suggests more efficient companies with gains passed on to consumers.

In contrast to the limited change in prices, we found indications of significant improvements in cost efficiency over the sample period, which is consistent with the contention that this rule-based regulatory regime, combined with private ownership, created strong incentives for cost efficiency. We focus on Chilectra, the largest and best-documented distribution company in Chile. Chilectra's costs, which we identified from public operating and financial statements, declined significantly in the 1990s. Energy losses fell by more than 60 percent, from 13.6 percent of sales in 1990 to just 5.4 percent of sales by 1999. Distribution costs measured by employees per customer served and by employees per unit of energy supplied decreased by 52 and 64 percent, respectively. To some extent this may reflect subcontracting, but costs from operations per unit of energy sold fell 56 percent.

When we combine this information on limited movement in prices and strong improvements in efficiency, we find, not surprisingly, that returns strengthened over this period. Chilectra's return on equity increased from 8 percent in 1988 to 32 percent in 1996–98. According to Fischer, Gutierrez, and Serra, "In the 2000 rate-setting process, rates were reduced by a further 18 percent, which led to lower profit margins at first. In response, Chilectra increased labor productivity substantially. . . . [T]he profit levels in distribution are much higher than those of the generating companies, which in any event are subject to greater risks, both for lack of a secure market (they operate under competition) and because of the potential for droughts."[17] Our own discussions with industry participants revealed a general impression of higher profitability in the electricity distribution sector relative to transmission and generation.

These changes in prices and efficiency took place in the context of a regulatory regime with higher degrees of commitment. In 1996, three Chilean electricity distribution companies filed lawsuits in response to the proposed reinitialization. The case illustrates both the regulator's attempts to use its discretion and the industry's attempts to use the courts to impose limits on regulatory discretion. Among other complaints, the distribution companies claimed that the regulator had abused its authority in designating sections of a distribution territory to be of higher density (and hence lower prices) and in setting coincidence factors. The distribution companies won most of the issues in the case in the appeals court, although the Supreme Court largely reversed this decision on technical grounds of whether the regulator had followed the terms of the statute. Regardless of the specific outcome, the court case itself

17. Fischer, Gutiérrez, and Serra (2003, p. 48).

suggests that the courts did limit regulatory discretion. Alejandro Jadresic, the Minister of Energy from 1994–98, noted the implicit constraints imposed on the regulator's ability to construct an efficient model company because of the threat of judicial review: "When building the model, you end up always looking at what happens in actual companies. The cost studies are subject to the challenge of verifiability in court; the model company could be regarded as pure ungrounded imaginary construction."[18] The constraint imposed by courts on regulatory discretion was also noted by Oscar Landerretche, the electricity regulator for the reinitialization in 2000: "Presently the courts play a big role, something I'm not altogether comfortable with. Courts aren't a way to resolve technical things."

Evidence that the rules mattered is found in firm behavior. Consultants and company executives note that despite the elaborate rules to divorce firms' reported costs from price determination, there is scope for firms to game the system aside from lobbying on coincidence factors. Sebastián Bernstein, of Synex Consulting Engineers, acknowledges such gaming: "Consultants hired by the regulators would sometimes take underground lines as overhead lines. They would inflate man-hours, quantities, quality, and costs of investment. For example, they never identified volume discounts, booking full price for every item even though we knew they were getting volume discounts." The chief executive of a distribution company pointed to similar practices: "In the technical studies, both sides cheat—everyone does this. If you didn't cheat, then you would be stuck with the superintendent's numbers, which simply aren't fair. Of course, hiding information is very difficult because after you do your NRC study, the inspector from the regulator comes. But the superintendence has poor people who don't like to do much work, so it works out. When Chilectra delivers information, they use a freight truck. The guys in the regulator's office get depressed when it comes."

Interview participants suggested a variety of strategies for shifting costs, such as booking all maintenance costs in the review period (which is the year prior to when the review actually takes place), when in fact they are incurred continually over a longer period; timing efficiency plans that involve redundancies to take effect after review periods; and planning investment programs to peak around review periods to maximize the capital base. The companies' investor relations personnel suggested that we focus on nonreview periods to get more accurate indicators of the firms' efficiency. Equity analysts and institutional investors similarly reported that they treated cost information

18. All quotes included in this section are from Di Tella and Dyck (2001).

differently during review and nonreview periods, because they understand that "bad news" in the year prior to the regulatory review is, in fact, a response to the incentives that firms face.

## Theory, Empirical Strategy, and Data

The extent to which the price cap is predicted to improve incentives and reduce costs depends on the degree of commitment. In price-cap regimes with limited commitment, like those that revert to rate-of-return regulation, investment incentives are distorted. The following three predictions are standard in price-cap models.[19] First, price caps provide strong incentives for cost reductions, because firms will be motivated to reduce costs if prices, not profits, are fixed in the regulatory regime. Second, the incentives to reduce costs will be strongest immediately after a reinitialization of price caps and weakest as the new rate review approaches. This prediction is based on the fact that cost reductions implemented farther away from review years will be enjoyed for longer periods, without threat of being confiscated by the regulator. Finally, firms have an incentive to increase reported costs during regulatory review periods, since cost revelations that are closer to a review year are most likely to affect future price caps.

To implement our empirical tests of these three predictions, we focus on the evolution of costs in the industry, rather than prices.[20] Our first hypothesis is that COSTS (defined as costs as a proportion of revenue) for company $i$ in quarter $q$ fall over time under a price cap. In other words,

$$\mathrm{COSTS}_{iq} = \phi + \alpha \mathrm{TIME}_q + \eta_i + \varepsilon_{iq},$$

where $\mathrm{TIME}_q$ is a time trend equal to one in the first quarter of 1989 and forty-four in the fourth quarter of 1999 (the end of our sample), $\eta_i$ is a company fixed effect, and $\varepsilon_{iq}$ is an error term.[21] The hypothesis suggests that $\alpha$ is negative. The inclusion of the company fixed effect accounts for possible differences in the initial level of costs based on a variety of factors such as

19. See, for example, Biglaiser and Riordan (2000); Cabral and Riordan (1989).

20. This approach contrasts with that of Mathios and Rogers (1989). If the version of the price-cap system used favors firms, the extent to which efficiency gains will show up in price reductions is unclear.

21. Part of the trend may initially reflect the reduction of electricity theft, which is unlikely to be replicable in later years. An alternative justification for a nonlinear trend is learning.

differences in the density of the distribution area or differences in local labor markets.

The second hypothesis we consider is that costs fall more early on in each of the four-year regulatory periods and rise later in the review period. The estimating equation is

$$COSTS_{iq} = \phi + \alpha TIME_q + \lambda EARLY_q + \delta EARLY_q^2 + \eta_i + \varepsilon_{iq},$$

where $EARLY_q$ is a variable indicating the stage in the review period; it takes a value of one in the first quarter after a review, two in the second quarter, and so on up to sixteen in the last quarter of the review year.[22] The hypothesis is that $\lambda$ is negative and $\delta$ is positive. Again, company fixed effects are included.

We generate an additional prediction if we assume that firms have private information about their costs and can either report the true information or shift cost reports from the quarter in which they are incurred to another quarter at a private cost to the firm (that is, cost padding). The regulator may incorporate these exaggerated cost reports in the new regulated prices, either because of capture or because there is some commitment in the system. One limit to such behavior is that the regulatory review can be reopened if profits are excessive (basically, because Chile is a sovereign country and because there are explicit provisions for doing so if the rate of return exceeds 15 percent). Any additional income that companies earn from leasing their lines to cable or telecom companies does not count toward their regulated income.[23]

The regulator's tendency to expropriate investments may have led to a system with little regulatory discretion, but this allows the firms to game the system. If the regulator were truly setting prices according to the efficient-firm construct, such padding should not affect the prices firms face (as in Shleifer's yardstick model).[24] To be legally enforceable by the courts, however, price caps must resemble actual costs, so the extent to which the system has achieved this separation is testable. The private costs of such behavior for the firm will probably increase as the extent of cost shifting rises.[25]

The third prediction states that the incentives for cost exaggeration will be stronger the closer the next review period, since cost revelations that are closer to a review year are most likely to affect future price caps. To explore

22. We do a robustness check excluding review years.

23. See Pollitt (2005).

24. Shleifer (1985).

25. For example, firms will want to limit the number of periods with inaccurate accounting information, to the extent that there are costs to keeping two sets of books or information is used both by managers inside the firm and by analysts outside the firm.

this prediction, we introduce a review period dummy in the above specifications for the year prior to the review year. To further explore how regulatory commitment (or lack of discretion) and strategic misrepresentation by the firm affect firm behavior, we consider the possibility that the interaction between the firm and the regulator is observed by a third actor—namely, the stock market. In a stable environment, the stock market probably already prices in any freedom that firms have to exaggerate costs in an effort to influence future rates. This may not be the case in Chile, however, given the relatively recent introduction of the system and the delicate political transition following the Pinochet regime. The stock market may be unsure of the extent to which firms will be willing and able to game the system, or how much regulatory latitude will exist for apparently exaggerated cost reports, or how tolerant the public will be of high utility rates. This suggests that review periods will be years of relative uncertainty, and that the stock market may respond positively to a high cost report.

To construct a simple test, we define what can be called naïve cost expectations as the cost that is expected by a market participant with the best available knowledge but with no information on the occurrence of regulatory reviews. We then define a cost surprise as the difference between the actual reported cost and this measure, and we define $\beta$ as the effect of cost reports that exceed naïve expected costs on abnormal stock market returns.[26] This setup generates the following four possibilities, depending on whether the stock market believes that the firm's announcement represents the truth or a strategic attempt to influence future price caps and whether the regulator incorporates the reports into the calculation of future caps (either because of capture or because the law allows no discretion) or ignores them (and uses wider sources of information in resetting price cap). See table 1.

The simplest case to consider is the one in which cost information is truthful and does not affect future prices, as the regulator uses a wider source of information than just the most recent cost information ($\beta \leq 0$). This is the normal situation for firms that operate in unregulated industries and for regulated firms in nonreview years; it corresponds to the top right quadrant of a truthful firm and a regulator that uses a wider source of information than just the most recent cost information. We predict that higher costs, which depress earnings and which are not translated fully into higher rates by the regulator, will lead to lower values of equity in this case.

26. An alternative approach is to use cost expectations that incorporate the information on the occurrence of review years and thus focus on the case of strategic firms as a benchmark.

**TABLE 1. Possible Effects of the Revelation of Higher-than-Expected Cost on Abnormal Stock Market Returns in a Review Year**

| | *Regulator incorporates reports* | *Regulator ignores reports* |
|---|---|---|
| Truthful firm—cost information reflects true costs | $\beta = 0$ | $\beta \leq 0$ |
| Strategic firm—cost information can be shifted | $\beta > 0$ | $\beta \leq 0$ |

This situation contrasts with that of a strategic firm and a regulator that incorporates this information into higher rates either because of capture or because the regulatory regime leaves little discretion in the hands of the regulator, which corresponds to the bottom left quadrant ($\beta > 0$). In this case, the stock market may interpret the cost revelations as the amount that the firm will propose to the regulator for the next review period, perhaps as its bargaining position with the regulator. Alternatively, the cost report may be interpreted as the amount that the regulator has hinted that it will accept. In these scenarios, the cost reports will increase future prices, and actual costs are expected to be lower than reported costs in the review period. Consequently, there should be a positive relationship between a regulated firm's cost revelations and its returns. Interestingly, the very same lack of discretion that allows efficient investments to occur without fear of confiscation also permits a captured regulator to use cost reports to the detriment of consumers and then argue that the system left no option.[27]

A third possibility is that the market believes the regulator will ignore the information produced by a strategic firm ($\beta \leq 0$). In this case, the market will accord little value to the information, so cost reports should have either no impact on stock prices or a negative effect if the market thinks that such cost padding is costly to the firm. Finally, the fourth possibility is that the regulator will incorporate the reports produced by a truthful firm. In this case, the cost revelation produces two offsetting impacts. First, the market believes these are real costs and thus responds in the traditional way, such that higher costs reduce equity value. Second, the market also believes the regulator will set a more generous price cap, leading to higher revenues in the future. In this case, the higher reported costs will not lead to lower stock market prices.

Empirically, we define the stock market response to information concerning each firm in each quarter as $\text{STOCK}_{itq}$, which is the cumulative abnormal

27. If costs are mean reverting, the regulator may set a price that is too high, delivering a positive coefficient for the relation between the cost surprise and the stock price of the company. This would have nothing to do with strategic behavior, however, as it results from the stochastic properties of the cost process and the regulatory framework.

return surrounding the window in which information about firm performance (costs and revenues) is revealed to the public and may be incorporated into equity prices. The subscript $t$ denotes a distinction between quarters that fall in review periods and those that do not. As our right-hand-side variable, we introduce $\text{COSTSURPRISE}_{itq}$, a measure of the difference between actual costs and expected costs under the assumption that regulatory periods are not different from nonreview periods. It is constructed by taking the actual level of $\text{COSTS}_{itq}$ and subtracting the best estimator of $\text{COSTS}_{itq}$, given all the available information at $t-1$ but excluding information on the occurrence of review periods. Finally, $\text{REVIEWYEAR}_{iq}$ is a dummy variable that takes the value of one during the year in which the information taken into account in the new prices is generated (specifically, the year prior to the change in regulated prices, which in our sample includes the years 1991, 1995, and 1999). The decision to include the full year prior to the review follows the information provided to us by the key informants and the institutional data available from the National Energy Commission.[28] In brief, data on company performance (which are used to evaluate the profitability of a model company) arrive at the regulator's office during different months of the prior year. The regulator calculates the new tariffs in the first half of the following year (the actual year in which the rates are changed, which in our sample includes 1992, 1996, and 2000), and these rates are put in place in July through October (the date follows Chile's historical practice).

The estimating equation is

$$\begin{aligned}\text{STOCK}_{itq} &= \alpha + \beta\text{COSTSURPRISE}_{itq} * \text{REVIEWYEAR}_{iq} \\ &\quad + \psi\text{COSTSURPRISE}_{itq} + \gamma\text{REVIEWYEAR}_{iq} + \varepsilon_{itq},\end{aligned}$$

where $\psi$ measures the effect of bad news on STOCK and is expected to be negative, $\gamma$ is the effect of review periods, and $\beta$ provides an estimate of the effect of cost surprises on stock market returns in a review year. We expect $\beta$ to behave as discussed earlier.

## *Data*

The electricity distribution companies in our sample account for 94 percent of total production in the central connected grid in Chile (based on 1991 data), from the time the companies were privatized (in most cases between

28. See (www.cne.cl). For example, in the latest available accounting period (2004), the information gathered concerns the model firm for 2003 and includes the wage information provided to us by Ernst and Young for December 2003.

1989 and 1991) to 1999. We use a broad measure of costs, taking the sum of the cost of goods sold and sales and administrative expenses. Since cost shifting occurs in many categories, this aggregate measure of costs should capture cost shifting if it does take place. These data are available on a quarterly basis from the financial statements that publicly traded utilities are required to file as part of their listing requirements, and this information is what equity analysts use.

We divide costs by revenues. This normalization has a number of attractive features relative to using raw cost data. The ratio is quite insensitive to cost and revenue changes of the same magnitude, which are common in the industry (that is, the system has a strong pass-through element). For example, according to the price-cap formula, prices automatically adjust to changes in the cost of purchased power (which can change every six months). They also adjust for known and expected cost drivers unrelated to company actions.[29] Implicitly, we are assuming that the ratio is driven primarily by cost changes. This is fairly accurate for Chile, where prices for the value added of distribution moved very little over the sample period.

Other cost measures and normalizations are possible, but they severely limit the number of firms and number of observations. These other possibilities include the cost information used explicitly in the VAD studies, controllable costs that exclude the costs of purchased power, costs per unit of output, costs per employee, and costs per customer. Cost information used explicitly in the VAD studies for firms, for example, is only collected once every four years, and it is not available to equity investors. Unfortunately, information on the volume of power purchases is only available after 1996 and then only on an annual basis.[30] Appeals to the office that regulates the electricity sector, individual companies, industry associations, and equity analysts only produced quarterly data for one company. Information on customers and employees was also only available on an annual basis, for limited time periods, and for a subset of companies. We used the information we were able to collect to verify that our findings are not sensitive to the choice of cost normalization. Specifically, our refined cost measures are highly correlated with our base measure and produce qualitatively similar results for Chilectra, the one company for which much of this information is available.

29. Specifically, the formula calls for prices to be adjusted based on the movement of a composite index (with the weights specific to each company) that includes increases in the consumer price index, the copper price index, the wholesale prices index, and an earnings index.

30. On the strategic use of power purchase expenses, see Baron and de Bondt (1979); Kaserman and Tepel (1982).

**TABLE 2. Summary Statistics**[a]

| *Variable* | *No. observations* | *Mean* | *Std. deviation* | *Minimum* | *Maximum* |
|---|---|---|---|---|---|
| COSTS | 399 | 0.832 | 0.052 | 0.696 | 1.030 |
| COSTSURPRISE | 377 | −0.001 | 0.036 | −0.100 | 0.161 |
| STOCK | 394 | 0.016 | 0.083 | −0.258 | 0.180 |
| EARLY | 399 | 10.138 | 5.113 | 1 | 20 |
| TIME | 399 | 23.521 | 12.530 | 1 | 44 |
| REVIEWQUARTER | 399 | 0.140 | 0.348 | 0 | 1 |
| REVIEWYEAR | 399 | 0.281 | 0.450 | 0 | 1 |
| POST_REVIEWQUARTER | 399 | 0.135 | 0.343 | 0 | 1 |
| POST_REVIEWYEAR | 399 | 0.271 | 0.445 | 0 | 1 |

a. The data definitions and their sources are given in appendix A.

Table 2 presents summary statistics for our variables, and table 3 lists their correlation coefficients. Among the firms in our sample, the average level of costs as a proportion of revenues is 83 percent. Costs as a percentage of revenues decline from a mean value of 89 percent in 1989–90 to just 78 percent in 1998–99. The next section reports the results of our empirical tests, in which we control for firm fixed effects, quarterly effects, and so forth, but visual inspection of the raw data is suggestive. Declines in costs appear to be concentrated immediately after rate reviews, and the rate of decline slows later in the period. The review periods are themselves distinct, with costs tending to spike in the final quarter of the reference year used for reinitializing rates.

Following standard event-study methodology, we measure the stock market's response through a firm's cumulative abnormal return around the window in which information is revealed. We construct a capital asset pricing model (CAPM) cumulative abnormal return. We first estimate the industry's beta using the industry's capitalization-weighted daily stock returns and the returns on the market index. The daily abnormal returns are the firm's daily returns less the industry's beta times the daily market return. We cumulate abnormal returns over the information window. For the date on which information is revealed to the market, we use the dates of the annual reports submitted to the Institutional Brokers' Estimate System (IBES) and the dates of the quarterly financial reports available in Michigan State University's Global Access Database.[31] Our window ends five trading days after

31. For the fourth quarter (annual) reports, we use the report dates in IBES. The report release dates vary across years and across firms, but most are released in late March. Global Access provides release dates for quarterly reports of a smaller set of companies, and we use these dates for the full sample. We assume the quarterly financial statements become public thirty trading days after the end of the quarter, except for the last quarter of each year.

**TABLE 3. Correlation Coefficients**[a]

| *Variables* | *COSTS* | *COST SURPRISE* | *STOCK* | *EARLY* | *TIME* | *REVIEW QUARTER* | *REVIEW YEAR* | *POST_REVIEW QUARTER* | *POST_REVIEW YEAR* |
|---|---|---|---|---|---|---|---|---|---|
| COSTS | 1.000 | | | | | | | | |
| COST SURPRISE | 0.625 | 1.000 | | | | | | | |
| STOCK | −0.028 | −0.040 | 1.000 | | | | | | |
| EARLY | 0.202 | 0.169 | −0.261 | 1.000 | | | | | |
| TIME | −0.725 | 0.021 | −0.003 | −0.115 | 1.000 | | | | |
| REVIEWQUARTER | −0.002 | 0.064 | −0.472 | 0.530 | 0.122 | 1.000 | | | |
| REVIEWYEAR | 0.027 | 0.083 | −0.163 | 0.700 | 0.135 | 0.643 | 1.000 | | |
| POST_REVIEWQUARTER | 0.041 | −0.111 | 0.302 | −0.516 | −0.103 | −0.142 | −0.221 | 1.000 | |
| POST_REVIEWYEAR | 0.096 | −0.086 | 0.202 | −0.620 | −0.206 | −0.232 | −0.361 | 0.611 | 1.000 |

a. The data definitions and their sources are given in appendix A.

this event, to allow for the information to be widely communicated and incorporated into prices. We use two starting dates for the window: five days before the announcement and twenty-five days before the announcement. Our discussions with market participants indicate that the wider window is more appropriate because it captures the possibility of information's being leaked to the market prior to the event.[32]

To estimate the COSTSURPRISE, we subtract predicted costs from reported costs. Operationally, we predict the value of COSTS using a regression of a company's COSTS on its lagged COSTS, a time trend, and seasonal dummies estimated on the full sample up to period *t*. Our results are robust to using measures of predicted costs from regressions that estimate the parameters using the full sample, as well as to simpler specifications that exclude the lagged term. We use the above specification as it yields the highest *R* squared.

Table 2 also provides summary statistics for abnormal returns (the variable STOCK) and cost surprises, which reflect the strong performance of the distribution sector. The average cumulative abnormal return in event windows is 1.6 percent, with significant variability (a standard deviation of 8.3 percentage points). The mean value of our cost surprise variable is zero, with a standard deviation of 3.6 percentage points.

## Empirical Results

Table 4 presents the basic results for our unbalanced panel. Our sample includes eleven electricity distribution companies, and we use quarterly data. We have an average of 39.9 observations per company, with a minimum of fifteen and a maximum of forty-four. Regression 1 shows that a time trend is a negative and significant determinant of costs for our sample, even after we control for company fixed effects and include dummies for the four quarters in the year to control for any seasonal effects that may be present. The estimated effects are economically significant. Since the data are quarterly, they suggest that reported costs as a proportion of revenues have dropped by 1.2 percent each year. Although our estimates cannot be interpreted as causal, given that other institutions may be causing the cost reductions, they do suggest that price-cap regulation has not stood in the way of cost efficiencies.

32. Our results are qualitatively similar, albeit less significant, in a much shorter window [−5, +5].

**TABLE 4. The Evolution of Costs over Time under a Price-Cap Regime, 1989–99[a]**

| *Explanatory variable* | (1) | (2) | (3) |
|---|---|---|---|
| TIME | −0.0030*** | −0.0032*** | −0.0030*** |
| | (0.0001) | (0.0005) | (0.0001) |
| $TIME^2$ | | 7.5e−06 | |
| | | (1.1e−05) | |
| REVIEWYEAR | | | 0.0142*** |
| | | | (0.0003) |
| Constant | 0.8933*** | 0.8948*** | |
| | (0.0041) | (0.0056) | |
| *Summary statistic* | | | |
| No. observations | 399 | 399 | 399 |
| No. companies | 11 | 11 | 11 |
| Seasonal dummies | Yes | Yes | Yes |
| Company fixed effects | Yes | Yes | Yes |
| $R^2$ | 0.55 | 0.55 | 0.57 |

***Statistically significant at the 1 percent level.

a. The dependent variable is COSTS, defined as reported costs divided by reported revenues. TIME is a time trend equal to one in the first quarter of 1989 and forty-four in the fourth quarter of 1999. $TIME^2$ equals TIME squared. REVIEWYEAR is a dummy variable equal to one in the year prior to when the regulatory review takes place, and zero otherwise. Robust standard errors are in parentheses.

Regression 2 includes a squared time trend to evaluate whether these cost reductions have weakened over time. We find no evidence for this possibility. The estimated coefficient increases slightly, implying cost reductions of 1.3 percent a year. Regression 3 incorporates review year dummies. We obtain similar results for the continued and significant improvements in cost efficiency. Notably, the review year dummy is positive and significant. This dummy implies that trends in cost reductions are reversed in review years, with costs on average 1.4 percent above those in nonreview years.

Table 5 explores our second hypothesis: namely, that costs fall more during the early phase of a review period. The intuition behind this prediction is that cost reductions that occur early in the review period provide benefits over more periods and are thus more desirable. Regression 1 in the table tests this hypothesis by including a variable (EARLY) that indicates how far into a regulatory period (of 4 years = 16 quarters) we are, EARLY, and its square, $EARLY^2$. The results favor the theoretical prior that cost reductions are strongest early in the regulatory periods, when the firm still has many future quarters in to benefit from the cost reduction. The estimated coefficients suggest that costs have a U-shaped distribution, with a minimum in the fifth quarter. Toward the end, costs equal the intercept, indicating that the firms reverse any earlier cost gains in the last quarters. The fact that firms

**TABLE 5. The Evolution of Costs within Review Periods, 1989–99**[a]

| *Explanatory variable* | *(1)* | *(2)* |
|---|---|---|
| EARLY | −0.0019 | −0.0020 |
| | (0.0014) | (0.0016) |
| EARLY$^2$ | 0.0002** | 0.0002 |
| | (7.6e−05) | (0.0001) |
| TIME | −0.0031*** | −0.0032*** |
| | (0.0001) | (0.0002) |
| Constant | 0.9096*** | 0.9058*** |
| | (0.0068) | (0.0074) |
| *Summary statistic* | | |
| No. observations | 399 | 287 |
| No. companies | 11 | 11 |
| Seasonal dummies | Yes | Yes |
| Company fixed effects | Yes | Yes |
| $R^2$ | 0.57 | 0.58 |

***Statistically significant at the 1 percent level; **statistically significant at the 5 percent level.

a. The dependent variable is COSTS, defined as reported costs divided by reported revenues. EARLY is a time trend equal to one in the first quarter of the four-year period between review years and sixteen in the fourth quarter of the fourth year. EARLY$^2$ equals EARLY squared. In column 2, review years are excluded. Robust standard errors are in parentheses.

record no cost gains toward the end of the regulatory period is consistent with the idea that late cost revelations may be an attempt to influence future price caps. To reduce the influence of the regulatory review periods, regression 2 repeats regression 1 excluding these periods. The results reveal a similar U-shaped pattern, although the effects are somewhat less precisely estimated.

Table 6 incorporates stock market information to further explore the effect of the price-cap regime. Regression 1 shows that cost reports that exceed our simple measure of expected costs have a negative influence on the cumulative returns to holding the firm's stock. The effect of cost surprises on STOCK is negative, although not significant. As suggested earlier, this specification could be mixing up observations for which the expected effect is negative with observations for which it is positive. Regression 2 in table 6 shows that the review period dummy (defined as the last two quarters of the year prior to the year in which a regulatory review is taking place) is negative and significant, suggesting that returns are 11 percent lower, on average, in quarters corresponding to a year in which regulatory reviews are taking place. A possible interpretation of this coefficient is that review years introduce a significant amount of uncertainty, which is not priced in by the market. When we study this phenomenon over time in table 7, we find that the negative effect is larger (that is, more negative) in the early review periods than in later

**TABLE 6. The Effect of Cost Announcements on Stock Returns in Review and Nonreview Periods**[a]

| *Explanatory variable* | *(1)* | *(2)* | *(3)* | *(4)* | *(5)* |
|---|---|---|---|---|---|
| COSTSURPRISE | −0.129 | −0.087 | −0.301* | −0.053 | −0.352 |
| | (0.143) | (0.142) | (0.169) | (0.141) | (0.224) |
| REVIEWYEAR | | −0.029*** | −0.030*** | −0.019* | −0.020* |
| | | (0.010) | (0.009) | (0.010) | (0.010) |
| REVIEWYEAR*COSTSURPRISE | | | 0.606** | | 0.665** |
| | | | (0.262) | | (0.297) |
| POST_REVIEWYEAR | | | | 0.032*** | 0.032*** |
| | | | | (0.011) | (0.011) |
| POST_REVIEWYEAR*COSTSURPRISE | | | | | 0.198 |
| | | | | | (0.307) |
| Constant | 0.017*** | 0.026*** | 0.025*** | 0.015** | 0.015** |
| | (0.004) | (0.005) | (0.005) | (0.006) | (0.006) |
| *Summary statistic* | | | | | |
| No. observations | 377 | 377 | 377 | 377 | 377 |
| No. companies | 11 | 11 | 11 | 11 | 11 |
| Company fixed effects | Yes | Yes | Yes | Yes | Yes |
| $R^2$ | 0.00 | 0.03 | 0.04 | 0.05 | 0.06 |

***Statistically significant at the 1 percent level; ** statistically significant at the 5 percent level; * statistically significant at the 10 percent level.

a. The dependent variable is STOCK, defined as the cumulative abnormal return of stocks inside a thirty-day window [−25, +5] around the dates on which the quarterly financial reports of each company are made public. REVIEWYEAR is a dummy equal to one for all four quarters of the year prior to the regulatory review. POST_REVIEWYEAR is a dummy equal to one in the four quarters of the year following the regulatory review. COSTSURPRISE is the forecast error of COSTS (costs/revenue). The best prediction of COSTS at time $q$ is assumed to be estimated by the data available up to $q$, according to the following specification:

$$\text{COSTS}_{iq} = \alpha + \beta\text{COSTS}_{iq-1} + \gamma\text{TIME}_q + \delta\text{SEASONAL\_DUMMIES} + u_i + \varepsilon_{iq}.$$

The forecast value of $\text{COSTS}_{iq+1}$ is based on the estimated coefficients, and the surprise is the positive or negative deviation of the real value from its forecast. The estimated coefficients change as more data become available over time. Robust standards are in parentheses.

review periods, suggesting that participants are learning about the workings of the system.

Regression 3 in table 6 provides some of our most important results, showing that cost surprises (that is, costs that exceed the naïve cost expectation) generally reduce stock market returns, and the effect is significant at the 10 percent level.[33] Importantly, review periods again have a negative and well-defined effect on prices. Cost surprises that take place in a review year tend to increase the firm's stock returns significantly.

The evidence in table 6 is consistent with the hypothesis that market participants believe, first, that the firm is behaving strategically and, second, that

33. The results are significant at the 5 percent level in table A-1 in appendix A.

**TABLE 7. Time Sensitivity of the Interactions of Cost Surprises with the Review Periods[a]**

| *Explanatory variable* | *First and second reviews (before 1996)* | *Second and third reviews (after 1992)* |
|---|---|---|
| COSTSURPRISE | −0.308 | −0.197 |
| | (0.223) | (0.233) |
| REVIEWYEAR | −0.019 | −0.031*** |
| | (0.013) | (0.010) |
| REVIEWYEAR*COSTSURPRISE | 1.327** | 0.226 |
| | (0.326) | (0.384) |
| Constant | 0.017** | 0.025*** |
| | (0.007) | (0.006) |
| *Summary statistic* | | |
| No. observations | 222 | 263 |
| No. companies | 9 | 11 |
| Company fixed effects | Yes | Yes |
| $R^2$ | 0.04 | 0.04 |

***Statistically significant at the 1 percent level; **statistically significant at the 5 percent level.

a. The dependent variable is STOCK, defined as the cumulative abnormal return of stocks inside a thirty-day window [−25, +5] around the dates on which the quarterly financial reports of each company are made public. REVIEWYEAR is a dummy equal to one for all four quarters of the year before the regulatory review. COSTSURPRISE is the forecast error of COSTS (costs/revenue). The best prediction of COSTS at time $q$ is assumed to be estimated by the data available up to $q$, according to the following specification:

$$COSTS_{iq} = \alpha + \beta COSTS_{iq-1} + \gamma TIME_q + \delta SEASONAL\_DUMMIES + u_i + \varepsilon_{iq}.$$

The forecast value of $COSTS_{iq+1}$ is based on the estimated coefficients, and the surprise is the positive or negative deviation of the real value from its forecast. The estimated coefficients change as more data become available over time. Robust standards are in parentheses.

the regulator will be forced to use these cost data to set the new prices for the following review period. It also suggests that the market is somewhat surprised by the extent of the cost reports. This effect falls over time, however, reinforcing the idea that the market learns to expect this type of interaction between the firms and the regulator (see table 7). Since individual reviews include only a limited number of years (the first review, in particular, only has two preceding years), table 7 partitions the sample into two subsamples, one containing the first and second review and the other containing the second and third reviews. Similar results emerge when we look at individual reviews.

Regression 4 in table 6 introduces a post-review-period dummy and finds that such periods tend to significantly increase stock returns. We find large average effects in stock returns considering the pre- and the post-review periods. Cost surprises in post-review periods do not have a significant effect on returns.

Table A-1 in appendix A uses a shorter measure inside the review period of just two quarters (the last two), with somewhat stronger results. Table A-2, again using the shorter review period, presents slightly stronger evidence in favor of the hypothesis that the effects fall over time. Cost shifting would be limited to and focused on the last few quarters if (as it is natural to assume) the private costs to a firm as a result of shifting increase with the number of periods of distorted information or with the time gap between reported and actual costs.

## Conclusions

Price caps have been a popular solution to the problem of regulating private monopolies. Virtually all of the countries that privatized their utilities in the 1990s adopted price-cap regimes. Partly as a result, there has been considerable interest in the theoretical properties of price caps. Some studies suggests that the system provides adequate incentives for cost reductions and can limit regulatory discretion. Others warn of potential inefficiencies, including distortions stemming from incorrect pricing, and the possibility of a sustained shift of returns to producers.[34] Little empirical work has been undertaken in the area, however, and most researchers refer to the empirical work of Mathios and Rogers and the case studies contained in Levy and Spiller.[35] Our paper seeks to contribute to the empirical understanding of price-cap regimes and, more generally, the costs of inflexible rules when firms behave strategically. It also complements the descriptions and analyses of the Chilean electricity sector, which, together with the experience of the British reforms, has been influential in shaping the profession's perception of how much can be achieved by good regulation of private monopolies.[36]

We study the performance of the electricity distribution industry in Chile in the 1990s under price-cap regulation, an institution that was put into place with the explicit objectives of increasing efficiency and limiting regulatory discretion at a time of considerable political uncertainty. Given that

34. See, for example, Beesley and Littlechild (1989); Breautigam and Panzar (1993); Levy and Spiller (1994); Schmalensee (1989).

35. Mathios and Rogers (1989); Levy and Spiller (1996).

36. On the British reforms, see Armstrong, Cowan, and Vickers (1994); Green and Newbery (1997).

the sector has undergone relatively few regulatory reviews to date, the evidence we present is only suggestive and should be interpreted in the context of broader studies of the industry.[37] We document reductions in the ratio of reported costs to revenues, on the order of 1.2 percent a year. This finding is consistent with strong incentives for cost reductions under a price-cap regime, as argued in the literature. We also find evidence consistent with strategic behavior by firms. The time profile of cost reductions within the four-year period between regulatory reviews is U-shaped, with most of the cost reductions taking place early in the process. We also find that cost reductions are reversed during the last year of each review period. A natural hypothesis is that firms are trying to influence the regulator. Although caps are supposed to ignore information from specific firms and reflect the costs of an ideal efficient company, as in the yardstick models, the regulator has a limited number of firms from which to draw the information in practice. Furthermore, the Chilean regulatory regime was designed with the objective of removing as much discretion from the hands of the regulator as possible, so a regulator that is captured by the industry and that incorporates inflated costs into future price caps can always claim not to have had the discretion to act differently.

We then propose a method that incorporates information generated by a third party (namely, the stock market) to evaluate the hypothesis that firms behave strategically. Our starting point is the finding that cumulative abnormal returns around the dates when firms announce quarterly results are negative during review periods, which suggests that there is considerable uncertainty that is not priced in by the market. Alternatively, the different actors may be learning about the workings of the new system. We then construct a measure of cost expectations that ignores information on the occurrence of review periods. We study the reactions of the stock market to firm announcements in nonreview years and compare them to market reactions in review years. Bad news (that is, cost reports that are higher than our measure of naïve cost expectations) depresses the returns to holding the firm's stock in normal times, but it increases these returns in review years. In a nonreview year, a one-standard-deviation (3.6 percentage point) unexpected increase in costs is associated with a negative cumulative abnormal return of 1.07 percentage points, whereas in a review year, a similar surprise increase in costs produces a positive cumulative abnormal return of 2.15 percentage points. Interestingly, the estimated effects fall over time. This evidence is consistent with firms' behaving strategically and the regulator's incorporating the infor-

37. See Fischer, Gutiérrez, and Serra (2003).

mation into future price levels, either because of capture or because the regulatory regime requires it.

In sum, the price-cap system seems to have promoted large efficiency gains. It also seems clear that the system has allowed producers to capture at least a part of those gains. More generally, our results suggest it may be worthwhile to complement regulatory procedures with stock market information.[38]

## Appendix A: Supplementary Tables

**TABLE A-1. The Effect of Cost Announcements on Stock Returns in Review and Nonreview Periods, Alternative Definition[a]**

| *Explanatory variable* | *(1)* | *(2)* | *(3)* | *(4)* | *(5)* |
|---|---|---|---|---|---|
| COSTSURPRISE | −0.129 | −0.034 | −0.283** | 0.046 | −0.218 |
| | (0.143) | (0.127) | (0.140) | (0.123) | (0.141) |
| REVIEWQUARTER | | −0.111*** | −0.114*** | −0.103*** | −0.107*** |
| | | (0.011) | (0.011) | (0.011) | (0.010) |
| REVIEWQUARTER * COSTSURPRISE | | | 1.067*** | | 1.016*** |
| | | | (0.273) | | (0.267) |
| POST_REVIEWQUARTER | | | | 0.067*** | 0.068*** |
| | | | | (0.013) | (0.013) |
| POST_REVIEWQUARTER*COSTSURPRISE | | | | | 0.329 |
| | | | | | (0.396) |
| *Constant* | 0.017*** | 0.034*** | 0.033*** | 0.026*** | 0.026*** |
| | (0.004) | (0.004) | (0.004) | (0.004) | (0.004) |
| *Summary statistic* | | | | | |
| Number of observations | 377 | 377 | 377 | 377 | 377 |
| Number of companies | 11 | 11 | 11 | 11 | 11 |
| Company fixed effects | Yes | Yes | Yes | Yes | Yes |
| $R^2$ | 0.00 | 0.22 | 0.25 | 0.28 | 0.31 |

***Statistically significant at the 1 percent level; **statistically significant at the 5 percent level.

a. The review period is defined as the last two quarters in the review year. The dependent variable is STOCK, defined as the cumulative abnormal return of stocks inside a thirty-day window [−25, +5] around the dates on which the quarterly financial reports of each company are made public. REVIEWQUARTER is a dummy variable equal to one for the last two quarters of the year before the regulatory review. POST_REVIEWYEAR is a dummy variable equal to one in the first two quarters after the end of each regulatory review. COSTSURPRISE is the forecast error of COSTS (costs/revenue). The best prediction of COSTS at time $q$ is assumed to be estimated by the data available up to $q$, according to the following specification:

$$\text{COSTS}_{iq} = \alpha + \beta\text{COSTS}_{iq-1} + \gamma\text{TIME}_q + \delta\text{SEASONAL\_DUMMIES} + u_i + \varepsilon_{iq}.$$

The forecast value of $\text{COSTS}_{iq+1}$ is based on the estimated coefficients, and the surprise is the positive or negative deviation of the real value from its forecast. The estimated coefficients change as more data become available over time. Robust standards are in parentheses.

38. See Di Tella and Kanczuk (2002).

**TABLE A-2. Time Sensitivity of the Interactions of Cost Surprises with the Review Periods, Alternative Definition**[a]

| *Explanatory variable* | *First and second reviews (before 1996)* | *Second and third reviews (after 1992)* |
|---|---|---|
| COSTSURPRISE | −0.316** | −0.114 |
| | (0.177) | (0.204) |
| REVIEWQUARTER | −0.130*** | −0.078*** |
| | (0.013) | (0.013) |
| REVIEWQUARTER*COSTSURPRISE | 1.327*** | 0.226 |
| | (0.326) | (0.384) |
| Constant | 0.032 | 0.029*** |
| | (0.005) | (0.005) |
| *Summary statistic* | | |
| Number of observations | 222 | 263 |
| Number of companies | 9 | 11 |
| Company fixed effects | Yes | Yes |
| $R^2$ | 0.34 | 0.13 |

***Statistically significant at the 1 percent level; **statistically significant at the 5 percent level.

a. The review period is defined as the last two quarters in the review year. The dependent variable is STOCK, defined as the cumulative abnormal return of stocks inside a thirty-day window [−25, +5] around the dates on which the quarterly financial reports of each company are made public. REVIEWQUARTER is a dummy variable equal to one for the last two quarters of the year before the regulatory review. COSTSURPRISE is the forecast error of COSTS (costs/revenue). The best prediction of COSTS at time *q* is assumed to be estimated by the data available up to *q*, according to the following specification:

$$\text{COSTS}_{iq} = \alpha + \beta\text{COSTS}_{iq-1} + \gamma\text{TIME}_q + \delta\text{SEASONAL\_DUMMIES} + u_i + \varepsilon_{iq}.$$

The forecast value of $\text{COSTS}_{iq+1}$ is based on the estimated coefficients, and the surprise is the positive or negative deviation of the real value from its forecast. The estimated coefficients change as more data become available over time. Robust standards are in parentheses.

**TABLE A-3. Data Definitions and Sources**

| *Variable* | *Definition* | *Source* |
|---|---|---|
| COSTS | The firm's reported operating costs over revenue | Chilean Securities and Exchange Commission (CSV) |
| COSTSURPRISE | Deviation of the reported cost per revenue from its forecasted value. The best prediction of COSTS at time *q* is assumed to be estimated by the data available up to *q*, according to the following specification: $\text{COSTS}_{iq} = \alpha + \beta\text{COSTS}_{iq-1} + \gamma\text{TIME}_q + \delta\text{SEASONAL\_DUMMIES} + \mu_i + \varepsilon_{iq}$ The forecasted value of $\text{COSTS}_{iq+1}$ is based on the estimated coefficients, and the surprise is the positive or negative deviation of the real value from this forecast | Estimated separately for each quarter and for each company using cost per revenue data from CSV |

(*continues*)

**TABLE A-3. Data Definitions and Sources (*Continued*)**

| *Variable* | *Definition* | *Source* |
|---|---|---|
| STOCK | Cumulative abnormal returns of company stocks inside a thirty-day [−25, +5] window around the dates that the quarterly financial reports become public | Calculated using stock price data from Datastream and date information from the Institutional Brokers' Estimate System (IBES) and Michigan State University's Global Access Database |
| TIME | The quarter number, which takes a value from one in the first quarter of 1989 to forty-four in the fourth quarter of 1999 | Author's definition |
| EARLY | Time trend equal to one in the first quarter of the four-year period between review years and sixteen in the fourth quarter of the fourth year | Author's definition |
| REVIEWYEAR | Dummy variable equal to one if the year is 1991, 1995, or 1999, and zero otherwise | Authors' definition. Note that regulatory reviews occur in 1992, 1996, 2000 |
| REVIEWQUARTER | Dummy variable equal to one if the quarter is one of the last two quarters of the year prior to the regulatory review and 0 otherwise | Authors' definition |
| POST_REVIEWYEAR | Dummy variable equal to one in the first four quarters of the year after the regulatory review, and 0 otherwise | Authors' definition |
| POST_REVIEWQUARTER | Dummy variable equal to one in the first two quarters after the end of the regulatory review, and 0 otherwise | Authors' definition |
| Seasonal dummies | A set of four dummies taking a value of one in the corresponding quarter, and zero otherwise | Authors' definition |

## Appendix B: Institutional Background and Regulatory Reforms

Chile's approach to regulating the power sector prior to 1982 was to use rate-of-return regulation for vertically integrated utilities dominated by state-owned firms, which resulted in the typical problems of political manipulation and asymmetric information.[39] The Electricity Law of 1931, amended in 1959, specified a maximum rate of return on fixed assets of 10 percent, with assets revalued annually. In the 1960s, prices were set so that firms did not even approach the maximum rate of return, and the financial situation deteriorated

39. For a thorough discussion of regulation in Chile, see Bustos and Galetovic (2002).

further under the Allende government (1970–73), when there were limited price increases despite hyperinflation. The Pinochet government responded in 1974–79 by adjusting prices upward to reflect revalued assets, but the companies clearly enjoyed advantages in having more intimate knowledge of their costs.[40]

The electricity reforms that produced the price-cap system for regulating distribution were designed to both increase efficiency and reduce political discretion over decisionmaking in the industry. Electricity reform began in 1978, when the National Energy Commission (CNE) was established and a committee was formed to make recommendations. It was formalized four years later, in the General Law on Electric Power Services of 1982 (DFL 1 of the Ministry of Mining).[41] The reforms moved to stimulate efficiency in electricity generation through the introduction of competition.[42] For distribution, the legislation called for a version of price-cap regulation.

The committee crafting the system had a clear understanding of the potential efficiency and political gains of a price-cap regime. Sebastián Bernstein, the head of the committee that drafted the 1982 law, describes the process as follows:

> Yardstick is a term we learned later, but in many ways that is an accurate way to characterize our model. The system was consciously designed to decentralize decisionmaking away from politicians and regulators. We had no reference books to turn to, but instead thought that the best way to regulate would be to simulate a market. In a market, you do not set prices—they are set by the most efficient company in the industry. This was a radical departure from what we had been doing looking at costs. We also knew that there were political troubles when prices had to be adjusted. We wanted to avoid politics by having a

40. Sebastián Bernstein, coauthor of the Electricity Law of 1982, noted, "We discovered that the book information didn't represent anything. At the time, we had an inflation rate of 500 percent a year. We were not sure what was in the books. It is very hard to go inside the company. They could convince you of anything. The main goal of managers at the time was to lobby to raise prices." See Di Tella and Dyck (2001, p. 4).

41. The stated objectives of the law are "to simplify the regulatory scheme and the tariff-setting process and to limit the discretionary role of government; to establish objectively measurable criteria for determining tariffs in a way which results in an economically efficient allocation of resources; to provide a competitive rate of return on investments in the sector to stimulate private investment; and to ensure availability of service to all who request it." Enersis S. A., "Form F-1: Prospectus for Sale of Shares," New York, 1993, p. A-10.

42. Spiller and Martorell (1996) provide a more detailed description of the generation sector. Some of its key components include the division of the electricity supply sector into a free market for large consumers (less than 2 megawatts) and a regulated market for small consumers. In the regulated market, prices for distributors are set twice a year based partly on expected short-run marginal costs over the next four years and partly on free market prices.

rule-based system with automatic adjustments. We had the idea that the efficient company should not be your company, and it shouldn't be based on reported costs. Our idea was to use replacement costs applied to the actual structure of the grid and impartial information on the costs of services.[43]

Formally, DFL 1 sets a maximum price for the markup distribution companies can charge consumers for their service (called the value added of distribution, or VAD). This price is fixed for four years subject to automatic adjustments, and it is then revised systematically in review periods using a specific formula. The maximum price is designed to cover selling, general, and administrative costs; maintenance and operating costs; a factor for distribution losses; and a 10 percent real return on investment, based on the new replacement value of assets employed in distribution. To reduce the incentive for firms to misreport costs, the costs considered are not those reported by individual companies, but rather the costs of a model efficient company (taking into account the three types of density of distribution networks and whether lines are overhead or underground).[44] The costs of the model efficient company are based on the costs of a single test company (or the area of a company). No firms are informed of the choice beforehand, and the regulator is allowed to improve the test company results if costs are viewed as imprudent. Between reviews, prices are to be adjusted solely based on interim automatic adjustments using a weighted average factor (with the weights defined separately for each company) that includes increases in the consumer price index (CPI), the copper price, wholesale prices, and the earnings index published by the National Institute of Statistics.

This price cap thus features the four properties proposed by Acton and Vogelsang: the use of price ceilings; the definition of the price ceilings based on a bundle of services; the periodic adjustment of the price ceilings using "a preannounced adjustment factor that is exogenous to the firm" in intervals of several years; and the review and possible adjustment of the baskets and weighting schemes used by the industry.[45] This particular price-cap system also meets Levy and Spiller's three tests of commitment, which focus on

43. Di Tella and Dyck (2001, p. 5).

44. As Bernstein states, "There were only small differences in costs as firms increased in size, so long as we accurately characterized their density. This gave us an important idea: we could provide just three standards that would completely characterize all firms in the industry. This parsimony was essential because it would allow us to avoid discussions company by company. We knew if that was the situation, we could never prevail. The company could always produce more information—literally they could provide us with meters of documents" (Di Tella and Dyck 2001, p. 5).

45. Acton and Vogelsang (1989, p. 370).

substantive restraints on discretion, formal and informal constraints on changing the system, and institutions to enforce these constraints.[46]

While the regulator can choose the test company (or area), DFL 1 requires that both firms and the regulator can solicit cost studies and guarantees firm-generated studies a weight in the final determination.[47] The regulator is not allowed to use its own staff to prepare studies (both firms and the regulator have to use independent consultants from an approved list, who are in turn required to operate according to detailed terms of reference), and cost studies are only allowed to focus on one year of data, with no inclusion of past data or data from other countries. The legislation also requires prices to be reset if this procedure produces a rate of return for firms that is below 6 percent.[48]

The legislature and the courts provided formal constraints on changing the system. Passage of a new electricity law would require approval of both houses of the bicameral legislature, where one party rarely holds a majority in both chambers. Firms have the right to take the regulator to court if they feel the regulator has overstepped its regulatory authority, and the previous prices would hold pending judicial determination. The Supreme Court was credited with independence based on past records of impartial responses.[49]

Informal constraints on changing the system arose from the privatization of distribution companies and the widespread ownership of these companies. By 1991, the electricity sector consisted of two integrated companies, eleven power generation and transmission companies, fourteen electric power cooperatives, and twenty-one electricity distribution companies.[50] Almost all distribution assets are owned by publicly traded companies (see table B-1).

46. Levy and Spiller (1996). Limits on political discretion are not a necessary feature of price caps. In the case of the United Kingdom's price-cap regime, for example, Beesley and Littlechild argue that regulators have significant discretion during the reinitialization of price caps, with no formal constraints on the level of prices in the reinitialization: "The U.K. regulator is deemed to be a person to whom public policy may be safely delegated, subject only to judicial review on the question of whether his actions are legitimate in terms of the act. In the U.K., neither government nor regulators have given detailed reasons for their decision on *X*. This reduces the bases for challenge (by company, competitors, or customers)" (Beesley and Littlechild 1989, p. 461).

47. In case of a dispute over the findings of the regulator, the VAD would depend two-thirds on the estimate of the government's consultants and one-third on the estimate of the firm's consultants.

48. The procedure needed to produce an estimated rate of return of between 6 and 14 percent.

49. Unlike the United Kingdom, there were no independent regulator's offices. In Chile, the electricity regulator is headed by a political appointee, staffed by regular civil servants, and located inside the Ministry of Energy.

50. Spiller and Martorell (1996).

**TABLE B-1. Electricity Distribution Companies in Chile, 1991**

| *System and company* | *Included in sample?* | *Publicly traded throughout period* | *Customers (in thousands)* | *Energy (GWh)* |
|---|---|---|---|---|
| Norte Grande Interconnected System | | | | |
| EDELNOR | No | No | 140 | 139 |
| Central Interconnected System | | | | |
| CHILECTRA Metro | Yes | Yes | 1,106 | 4,741 |
| CGEI | Yes | Yes | 365 | 1,138 |
| Rio Maipo | Yes | Yes | 285 | 1,119 |
| SAESA | Yes | No | 114 | 328 |
| EMEC | Yes | Yes | 110 | 289 |
| FRONTEL | No | No | 107 | 184 |
| CONAFE | No | No | 94 | 271 |
| EMEL | Yes | Yes | 91 | 195 |
| ELECDA | Yes | Yes | 84 | 187 |
| EMELAT | Yes | Yes | 46 | 187 |
| EMELARI | Yes | Yes | 39 | 90 |
| ELIQSA | Yes | Yes | 35 | 90 |
| EE DEL SUR | No | No | 16 | 29 |
| EE PTE ALTO | No | No | 14 | 26 |
| CE LITORAL | No | No | 13 | 14 |
| Other | | | 12 | 22 |
| Total | | | 2,531 | 8,932 |
| Aysen Isolated System | | | | |
| EDELAYSEN | No | No | 14 | 148 |
| Punta Arenas Isolated System | | | | |
| EDELMAG | Yes | Yes | 36 | 72 |

Source: Authors' compilation, based on Spiller and Martorell (1996).

Shares in distribution companies are held by employees, management, foreigners (through the cross-listing of company shares on U.S. stock exchanges as American Depositary Receipts, or ADRs), and indirectly by a wide cross-section of the Chilean population through the Chilean private pension funds created in 1982. This ownership structure meant that tough regulatory decisions could hurt the private pension scheme and Chilean firms' standing in international markets, factors which the regulator was unlikely to be able to ignore. Interestingly, the presence of foreign funds has increased over time.

# Comments

**Alexander Galetovic:** Many think that price-cap regulation was conceived and first used in the United Kingdom in the late 1980s, as part of the privatization of British Telecom. In fact, it was invented in all but name nearly a decade earlier in Chile, first applied to set the tariffs of Chilectra, a publicly owned electricity distribution firm, in October 1980 and later made official in a 1982 law that radically reformed the regulation of electricity.[1] When generation and distribution companies were privatized in the second half of the 1980s, a clear set of rules had been in place for several years. These rules have remained essentially unchanged for more than a quarter century and presided over a massive expansion of generation, transmission, and distribution capacity during the golden years of Chilean growth. All in all, Chile's regulation has been quite successful.

Relative success does not imply perfection, however, and it is fair to say that the list of shortcomings is rather long. One of these shortcomings is that distributors have made substantial efficiency gains while tariffs have lagged behind.[2] Distribution companies systematically earn high returns, well above the 10 percent real rate granted by regulatory rules. It thus seems that the regulator has been unsuccessful in passing efficiency gains to consumers.

Pundits have offered many explanations. One is that distributors wield formidable lobbying power over a weak regulator. Another culprit is deficiencies of the so-called efficient-firm standard as a regulatory technique. Cost padding and exaggeration surely also play a part, especially in view of the rather silly "arbitration" rule that averages the regulator's and the firms' cost estimations of the efficient firm. But while a lot has been said and anecdotes abound, little empirical work has tested these beliefs. For this reason, Di Tella and Dyck's interesting paper is a welcome evaluation of the workings and performance of

1. Sebastián Bernstein (personal communication).
2. See Fischer, Gutiérrez, and Serra (2005); Fischer and Serra (2007).

the Chilean distribution price cap. They confirm—this time with evidence—that no matter how hard you try, you cannot regulate without looking at the costs of the real firm. They also provide a clever method for figuring out whether firms influence their tariffs by exaggerating costs.

It is useful to put the Chilean price cap into perspective, both conceptually and historically. Any price-cap regime has at least three parts: a pricing rule, a valuation source, and the price cap. The Chilean price cap is quite standard in that tariffs are set every four years, and between review years prices only change in response to variations in exogenous variables (namely, the inflation rate and the price of key inputs like copper).[3] The pricing rule and valuation source, however, are quite peculiar to Chile.

Consider first the pricing rule, which maps costs into a tariff. In Chile, the price of distribution (the so-called value added of distribution, or VAD) equals the intertemporal average cost of one kilowatt of distribution capacity. Formally, assume that the distributor must supply $Q$ kilowatts, requires $K(Q)$ units of capital, which have a useful life of $T$ years, and spends $c$ pesos per kilowatt every year in operation and maintenance costs. The Chilean tariff per kilowatt of distribution capacity then equals

$$p = c + \frac{K(Q)}{Q \cdot R},$$

with $R \equiv \int_0^T e^{-rt}\, dt$, where $r = 10$ percent real by law. A pricing rule such as the above equation has several desirable properties. In particular, it is the Ramsey-Boiteaux tariff when capital costs have to be recovered over time, and it is thus allocatively efficient subject to the firm's self-financing constraint. Nevertheless, this pricing rule is somewhat peculiar. In most price-cap regimes around the world, tariffs are not equal to the intertemporal average cost, but are instead quite arbitrary.[4]

The second peculiarity of the Chilean price cap is the valuation source. The law mandates that the regulator is to obtain all the technical parameters and unit costs that determine $c$ and $K(Q)$ by designing and valuing an efficient firm from scratch each time tariffs are set. The efficient firm is, in principle, a completely independent entity with no direct relation to the actual firm, as it operates with the best available technology and serves actual demand at least cost. It is not a fantasy, however, for it is designed obeying the topographic,

3. By contrast, no allowance is made for exogenous productivity improvements—the $X$ factor is set equal to zero.

4. See Newbery (1997); Bustos and Galetovic (2007).

demographic, and technological constraints faced by the actual firm. In other words, the efficient firm operates at minimum cost with the best technology available at the time of the tariff review, but it is adapted to the properties of actual topography and demand.[5]

Of course, almost three decades of information economics might suggest some naïveté on the part of Chilean lawmakers. How can a regulator expect to know what is efficient? Here, a little historical context is useful. Efficient-firm regulation was conceived in the late 1970s, when all distributors were public firms controlled de facto by managers and unions. Until then, no agency in the central government was capable of evaluating the cost estimates that utilities presented to justify their tariffs. Tariffs were reviewed by the government's budget office, which, lacking the skills to confront an informed agent, routinely rubber-stamped whatever the distributors proposed. This led to large allocative and productive inefficiencies that were prompted by overinvestment, overstaffing, above-market wages for most workers, and relaxed working conditions. Consequently, the National Energy Commission was created in the late 1970s with the specific mandate of overseeing public utilities and fixing their tariffs. The efficient-firm standard was part of a package of reforms meant to inform an up-to-then very poorly informed regulator, detect gross inefficiencies, and control managers; it wasn't meant to substitute for knowledge about the actual firm.

Be that as it may, the efficient-firm standard is almost ideal for testing whether distributors inflate costs and successfully influence regulators. If the standard is fully exogenous and tariffs are independent of the actual firm, higher-than-expected costs (that is, a negative cost surprise) should always make returns fall. Even better, if the regulator ignores the real firm while setting tariffs, strategic cost surprises are useless and should not be observed in the first place. By contrast, if the actual firm influences the regulator, strategic cost surprises may inform the market that tariffs will be set higher than expected. Indeed, Di Tella and Dyck's regression 3 in table 6 implies that a one-standard-deviation negative cost surprise during a year before the tariff review (1991, 1995, and 1999 in their paper) increases returns by 220 basis points.[6] By contrast, a negative cost surprise reduces returns by 110 basis points if it does not occur during the year before a review takes place. The

5. On the efficient-firm standard and its application to regulate Chilean distributors, see Rudnick and Donoso (2000); Bustos and Galetovic (2007).

6. The authors call 1991, 1995, and 1999 review years, although the reviews took place in 1992, 1996, and 2000. In any case, 1991, 1995, and 1999 are the correct dates to insert interaction dummies, as I argue below.

efficient-firm standard thus does not seem to be exogenous after all. Moreover, Di Tella and Dyck seem to have found the smoking gun: distributors exaggerate costs during review years to get higher tariffs.

But did they really find the smoking gun? The paper's thesis is that strategic cost surprises generate abnormally high returns because they raise tariffs. To test this, the interaction dummies must be inserted in the exact quarters in which negative cost surprises can plausibly influence the regulator. Di Tella and Dyck rightly choose the four quarters of the year before the review year. To explain why, let me briefly review the timing of each tariff review. Since October 1980, distribution tariffs are set in Chile every four years in either late October or early November.[7] Six months before, in late May, the National Energy Commission publishes the methodology that must be used to calculate the value added of distribution, and both the regulator and distributors then have four months to conduct their study. For example, in the 1992 review, the tariff-setting process started in mid-May 1992, and tariffs were then set on 27 October.

On the face of it, one might think that the authors should have inserted interaction dummies for the first three quarters of 1992, 1996, and 2000, instead of the four quarters of 1991, 1995, and 1999. As practitioners and stock analysts know, however, the distributors report to the regulator their costs of the year before a tariff review takes place—in this case 1991, 1995, and 1999. Thus, the interaction dummies were inserted precisely in those quarters in which the information likely to be considered by the regulator is generated. Moreover, the results are even stronger when the authors only insert dummies for the last two quarters of 1991, 1995, and 1999 (as column 3 in table A-1 shows, the effect nearly doubles). It seems reasonable to believe that information generated toward the end of the year will give the market a sharper idea of what the regulator will see while setting tariffs.

The only doubt I am left with concerns strategic cost surprises. Di Tella and Dyck should have reported each of the forty-four quarterly cost surprises they computed. Results would be strengthened if one finds that cost surprises were systematically negative and large in 1991, 1995, and 1999, but did not exhibit any systematic pattern in irrelevant quarters. By contrast, if they are not systematically negative in the key quarters, then one would wonder whether distribution firms act strategically after all, for what would be the point of strategically reporting costs that are lower than expected?

7. Thus there have been seven reviews to date, and this paper considers three—1992, 1996, and 2000.

All in all, this is an important paper. The evidence is convincing, and the authors have developed an interesting method for testing whether firms use strategic cost surprises to influence regulators. A straightforward but important lesson is that regulators should examine the evolution of costs over the entire period between tariff reviews and be particularly skeptical of cost increases that occur right before the tariff review begins. While this may sound obvious after reading Di Tella and Dyck's paper, I doubt that most regulators are aware of it, much less that they do anything about it.

**William W. Hogan:** Di Tella and Dyck address the incentive regulation scheme applied to the Chilean electricity distribution system, covering the period between 1989 and 1999. Chile was an innovator in restructuring the electricity system to allow for greater reliance on competition and markets. Previous studies focus on policies for generation competition through a wholesale market design built on principles of economic dispatch. The wholesale market is an interesting topic, but it leaves out the important transmission and distribution sectors. The case of high voltage transmission is a separate and separable topic, with many debates about the best approach to regulating transmission systems. There is little controversy, however, about the character of electricity distribution systems, which comprise the local collection of wires and meters that connect final customers to the high voltage grid. The distribution system is generally deemed to be a natural monopoly. As such, it lends itself to various forms of incentive regulation that have been much discussed and debated in the literature.

Joskow provides a recent overview of the theory and much of the practice in the case of electricity.[1] In a world of assumed uncertainty and asymmetric information between regulator and firm, the fundamental tension is to ensure the firm's financial viability while balancing the trade-off between the goals of providing high-powered incentives for efficiency and ensuring a maximum rent extraction from the regulated company. For example, an idealized price-cap model with fixed prices set independently of the firm's performance would provide very strong incentives for cost reductions. Traditional cost-of-service regulation emphasizes setting prices equal to the firm's reported costs for the maximum in rent extraction, but it provides poor incentives for efficiency. There are many alternatives in between these two extremes. Theoretical and empirical work seeks to analyze and evaluate the incentives induced and the results produced by alternative implementations of the idealized models.

1. Joskow (2006).

The case of Chile and the research of Di Tella and Dyck raise general questions that could be addressed in other countries. As part of their research, Di Tella and Dyck collected quantitative data supplemented by interviews in 1999 that add insight to the numbers and the models. One of the interesting features of the Chilean experience is that the innovative models were developed independently in Chile, without apparent reference to work on similar problems in other countries. The authors quote Sebastián Bernstein, who headed the committee drafting the 1982 reform law: "Yardstick is a term we learned later, but in many ways that is an accurate way to characterize our model. The system was consciously designed to decentralize decisionmaking away from politicians and regulators. We had no reference books to turn to, but instead thought that the best way to regulate would be to simulate a market." Based on this alone, the Chilean innovations are impressive.

There is a political economy story here about limiting the discretion and political control of regulators. The basic idea was to create a model distribution company in each of five zones and then optimize this company based on a comparison with other distribution companies in Chile, to produce an efficient-standard company that would provide the regulatory yardstick for setting the distribution prices of the real regulated company. This is one form of benchmarking.[2] Although benchmarking has many obvious attractions as a management tool used to point to opportunities to improve company operations, it can be much more problematic in setting prices for regulated companies.[3] Yardstick competition based on the performance of other identical companies has great theoretical appeal, as long as the yardstick derives from identical companies. The fundamental difficulty arises in dealing with real companies, which are never identical. In the case of Chile, "the methodology has been complex to apply, with bitter disputes among the parties involved."[4]

Di Tella and Dyck complement their research with an effort to theorize and examine the data to answer a number of interesting questions about the performance of this particular model. The paper addresses four broad questions. First, are the incentives sufficient to produce cost reductions? Based on the interviews and case studies included in the paper, the broad answer is probably yes. As Di Tella and Dyck observe, however, the evidence is consistent with induced cost reductions, but it is not dispositive because there is no real control group for comparison.

2. Farsi, Fetz, and Fillipini (2007).
3. Shuttleworth (2005).
4. Rudnick and Donoso (2000).

Second, does this yardstick competition provide an effective means of rent extraction and lower prices for customers? Apparently, the broad answer is no. Although there is evidence of material reductions in costs, the data and the interviews suggest that relatively little of the improved efficiency has been translated into prices.

Third, does the Chilean scheme conform to the theory of yardstick competition, according to which prices are set independently of the observed costs of the regulated firm, or do firms behave strategically to influence the yardstick? This is perhaps the most interesting part of the paper. Di Tella and Dyck collect data on company cost performance and stock prices. They present a theoretical model and hypotheses, which they explore using econometric estimates based on pooled data for companies in Chile. The collective results support the hypothesis that a company's own actions have a direct impact on the estimates that will be developed in a review period when the yardstick is reset. Compared to a naïve model, actual costs decline more until the review period and then decline less. For stock prices, Di Tella and Dyck use an event model analysis to show a positive impact on stock valuation as a result of a cost surprise increase above a simple trend, but only during the review period. It is hard to see how these results could be squared with any theory that does not include regulators' and consultants' peeking at the company results in the interest of producing yardsticks that are not unreasonable. This peeking, of course, undermines the incentive properties of yardstick competition and presents the opportunity for strategic behavior by the regulated firm.

Figure 1 of the paper reveals a troubling feature of this implementation of yardstick competition. The data show the yardsticks calculated by two different sets of consultants, one hired by the regulator and one hired by the company. Any delusion that there is a simple way to set the yardstick is quickly dispelled by these figures. The price differences are substantial, and the bias is clear, with the regulator's consultants coming in low and the companies' consultants coming in high. This does not look like objective yardstick calculation. The presence of fixed weights for averaging the two estimates gives little comfort for those who hope objectivity in the yardstick is producing strong incentives.

Finally, what are the other incentive effects of the optimized model-company yardstick regulation? Di Tella and Dyck suggest that yardstick competition in Chile probably reduced costs as measured over this period, but the strategic behavior of firms runs against this conclusion. Furthermore, other incentive effects may be even more important in the long run. For example, the Chilean model-company approach is very similar in spirit to the "optimal deprival value" price regulation found in New Zealand. In the face of uncertainty, this form of regulation creates an ex post asymmetry that provides a bias against capital investment. The difficulty is that repeated optimization of the model company to set the price cap in effect always assumes that investments are made with perfect foresight. If the allowed return is set in the usual ex ante way, as is typically the case, the earned return can never be more than the allowed return and will usually be less. This creates a slow bleed with a bias against capital investment, until the situation becomes dire and the rules are changed. It would be interesting to explore whether the Chilean data could be applied to further empirical work addressing this long-term incentive effect.

If such work is undertaken, it would be useful to reconsider the cost measure employed in the econometric model. Di Tella and Dyck argue that normalizing total costs by total revenues provides the best measure for their purposes, and this choice expands the available data for the statistical analysis. However, what is being measured is a combination of cost reductions and revenue increases, which confuses the interpretation of the efficiency results. A more appealing approach would be to normalize for numbers of customers and quantities of delivered energy. Rudnick and Donoso use the latter approach to compute their benchmarks.[5] Their model and data set may provide additional leverage for Di Tella and Dyck's analysis.

This concern about the cost measure does not extend to the stock price analysis. Assuming the cost variable is defined the same way (that is, costs as a proportion of revenue), increases in this variable should reflect either higher costs or lower revenues, both of which should result in lower, not higher, stock valuations. The impressive stock market results thus seem to provide robust evidence of assumed strategic behavior, or at least behavior that leads the stock market to believe that the company's performance affects its own yardstick.

5. Rudnick and Donoso (2000).

## References

Acton, Jan Paul, and Ingo Vogelsang. 1989. "Introduction: Symposium on Price-Cap Regulation." *RAND Journal of Economics* 20(3): 369–72.

Armstrong, Mark, Simon Cowan, and John Vickers. 1994. *Regulatory Reform: Economic Analysis and British Experience.* MIT Press.

Averch, Harvey, and Leland L. Johnson. 1962. "Behavior of the Firm under Regulatory Constraint." *American Economic Review* 52(5): 1053–069.

Baron, David P., and David Besanko. 1987. "Commitment and Fairness in a Dynamic Regulatory Relationship." *Review of Economic Studies* 54(3): 413–36.

Baron, David P., and Raymond R. de Bondt. 1979. "Fuel Adjustment Mechanisms and Economic Efficiency." *Journal of Industrial Economics* 27(3): 243–61.

Beesley, Michael E., and Stephen C. Littlechild. 1989. "The Regulation of Privatized Monopolies in the United Kingdom." *RAND Journal of Economics* 20(3): 454–72.

Bernstein, Sebastián. 1995. "Pragmatic Privatization." *Independent Energy* 25(2): 30–36.

Biglaiser, Gary, and Michael H. Riordan. 2000. "Dynamics of Price Regulation." *RAND Journal of Economics* 31(4): 744–67.

Blank, Larry, David Kasserman, and John Mayo. 1998. "Dominant Firm Pricing with Competitive Entry and Regulation: The Case of IntraLATA Toll." *Journal of Regulatory Economics* 14(1): 35–53.

Braeutigam, Ronald R., and John C. Panzar. 1993. "Effects of Change from Rate-of-Return to Price-Cap Regulation." *American Economic Review* 83(2): 191–98.

Bustos, Alvaro, and Alexander Galetovic. 2002. "Regulación por empresa eficiente: quién es realmente usted?" *Estudios Públicos* 86 (otoño): 145–82.

———. 2007. "Monopoly Regulation Chilean Style: The Efficient Firm Standard in Theory and Practice." In *Regulatory Economics and Quantitative Methods: Evidence from Latin America,* edited by Omar O. Chisari. Cheltenham: Edward Elgar.

Cabral, Luis M. B., and Michael Riordan. 1989. "Incentives for Cost Reduction under Price Cap Regulation." *Journal of Regulatory Economics* 1(2): 93–102.

Di Tella, Rafael, and Alexander Dyck. 2001. "Strategy of the Firm under Regulatory Review: The Case of Chilectra." Case 9-701-044. Harvard Business School.

Di Tella, Rafael, and Fabio Kanczuk. 2002. "Good Regulation through Stock Market Prices." Harvard Business School.

Dnes, Antony, and others. 1998. "The Regulation of the United Kingdom Electricity Industry: An Event Study of Price-Capping Measures." *Journal of Regulatory Economics* 13(3): 207–26.

Farsi, Mehdi, Aurelio Fetz, and Massimo Fillipini. 2007. "Benchmarking and Regulation in the Electricity Distribution Sector." CEPE Working Paper 54. Zurich: Centre for Energy Policy and Economics.

Faure-Grimaud, Antoine. 2002. "Using Stock Price Information to Regulate Firms." *Review of Economic Studies* 69(1): 169–90.

Fischer, Ronald, and Pablo Serra. 2000. "Regulating the Electricity Sector in Latin America." *Economía* 1(1): 155–99.

———. 2007. "Efectos de la privatización de servicios públicos en Chile." University of Chile.

Fischer, Ronald, Rodrigo Gutiérrez, and Pablo Serra. 2003. "The Effects of Privatization on Firms and on Social Welfare: The Chilean Case." Research Network Working Paper R-456. Washington: Inter-American Development Bank.

———. 2005. "The Effects of Privatization on Firms: The Chilean Case." In *Privatization in Latin America: Myths and Reality,* edited by Alberto Chong and Florencio López-de-Silanes. Stanford University Press.

Galetovic, Alexander, and Ricardo Sanhueza. 2002. "Regulación de servicios públicos: hacia dónde debemos ir?" *Estudios Públicos* 85 (verano): 101–37.

Gilbert, Richard J., Edward P. Kahn, and David M. Newbery. 1996. "International Comparisons of Electricity Regulation." In *International Comparisons of Electricity Regulation,* edited by Richard J. Gilbert and David M. Newbery. Cambridge University Press.

Gilbert, Richard J., and David M. Newbery. 1994. "The Dynamic Efficiency of Regulatory Constitutions." *RAND Journal of Economics* 25(4): 538–54.

Gómez-Ibáñez, José A. 1999. "Commitment and Flexibility: Strategies for Regulating Privatized Infrastructure." Discussion Paper. Harvard University, Kennedy School of Government, Taubman Center for State and Local Government.

Green, Richard, and David M. Newbery. 1997. "Competition in the Electricity Industry in England and Wales." *Oxford Review of Economic Policy* 13(1): 27–46.

Hachette, Dominique, and Rolf Lüders. 1993. "Privatization in Chile: An Economic Appraisal." San Francisco: ICS Press.

Joskow, Paul. 2006. "Incentive Regulation in Theory and Practice: Electricity Distribution and Transmission Networks." Working Paper in Economics 0607. University of Cambridge.

Kaserman, David L., and Richard C. Tepel. 1982. "The Impact of the Automatic Adjustment Clause on Fuel Purchase and Utilization Practices in the U.S. Electric Utility Industry." *Southern Economic Journal* 48(3): 687–700.

Kridel, Donald J., David E. M. Sappington, and Dennis L. Weisman. 1996. "The Effects of Incentive Regulation in the Telecommunications Industry: A Survey." *Journal of Regulatory Economics* 9(3): 269–306.

Levy, Brian, and Pablo T. Spiller. 1994. "The Institutional Foundations of Regulatory Commitment: A Comparative Analysis of Telecommunications Regulation." *Journal of Law, Economics, and Organization* 10(2): 201–46.

———, eds. 1996. *Regulation, Institutions, and Commitment: Comparative Studies of Telecommunications.* Cambridge University Press.

Mathios, Alan D., and Robert P. Rogers. 1989. "The Impact of Alternative Forms of State Regulation of AT&T on Direct-Dial, Long-Distance Telephone Rates." *RAND Journal of Economics* 20(3): 454–72.

Newbery, David M. 1997. "Determining the Regulatory Asset Base for Utility Price Regulation." *Utilities Policy* 6(1): 1–8.

Pollitt, Michael G. 2005. "Electricity Reform in Chile: Lessons for Developing Countries." Working Paper in Economics 0448. University of Cambridge.

Posner, Richard A. 1971. "Taxation by Regulation." *Bell Journal of Economics and Management Science* 2(1): 22–50.

Rose, Nancy L. 1985. "The Incidence of Regulatory Rents in the Motor Carrier Industry." *RAND Journal of Economics* 16(3): 299–318.

Rudnick, Hugh, and Jorge A. Donoso. 2000. "Integration of Price Cap and Yardstick Competition Schemes in Electrical Distribution Regulation." *IEES PES Transactions on Power Systems* 15(4): 1428–33.

Rudnick, Hugh, and Sebastian Mocarquer. 2007. "Benchmark Regulation and Efficiency of Electricity Distribution: Strengths and Weaknesses." Working Paper 07GM0943. Piscataway, N.J.: IEEE.

Salant, David J., and Glenn A. Woroch. 1992. "Trigger Price Regulation." *RAND Journal of Economics* 23(1): 29–51.

Sappington, David E. M. 1980. "Strategic Firm Behavior under a Dynamic Regulatory Adjustment Process." *Bell Journal of Economics* 11(1): 360–72.

Sappington, David E. M., and David S. Sibley. 1992. "Strategic Nonlinear Pricing under Price-Cap Regulation." *RAND Journal of Economics* 23(1): 1–19.

Schmalensee, Richard. 1989. "Good Regulatory Regimes." *RAND Journal of Economics* 20(3): 417–36.

Schwert, G. William. 1981. "Using Financial Data to Measure Effects of Regulation." *Journal of Law and Economics* 24(1):121–58.

Shleifer, Andrei. 1985. "A Theory of Yardstick Competition." *RAND Journal of Economics* 16(3): 319–27.

Shuttleworth, Graham. 2005. "Benchmarking of Electricity Networks: Practical Problems for Its Use for Regulation." *Utilities Policy* 13(4): 310–17.

Spiller, Pablo T., and Luis Viana Martorell. 1996. "How Should It Be Done? Electricity Regulation in Argentina, Brazil, Uruguay, and Chile." In *International Comparisons of Electricity Regulation,* edited by Richard J. Gilbert and Edward P. Kahn. Cambridge University Press.

Whinston, Michael D., and Scott C. Collins. 1992. "Entry and Competitive Structure in Deregulated Airline Markets: An Event Study Analysis of People Express." *RAND Journal of Economics* 23(4): 445–62.

## Erratum

The following correction should be noted for "Electoral Campaign Financing: The Role of Public Contributions and Party Ideology," by Adriana Cuoco Portugal and Mauricio Bugarin, in *Economía* 8, no. 1 (Fall 2007): 143–73.

Equation 4 on p. 154 is corrected as shown below:

$$\pi^A = \sum_J \alpha^J \left[ \sigma^J + \frac{1}{2\phi} \right] \phi = \frac{1}{2} + \phi \sum_J \alpha^J \sigma^J$$